Dress Code

Dress Code

Unlocking Fashion
from the New Look
to Millennial Pink

Véronique Hyland

HARPER ● PERENNIAL

NEW YORK ● LONDON ● TORONTO ● SYDNEY ● NEW DELHI ● AUCKLAND

HARPER ● PERENNIAL

HarperCollins books may be purchased for educational, business, or sales promotional use. For information, please email the Special Markets Department at SPsales@harpercollins.com.

FIRST EDITION

Designed by Jen Overstreet

Library of Congress Cataloging-in-Publication Data has been applied for.

ISBN 978-0-06-305083-9

22 23 24 25 26   LSC   10 9 8 7 6 5 4 3 2 1

For my mother, the only "It" girl I recognize.

Contents

Introduction

WHEN I WAS fourteen, I made a pilgrimage—to see a dress. It was by Yohji Yamamoto, a white gown dubbed "the Secret Dress," with a hoop skirt and zip-away compartments from which the runway model unfurled a cardigan, hat, and gloves. I just wanted to look at it up close, as a piece of engineering. The salespeople could tell that I wasn't exactly in the market for the dress—I looked about eleven years old at the time. They made the quick calculations that I was probably *not* a wealthy avant-garde child bride, and very politely asked me to take a large step back.

It was my first close encounter with runway fashion that didn't come through either the pages of a magazine or a computer screen. I've always been fixated on this strange, perverse little world, to the point where I made a career out of it. I'm probably, at this point, an incurable case. I never really know what to say when people tell me they don't care about fashion, or that it doesn't affect them: They wear all black. They just wear hoodies, or yoga pants, everywhere. They can't be bothered!

The first assertion may be true—you certainly don't *have* to care about fashion, the same way you don't have to care about contemporary fiction, the art world, SoundCloud rap, or making your own sourdough bread. The difference between those realms and fashion, of course, is that with fashion, you have no choice *but* to opt in—even if you're reading this in a nudist colony, you'll probably have to put on clothes at some point to, like, go to the DMV. And yet, fashion is still too often seen as superficial, as trivial, or only taken seriously as an art form when it's the most rarefied of couture.

Even if your wardrobe is as dark as Lydia Deetz's soul, even if you exclusively wear athleisure, even if you consciously don't put a lot of thought into what you put on your body—which, to be clear, is perfectly fine—I am here to tell you that you are making a statement of some kind. Even being anti-fashion is, in itself, a fashion statement. Ultimately, fashion isn't so much a choice as a system that we all live under and are behaving in reaction to—like the weather, the Kardashians, or late capitalism.

Some of the dismissal of fashion comes from a place of sexism, mixed with homophobia—straight men are by far the most likely to tell me that they think fashion is for shallow people. No one thinks it's shallow to care about sports, cars, or video games, but fashion is still seen as a frivolous domain, mainly because it's long been considered the domain of women and gay men. Thankfully, that attitude is dying out, and more and more straight men are embracing *la mode*. (Have you seen the lines outside Supreme?)

The other, more defensible critique is that it's a shallow and elitist industry that, like the snottiest of high school cliques, excludes people who don't fit in. And that is . . . not entirely false. The industry as a whole has a long way to go when it comes to fully embracing racial and size diversity, among many other forms of diversity. The clothes shown on runways are often expensive and can seem irrelevant to one's everyday life. Trying to emulate the trends seen there can be intimidating—what if I'm wearing the wrong thing? What if I make a mistake? Do these culottes look dumb?

At one point in my life, shortly before the Yohji pilgrimage, I shared this view. In high school, I was a) an avowed Marxist, b) heavily involved in the experimental theater world, and c) insufferable (see a and b). But when I wasn't doing things like founding a "people's theater group" as an alternative to my school's existing theater club, I started taking trips to the library to pore over fashion magazines and following Fashion Week from afar on sites like Style.com. I was still reconciling my politics with my consumerist urges, and while I might have disapproved of capitalism, and still do, and shopped mainly at thrift stores, it didn't mean that I wasn't interested in capital-F fashion. It just felt very remote—I didn't know anyone who worked in design or media, and no one really seemed to care about the designers I was interested in.

What ultimately made me fall in love with fashion was the creativity, inclusiveness, and progressive viewpoints I have found there. Caring about how you dress and following the runway shows doesn't have to mean, as I once feared, being shallow and elitist. My favorite designers—people like Rei Kawakubo, Miguel Adrover, and Alexander McQueen—didn't come from a place of on-high privilege, but instead set their sights on dismantling our expectations about what beauty and "cool" could look like. At its best, fashion still has the power to be revolutionary and world-changing, and it's a stage that allows us to experiment with who we want to become. Even if you're a total skeptic, you can appreciate that power.

The way fashion works is changing, too, and many of the old signifiers are falling away. We've been told that millennials favor experiences over things, but things still indubitably matter. Now elitism can look like a hoodie and track pants, depending on the context (like in Silicon Valley, for example). In the essays that follow, I'll examine what status and luxury mean to a generation that sees those concepts in an utterly different way than their precursors did.

Even those of us who purport to not spend much mental energy on it ultimately care about how we dress and how we present ourselves. Style gives us clues about everything from class to which in-group we belong to, and we dismiss it at our peril. I want to take it seriously as a force in everyone's lives and examine why it is, ultimately, so crucial to our self-actualization.

Everything—from societal changes to the progress (or lack thereof) of women's rights to the hidden motivations behind what we wear to align ourselves with a social group—can be tracked through clothing. As I say later in these pages, style reveals a society's hidden obsessions, including ones we might not be attuned to. When we buy something, what are we really buying into? How does fashion intersect with late capitalism and technology? And how are values like feminism, empowerment, and individuality being appropriated to sell us things?

These essays will examine the way that fashion overlaps with our daily lives—not the dizzying heights of a runway show, but the clothing we actually wear: what it reveals about how we see ourselves and how others see us. They will also look at how the fashion imagery we see every day shapes our identities.

Over the course of the narrative, I'll examine questions like: Why has the "French girl" persisted as our most undying archetype? As a woman, what does "dressing for yourself" really mean? How should a female politician dress? Will gender-differentiated fashion go the way of the dinosaur? How has social media affected and warped our sense of self-presentation when it comes to fashion, and how are we styling ourselves expressly for it?

My premise here is that fashion is a key—it unlocks questions of power, sexuality, and class, tapping into history and sending signals to the world around us. It means something. Even if you're "just" wearing jeans and a T-shirt.

Dress Code

PART I

Underpinnings

Why We Wear
What We
Wear

CHAPTER ONE

Think Pink

IN THE SUMMER of 2016, I started to see a predominant shade bubbling up on everything that was marketed to me. Rather than being some dictated-from-on-high runway "color of the season," this was something aimed at the masses, backgrounding subway ads and fronting book covers as well as the windows of high-end boutiques.

It was a variation on the pink shade I'd always associated with girlhood, not necessarily *my* girlhood, but the concept at large. But instead of being the saccharine Barbie pink that brings to mind a disembodied squeal of "Accessories sold separately!" it was a weirdly desaturated hue that seemed stripped of all associations with bubblegum and *Sweet Valley High* book spines. I saw it on tubes of Glossier makeup, on the walls of the newly sprouted women's club The Wing, and on what felt like every Instagrammable book aimed at women in my cohort—late twenties and early thirties—from *Sweetbitter* to *#GIRLBOSS*.

The color seemed to defy the generally accepted order of fashion, where a trend trickles down from high to low (think of the famous "cerulean speech" from *The Devil Wears Prada*) or trickles *up* from low to high (think of high fashion's recent embrace of everything from sweatsuits to Crocs). Instead, it came from seemingly nowhere, and quickly blanketed every tier of design. Everything from the high-end Swedish brand Acne Studios to subway ads for Thinx period underwear used some variation of this shade.

After my then-coworkers at The Cut, *New York* magazine's women's vertical, started discussing the phenomenon, I wrote an essay for the site examining the idea, attempting to separate this strain of the color from the pure Elle Woods version. "The titration of actual pinkness varies a little, but it's still a fairly narrow spectrum—from salmon mousse to gravlax," I wrote. "It's a non-color that doesn't commit, whose semi-ugliness is proof of its sophistication." I was just trying to tease out a cultural curiosity, but along the way, I ended up stumbling into coining the term "millennial pink," a phrase that has gone on to make untold millions for . . . people who are not me.

In the story, I traced the phenomenon to a generational mood of "ambivalent girliness." Women my age were starting to embrace the gendered tics we'd been told would hold us back in the workplace, like vocal fry or punctuating phrases with "like" and "um." Now we could take pleasure in makeup—provided it was the kind that skimmed, rather than spackled, a canvas of perfect skin, and that came with collectible stickers. We could be bosses, though we'd probably use the awkward portmanteau "girlboss," so as not to threaten anyone. We could lead while wearing sweatshirts and sneakers and nail art in that hyper-identifiable shade of curdled pink.

The designer Rachel Antonoff has made a point of dressing cool, feminist women like Aubrey Plaza, Jenny Slate, and Alia Shawkat (often in pink), and has held fashion shows with sleepover and school-dance themes that explicitly reference girlhood. Antonoff told me she sees this new wave of pink as a way of "reclaiming something that . . . was maybe thought of before as too girly." When she was younger, "it was imprinted on me that it was cool to be one of the guys and to not be girly . . . to not be too feminine. A phrase that I have been thinking a lot about lately, which is just rife in pop culture and films, is a man [saying] to a woman: 'You're not like other girls.' And that drives me fucking insane. Let me tell you who I'm exactly like: Every girl I ever thought was cool or smart or fun or funny. Why is that a compliment? Because that's not a compliment that women give to men." She sees this wave of pink as a way to "reclaim these things that we thought made us less serious, less to-be-reckoned-with . . . and say 'No, we can be serious and like pink.' "

There are certainly things to embrace about this color, but a lot of its more questionable aspects got power-washed away by the frantic media coverage. Most people who've used the phrase "millennial pink" did not learn about it from my essay, but even I was surprised at how divorced the term became from its origin. I saw little analysis of its negative connotations. It had been reduced purely to its consumerist id: "Here are more things to buy in this color you love!"

Only a few months after I wrote the story, the phrase, which I'd initially used to define a much narrower color range, had entered the lexicon, like "normcore" before it. It had come to encompass everything from straight-up pastel pink to Fran Drescher magenta. My lazy coinage had gone viral, and pink's hegemony was complete. My life quickly became a chromatically themed *Groundhog Day*. I got daily press releases pointing me to the best "millennial pink" artwork, snacks, Airbnbs, and blushes. People at parties explained the definition to me, usually incorrectly. I went to a pink-branded Pilates studio that, like so many things in this hue, seemed to exist mostly for Instagram; its wan rosy lights, embedded in small, shrine-like structures in its walls, lit us as we studiously planked. I went to an all-pink restaurant in Nolita where the food was, mercifully, not pink. (At least, I remember thinking, my insides could be shielded from this scourge.) Even when I went to Disneyland, not my idea of a hotbed of bleeding-edge cool, they were selling millennial pink Mickey ears, which might have been the breaking point for me. Everywhere I turned, I was swaddled in pink, as sticky with it as though I'd stepped in bubblegum, longing for the embrace of a cool blue or green.

It had started to feel as though the color itself was a shorthand directed at an entire generational cohort, shrieking "Buy me!" And as with any trend, there were hangers-on, too: attempts to make millennial teal, purple, and even something called "Gen Z yellow" happen. As far as I can tell, they didn't. We've cycled through the many spokes of the color wheel, but pink has hung on, trapping us all in sickeningly sweet stasis. Like people on an endless layover, we're stuck here for a while.

Who is "we"? Well, there have been other color trends that swept an entire generation: the baby blue of Hard Candy's Sky nail polish that dominated the mid-'90s, the aerobics-evoking neons of the '80s. But I've rarely encountered a visual phenomenon that felt so generically aimed at an entire demographic. Like pinstripes to a yuppie or a Lacoste croc to a prepster, the shade came to stand for an entire generation's and gender's worldview—the Lena Dunham of colors.

The color pink didn't always telegraph "girl." It was only in the 1940s that parents began to differentiate boys' and girls' clothes by color, and not till the '80s and '90s, when millennials were growing up, that various shades of pink ran riot on every holiday season's It toy aimed at girls (see: Pretty Pretty Princess, Little Miss Makeup, Dream Phone, Mall Madness. For Barbie, a special Pantone shade, #219C, was copyrighted). But by the time I was a young adult, pink had full-fledged connotations of not just female, but *young*. Vapid. Incompetent. Clueless (in the Horowitzian sense). It was not a color you'd wear to be taken seriously at your job. Elle

Woods wore it. So did the Plastics (on Wednesdays, at least). So when it came creeping back into our consciousness, pink had an almost return-of-the-repressed quality, oozing through the brick wall of social conditioning, defying the demand that it be put away like so many other childish things.

Its semi-familiarity was part of its appeal. Think about the trappings of millennial pink culture—the stickers, the crop tops, the high-end jelly shoes, the many gingham things. What are they but our childhood favorites, repackaged into something palatable to our adult selves?

Revisiting my original story, the whole phenomenon feels more insidious than I once thought, especially as I consider how the past few years have unfolded. When I first wrote about millennial pink, I thought it represented a kind of half step on the part of women toward embracing, not apologizing for, our gender—an improvement on cloaking ourselves in shoulder-padded blazers and trying to be permanently in corporate costume, the way our mothers' generation did in the '80s. It was a rebuff to the *Lean In* school of feminism, which encouraged us to subsume those feminine-coded traits in service of climbing the ladder. Now, I'm not so sure.

The color came to stand in for a softer, non-confrontational strain of feminism, wherein women proclaimed their inclusivity while joining exclusive clubs and buying expensive signifiers of sisterhood, like a $650 sweater with a patch that reads RADICAL FEMINIST. How different, really, were these items from the dolls and tutus and teacups we were sold as children? And if we were so committed to wholeheartedly loving pink, why did we still swerve away from the saccharine side of it?

I think the association with childhood is crucial here. For many women in their twenties and thirties, adult life has not delivered on CEO Barbie's promises. Those of us who graduated from college are mostly saddled with student loans, underpaying gig-economy jobs supplemented by side hustles, and limited prospects for the future. (And that's if we're lucky!) Add to that the challenges of succeeding as a woman in the workplace, from the pernicious (sexual harassment, the gender pay gap) to the everyday irritants (men taking credit for our ideas). Meanwhile, we're being told we can achieve anything, and that if we haven't achieved all we wanted, it's our fault for being weak or unmarketable or insufficiently self-promotional. Why don't we have more Instagram followers or a more finely honed personal brand? We are transitional figures, vessels stuffed with empty empowerment, launched into an environment that hasn't caught up to that idealized vision of gender equality.

With all this in mind, who wouldn't long for the prosperous years of our childhoods, and instinctively be drawn to anything reminding us of them? The color's popularity can be read as the incomplete embrace of full-on femininity. No, we shouldn't be ashamed of being girls. But we also shouldn't be ashamed of being women.

Fashion and consumption can bring legitimate joy, and I don't necessarily begrudge anyone their millennial pink bucket bags. It's fun to have what everyone else has, and even smart people secretly enjoy being marketed to. But I wonder if this period in fashion history, with its toothless pastels and sweet, ruffled, Regency-style minidresses, will come to be seen as analogous to the '80s fashion backlash against strong-shouldered power suits worn with sneakers.

If you're young enough to be getting millennial pink nail art, you weren't sentient for this moment. But if you're older, you may remember that fashion reached a crisis point in the early half of that decade. Women began buying less clothing, preferring to budget for practical line items like homes and cars. Into this void came designers like Christian Lacroix, who began offering enormous, restrictive gowns complete with bustles, with prices topping out in the mid-five figures. Susan Faludi, writing about Lacroix's collections in *Backlash*, her seminal work about the one-step-forward-two-steps-back landscape of 1980s feminism, called the style High Femininity. Lacroix said he designed for women who want to "dress up like little girls." Faludi, being a third-waver, preferred the phrase "punitively restrictive clothing."

As with today, the trend was accompanied by a political rollback of women's freedoms, bent on legally reducing them to impotent childhood. But the difference is that back then, the infantilization thing did not play. Yes, socialites swanned around in Lacroix's designs, enjoying their Marie-Antoinette-at-the-*hameau* quality. But women, for the most part, did not want to dress up like Little Bo Peep, and the mass-market versions of Lacroix's confections lingered on department store racks.

Now, we've entered the stealth sequel to this period, what you might call High Femininity 2.0. But this time, the crucial difference is that women are buying in: to ruffles, to rompers, to all manner of smocked things straight out of an '80s Laura Ashley catalog. If there's a loose equivalent of Lacroix in these times, it would be the designer Batsheva Hay, who makes Laura Ingalls Wilder–esque dresses apparently designed for traversing the plains of Williamsburg and fording the Gowanus Canal. Like Lacroix's Marie Antoinette–evoking frippery, they look back to vague memories of a simpler, "less complicated" time. There's no frontier left, but her designs are a form of frontier nostalgia; to some commentators, they have evoked homesteading or Fundamentalist Latter-Day Saints (FLDS) garb.

These looks have a kind of hazy, appealing familiarity, too. They harken back to the vogue for lacy, frilly Gunne Sax and Jessica McClintock dresses that peaked in the late '80s and early '90s along with the craze for American Girl dolls—again, the formative years of so many millennials. On Instagram, Alexa Chung called her high-necked, ruffled look "A throwback Friday, if you will (to the 1800s.)" Molly Fischer, writing in *New York* magazine, said that trendy prairie dresses "offer conventional girliness drained of any prettiness, any elegance, any beauty: a gender norm codified as its homeliest possible husk." Sounds like the sartorial version of millennial pink.

The prairie look has come back at a time when the ironic distance between dress-up and reality has narrowed. Abortion rights are being rolled back; the gender pay gap has barely budged. In a more progressive time, reverting to signifiers of old-fashioned repression might feel like an interesting choice; right now, it's getting harder to separate the hipsters from the handmaids.

We're in a time where traditional femininity has been repackaged as cool, as chill, as "woke." The all-things-pink beauty brand Glossier commands us to be a body diversity–embracing "Body Hero" as part of its lotion campaign; The Wing (with an influx of series B funding from corporate giant WeWork) was touted to be "reviving the radical women's club movement," according to a *Vice* story. (What, exactly, is radical about an institution that costs more than $2,000 a year?) One of the most confounding things about the pink-tinted economy is the way it's selling back existing things to us and making them "new," painting them as essentials of self-actualization and empowerment. An elite women's club isn't new. Nor is makeup. Nor is a modest floral garment. Nor is pink. What we have here is a rebranding of the reactionary.

This kind of virtue signaling, in tandem with a lack of real progress, is part and parcel of the pink-tinted economy. The railroad barons of the Gilded Age would never have said, "We're building cross-country rail lines to make connections and bring like-minded people together." But now, especially in the world of tech, their contemporary heirs make these kinds of faux-philanthropic statements as a matter of course. And while these companies might align themselves with values you agree with, at the end of the day they still just want to sell you a ticket. The CEOs of supposedly female-friendly companies are—whoops!—sometimes still guilty of denying employees maternity leave. Meet the new girlboss, same as the old boss.

The writer Ann Friedman has talked about the insidiousness of this idea, coining the phrase "millennial pinkwashing," which she defined on Twitter as "when you take an established feminist concept and drape it in pale-pink startup branding and sell it off to sponsors, ideally companies that are selling women fitness, beauty products, or corporate advancement." Friedman and the writer Aminatou Sow had coined the term "shine theory," which they define as "a commitment to collaborating with rather than competing against other people—especially other women" back in 2013, and Friedman explains that she was frustrated that a phrase they came up with had been co-opted without credit by various corporate entities. (I can relate.)

I called Friedman to ask more about her thinking. "I started noticing more recently that [millennial pink] has become the signifying color of choice for what I would call 'empowertising' organizations," she said, noting that that term is itself a coinage by the writer Andi Zeisler. "It's not like I'm the first person to say, 'Look at the ways capitalism is taking feminism and using it to sell stuff.' But the color is strongly associated with the kinds of companies, conferences, platforms that market themselves to creative-slash-entrepreneurial millennial women and promise information about getting ahead in your career . . . Ultimately they're selling brand integrations, brands that want to be in front of young women whose earning power is increasing. But it's framed very much as, 'We're doing this for feminism.' It's kind of the background color for quotes about getting what's yours."

Friedman quickly clarifies that she doesn't have a problem

with being a feminist who wants to learn how to advance her career. But "when you frame advancing your individual career as some sort of movement work, I get a little prickly about it," she says. "The kind of women who are likely to be in the demo for platforms like this are probably attracted to certain Instagram design tropes that you and I are both very familiar with, and this color is a big part of it." She draws a comparison to the pink ribbon—branded merchandise that is used to advertise breast cancer awareness, sometimes by companies who are contributing to that very disease with carcinogen-ridden products. Their philosophy seems to be, "Hey, if we put this color on it, it's good for women—and don't ask any more questions."

Beyond the corporate appropriation of the color, there's also what it has come to signify in terms of politics. Millennial pink came along at a strange time. It began cresting toward the end of the optimistic Obama era, but after Trump's election and the formation of the "resistance," it became interwoven with, and sometimes a stand-in for, a kind of muffled dissent. I'll never forget visiting LA in November 2016, right after the election, and browsing through the woman-owned boutique Otherwild with a friend. We picked through the sweatshirts reading THE FUTURE IS FEMALE, which suddenly felt like a callow phrase, and the assorted pins and T-shirts and overpriced pink signifiers of the newly awakened. Nearly half of white women voters went for Trump, and this merch seemed like an expensive way to telegraph that you were not one of them. *Was this*, I thought, *protest?*

If you want further proof that High Femininity 2.0 has officially entered the political sphere, just look at the most notable fashion moment the resistance produced. Resistance movements have always incorporated fashion, but unlike with past protest waves, the signature look of the mainstream resister isn't riot gear, a balaclava, or even a slogan T-shirt. It's the cute, twin-eared "pussyhat" worn by Women's March protesters—cuddly, marketable, and, yes, bright pink.

The hordes who came out to march in their knitted headwear weren't described as angry or radical, the way Black Lives Matter protesters often were; they weren't ridiculed as wacky lefties or layabouts, the way Occupy Wall Street had been some years before. That was, in part, because the crowd was largely white, upper-middle class, and new to protest. (Note the much-circulated photo of Los Angeles protester Amir Talai with a sign that said, "I'll see you nice white ladies at the next #BlackLivesMatter march, right?") But it was also because of their accessories: hats that served as a homespun repudiation of 2016's other political headwear, the standard-issue Make America Great Again caps. With the home-knitted headwear, as folksy and old-fashioned as a Batsheva smock, protesters turned a dialogue about President Trump's misogynistic statements bragging about sexual assault on women into a craft project. In a way, this felt like the ultimate triumph of pinkwashing. Just like a salmon-hued conference backdrop, a corporate salute to International Women's Day, or the Fearless Girl statue—put in place by an investment management firm—confronting Wall Street's famous bull, a mass outcry against our government had been crystallized within the form of something tame, purchasable, and—what else?—pink.

What changed between the eras of High Femininity 1.0 and 2.0? For one thing, we've never consumed in such a visible way before. Clothes and makeup used to be the primary products with which we expressed ourselves. Instagram exploded that notion. Things previously only known to close friends or significant others, like the brand of underwear you wear, the plants in your home, your workout regimen, the freelance workspaces you choose, or the bath accoutrements and night cream you use, are now public, potentially politically freighted pieces of information. They're the particles that form the atomic structure of your personal brand. And God forbid you're sleeping on a non-woke mattress or using an electric toothbrush that doesn't stand in support of Elizabeth Warren's policies.

It might seem that we're freer now, but we are being asked to measure up in more ways. To keep up with the digital Joneses, we now have to buy and perform self-care, social responsibility, and empowerment. And politics and ideology have never intersected so much with, well, our stuff.

If you're a certain kind of liberal, coastal millennial, the protest you go to is of a piece with the sheet mask you use. Both are signifiers of the person you profess to be—socially aware, practicing self-care but not to the point of self-involvement, up-to-the-minute in terms of both skincare and politics. Consider it the "pics or it didn't happen" approach to personal growth.

The status signifiers of today may not be as obvious or as luxe as they were in the Gilded Age, but when social currency requires constant self-reinvention and measuring up, it takes effort to have the perfectly curated bookshelf, the photo-ready medicine cabinet, and the time to spend on self-actualization and self-improvement. For people in this privileged class, social media has become an opt-in surveillance state where how pretty and how good you are are constantly conflated. There have never been so many ways to express yourself—but there have also never been so many ways to be uncool and inadequate.

Of course, keeping pace with this parallel self, who is always morally correct and always perfectly lit, becomes a form of toil in itself. And constantly striving to make the "right" consumer choices arguably distracts us from the unglamorous, real work of changing the world.

Remember the you-go-girl ads for Virginia Slims cigarettes? They feel light-years removed from the campaigns of today, and not just because they're for a product we all know is carcinogenic. The template was simple: sepia photo of oppressed woman from the past—usually wearing some kind of bustle—overlaid with a full-color shot of the present-day, liberated babe. "First, you got the right to vote, and now you've got a cigarette all your own," was one caption, in which suffrage and the "right" to buy a product are weirdly conflated. Of course, other than their modish thinness, they were basically the same as standard cigarettes. ("Cancer—but for GIRLS!") Even the tagline—"You've come a long way, baby."—fell somewhere between gruff admiration and infantilizing condescension.

That broad approach wouldn't work today; we would see right through it. But it formed the playbook for today's millennial pink-washing. Is the empowertising we see now really that different from what came before it? We live in a world of feminist underwear that wants to salute *you* on International Women's Day and empowered razors whose makers think it's totally cool, actually, if you prefer to grow out your body hair, even if it cuts into their bottom line. It seems we haven't come such a long way (baby) after all.

Even the social justice movement recently took a page from this playbook, employing pastel-hued Instagram tiles that outlined steps to, say, defund the police. Abstruse concepts were made palatable through design, in a process akin to embedding spinach in a cupcake. You needed to squint at your screen to tell the difference between a direct-to-consumer deodorant brand and an instruction manual for dismantling the police state. Whatever the content of these infographics—some were clear and concise, while others possessed only a distant-cousin relationship to facts—it was as though the intended audience for these messages could no longer absorb them unless they were presented *like this*, swathed in the fondant of peachy backdrops and swooping serif fonts. The medium wasn't just the message; it had swallowed the message whole.

I had long thought the neoliberal version of this aesthetic, steeped as it was in a wishy-washy, consumerist centrism, was irritating enough. Then, a Faludi-esque backlash swept this array of dim pastels along with it, and they began turning up in decidedly-not-progressive quarters. When some NBC employees tried to unionize, an Instagram account, purportedly created by a group of anti-union staffers, popped up. The artist Molly Crabapple summed up the vibe as "Millennial Pinkerton," referring to the agency hired by employers to infiltrate labor strikes beginning in the late 1800s. The posts included an illustration of women's hands, in different skin tones, all forming the peace sign against a calm salmon backdrop and the slogan "Women's Healthcare." It looked, at first glance—and, in this context, first glance was all that counted—like an ad for a woke gynecologist's office, but it was actually trying to stoke fears that a union would take away benefits like maternity leave.

The moment I realized we were officially living in a simulation was when millennial pink and its siblings on the color wheel began being used to launder QAnon conspiracy theories pushed by lithe influencers of the yoni-egg variety. This sensibility was pervasive enough that academic Marc-André Argentino coined the term "pastel QAnon" to describe it. The inverse of bellicose masculine aesthetics, none of these posts featured warlike eagles or brightly colored flags. Instead, they'd been polished to a high gloss, rendered as colorful and gulpable as a gummy vitamin. They were designed to appeal to a young, female audience poised to lap up wellness tips, parenting content—and the occasional Pizzagate conspiracy, child-trafficking theory, or anti-vax screed along with them. In one typical example cited by Argentino, an arrangement of pink and white balloons, the kind you might see at a baby shower, spelling out "COVID IS OVER" (it wasn't), stands against a millennial pink background. The accompanying text urges us to "Open up our country" and insists on "No masks." The image was persuasive to its intended audience in a way that a cardboard sign bearing the same message in Sharpie would not be. Another said, in the kind of curvy, slightly groovy orange font that might once have adorned the cover of a '60s consciousness-raising manual, "wayfair scandal" (capital letters would evidently have been too strident) followed by "What You Need to Know," before devolving into the child-trafficking conspiracy centered around a popular furniture website.

Mimicking the structure and design of social justice posts that broke down, say, "10 Steps to Non-Optical Allyship," this imagery seemed aimed at an audience that might consider themselves liberal, or simply apolitical, but was open to "just asking questions." Its populist success coasted on the wake of similarly designed graphics featuring morally good-to-neutral things. I had assumed the style would just fall out of favor eventually, not metamorphose into something troubling. But now completely opposed ideologies had visually melted into one another in a way that made me think about the banality of evil. It wasn't that the aesthetic itself was evil, of course; it was that, like all aesthetics, it had gone from novel to trite, and its newfound banality was able to cloak any horrors that might be smuggled into it. We had now arrived at a point where everything looked alike, regardless of what it meant.

Stumbling across one of these posts always resulted in a thunderclap of cognitive dissonance. Ultimately, millennial pink under some other name would have triumphed without my input. I felt no ownership of, or claim to, the color; I was merely there as a chronicler. Yet I did feel strangely culpable every time I saw the next step in its evolution, from stealth capitalism to earnest neoliberalism to stealth fascism; it was like watching a dimly remembered classmate cycle through a series of increasingly incoherent ideologies before landing squarely on the worst one. When a group of people espousing assorted far-right views succeeded in battering their way into Congress, I saw a number of women among them, and wondered how many had been radicalized by something they saw in a pastel square.

CHAPTER TWO

The Kids Are Alright

W HEN I STARTED high school, I first encountered a New York–suburb variant of preppy style—a North Face puffer open over a Ralph Lauren polo shirt or Abercrombie & Fitch T-shirt. In college, I met its New England ancestor—irony-free Nantucket red slacks, whale accoutrements, and liberal usage of grosgrain. Prep did not strike me, at the time, as a style in itself. It felt like the default setting—something to rebel against. The only problem with constructing the perfect anti-prep identity was this: I didn't really know who I was, other than not a WASP and not rich. So I teetered through fashion phases: the anarchist with duct-taped jeans, the neo-hippie in crochet, the emo kid in gloves made from cutoff argyle socks. I salvaged clothes from the floor of a Boston establishment called Dollar a Pound, cut them up, dyed them, and turned them into costumes for my itinerant identity. I may have spent less in actual dollars than my nattily attired classmates, but in terms of labor—the fashion equivalent of a vinyl snob's crate-digging—

I was expending more. I put more effort into my anti-fashion than my supposedly fashionable peers.

I know I'm far from alone in this—adolescence is made for shrugging on different identities, and clothing is the easiest way to express those identities. Unless you're Madonna, most of us don't get to reinvent ourselves over and over again in adult life. For many of us, high school is our first fashion battleground, and the first time that class really starts to impact our dressing choices. Every American high school movie worth its salt has a scene in the cafeteria, that teenage agora, where a school's ecosystem is skimmed and summed up, its cliques and rivalries revealed through fashion. In *Mean Girls*, part of the joke was the hyper-specificity of each group: cool Asians, sexually active band geeks, and so forth. A 2019 Twitter meme showed a cartoon cafeteria and asked, "Where are you sitting?" based on your taste in everything from emo music to runway fashion. Most of the people participating were not currently in high school.

The idea of cliques persists, even after graduation. One of the ways those cliques define themselves in relation to, and sometimes against, one another is fashion. Style has always been an easy way of setting yourself apart and forging an alliance with others. And youth fashion subcultures, from hippie to punk to grunge (and all the infinite mini-categories within those categories), have been a way to assert oneself, to push gender and class boundaries and highlight the generational divide.

The idea of teenage-specific clothing is a relatively recent invention. For most of human history, you were a child, then you were an adult, with the attendant uniforms. "Teenager" became a category of person, requiring specific clothing, after World War II, when teen idols like Ricky Nelson and Annette Funicello began to model different kinds of teen-specific style and entertainment. A youth monoculture began to coalesce, and with it a number of opposed youth subcultures—Mods, rockers, and later, punks, goths, metalheads, and emo/"scene" kids among them. The history of teen style is really two parallel histories—the dominant culture doggedly pursued by a number of opposed subcultures.

Let's start with the former. Teen style, first dominated by T-shirts, jeans, and varsity jackets, made a quick detour into the aspirational. In the '80s, preppy labels like Ralph Lauren and Lacoste dominated. True preps had their own ways of distinguishing themselves; an advanced preppy move was to rip out the crocodile logo on your Lacoste polo, leaving only the outline—the ultimate sign that you didn't care about status, except you still did, because everyone could see what had once been there.

Abercrombie & Fitch, an outdoor outfitter founded in the 1890s, became the preppy teen brand of choice in the '90s, under then-CEO Mike Jeffries, and crested in the early 2000s, becoming almost synonymous with the era's teen style. The new Abercrombie bore virtually no resemblance to the original. Instead of clothes for horseback riding and hunting, there were now uniforms for mall cruising. The store published a magazine, *A&F Quarterly*, complete with homoerotic photo shoots by Bruce Weber and highbrow contributors: The philosopher Slavoj Žižek contributed display copy to one issue.

The brand wasn't shy about the fact that, like high school cliques, it was built on exclusion. "In every school there are the cool and popular kids, and then there are the not-so-cool kids," Jeffries told Salon's Benoit Denizet-Lewis. "Candidly, we go after the cool kids. We go after the attractive all-American kid with a great attitude and a lot of friends. A lot of people don't belong [in our clothes], and they can't belong. Are we exclusionary? Absolutely." He added that the brand only hired "good-looking" people. "Good-looking people attract other good-looking people, and we want to market to cool, good-looking people. We don't market to anyone other than that." Abercrombie's Look Policy contained specifications about employees' hair, makeup, and nails. The store's definition of "All-American" looks seemingly did not encompass non-white people at the time. A 2003 lawsuit alleged that employees of color were relegated to working in the stockroom as opposed to the sales floor. A later suit, which went all the way to the Supreme Court, concerned a young Muslim woman who was not hired by the store after being told her hijab violated its Look Policy.

A&F also courted controversy with a series of T-shirt slogans, notably in 2002 when it was forced to recall a T-shirt that read WONG BROTHERS LAUNDRY SERVICE—TWO WONGS CAN MAKE IT WHITE, after an outcry from Asian-American groups. Unbelievably, Abercrombie's spokesman responded, "We personally thought Asians would love this T-shirt. . . . We never single out any one group to poke fun at. We poke fun at everybody, from women to flight attendants to baggage handlers, to football coaches, to Irish Americans to snow skiers. There's really no group we haven't teased." Somehow, you got the sense that snow skiers were not really the primary group they were trying to exclude.

Today we still have brands that replicate that exclusionary mood. The "one-size-fits-most" emporium Brandy Melville is a perfect example. While it originated in Italy, the brand has an American, Southern California vibe—abetted by the actual teens who make up its "product research team." With a lack of size diversity (items are labeled "one size" or "small") and racial diversity (the girls showcased on its Instagram account are predominantly white), the store predicates itself on exclusion—if you're not one of the "most," you can, as the catty *Mean Girls* line goes, always try Sears. Also like Abercrombie & Fitch, they've been accused of shady hiring practices. A post on Glassdoor read: "Your pay rate is 100% determined by looks."

The label also seems to have a fascination with, of all people,

Ayn Rand. You might be thinking, What does the author of *Atlas Shrugged* have to do with Lilliputian tube tops? Well, Brandy Melville once had a sister brand named John Galt, after the hero of *Atlas Shrugged*, and according to a story in The Cut, "Early stores apparently sold copies of *Atlas Shrugged*, *Commentary* magazine, and publications from the Heritage Foundation and Cato Institute—a little libertarian, freedom-of-choice ideology slipped ironically in between lavender bike shorts and plaid miniskirts that only come in a single size." A cropped T-shirt sold by the brand in 2014 featured, in the kind of font that usually proclaims "Live, Laugh, Love," the quote THE QUESTION ISN'T WHO IS GOING TO LET ME; IT'S WHO IS GOING TO STOP ME.—AYN RAND. (This rousing slogan turns out to be a misquote jumbled together with dialogue from Rand's other major work, *The Fountainhead*.) The Rand fixation does make a bizarre kind of sense, given that her Objectivist ideology prioritizes "rational egoism" above concerns about fairness. In this dominant teen culture, if you're not among the favored "most," you're out of luck.

As this style monoculture has unfolded, multiple subcultures have been running in opposition to it. The inherent contradiction of a style subculture is that you're rejecting the monoculture by dressing differently, but within your group you're also dressing alike—there is a sense of belonging and family, of "us against the world." A style subculture isn't an individual pursuit—it's a microcosm of the larger culture, defined in opposition to it and in some sense defined *by* it. Which is why sometimes the rebellion involved can feel reflexive. In the 1953 movie *The Wild One*, someone asks Marlon Brando's tough biker character, "What are you rebelling against?" and he responds, "Whaddaya got?"

As teen culture rose, so did subcultures that were meant to oppose the "straight" world, self-sustaining biospheres with their own accompanying music, slang, drugs, and, of course, fashion. Despite their rebellious nature, these groups exhibited a kind of conformity among their members that felt similar to the dominant culture. More than that, belonging to a group—even if the group is "those weirdos who wear safety pins on everything"—takes the pressure off its members to do the much harder work of figuring out who they *really* are.

In the '50s, the beatnik subculture was born of a postwar weariness. "[Beat] implies the feeling of having been used, of being raw," John Clellon Holmes wrote in a 1952 *New York Times* story, a kind of proto-explainer on the culture. Beatniks made an intellectual anti-fashion (or really "above-fashion") statement: They dressed in monotone clothing that was a rejection of the cheery, colorful, hourglass-fitted 1950s norm. They wore their hair long and unstyled, in opposition to the helmetlike salon hairdos of the era. Everything they did, in fact, went against the prevailing '50s tastes: They favored jazz over radio hits, poetry over teen magazines, and marijuana over a can of beer. They cherry-picked facets of Black culture to adopt, particularly jazz and bebop, and co-opted the teachings of Eastern religions. Soon enough, the term became a marketing tool aimed at those trying to emulate the beatnik's countercultural cachet. Joyce Johnson recalls in her Beat memoir, *Minor Characters*, that the term "sold books, sold black turtleneck sweaters and bongos, berets and dark glasses, sold a way of life that seemed like dangerous fun—thus to be either condemned or imitated."

Meanwhile, in the UK, a raft of subcultures was about to form: Mods, rockers, and teddy boys. Rockers emulated Brando's character in *The Wild One*, with leather jackets and motorcycle boots. Teddy boys dressed like Edwardian-style dandies, while Mods played with traditional British iconography like the Union Jack. The Mods' rebellion took the form of putting "square" business clothing into a new context, reimagining it for their own working-class lives, and using the Establishment's props to subtly protest it. Hippies were another subculture that borrowed stylistically from the past, especially from the Renaissance era. In a time of war and up-heaval, they made a nostalgic turn to billowing sleeves and tapes-try prints, often bought secondhand. That salt-of-the-earth style soon became fodder for plenty of high-end designers, including Yves Saint Laurent and Halston, who incorporated it into their col-lections.

Punk took that bricolage of different eras a step further. Dick Hebdige's landmark book *Subculture: The Meaning of Style* came out during the height of the punk movement, when kids everywhere were ripping up their T-shirts and festooning them with safety pins and buttons. These everyday objects, he wrote, "warn the 'straight' world in advance of a sinister presence—the presence of differ-ence." By making the quotidian look, as he put it, "sinister" in this new context, they were making clear their rejection of mass culture. They were also grappling with personal and national disruption by expressing it through clothing. Punk came about in a time of eco-nomic recession and youth uncertainty in England, and later took hold most strongly in places that were experiencing austerity, like late-'70s Los Angeles and post-Franco Spain. Its chaotic approach helped express the chaos in the larger world. "Behind punk's fa-voured 'cut ups' lay hints of disorder," Hebdige writes, "of break-down and category confusion: a desire not only to erode racial and gender boundaries but also to confuse chronological sequence by mixing up details from different periods." I realize it's not very punk to explicate this.

The punk ethos held within it a contradiction: To rebel, you have to, unlike Brando's biker, know what you're rebelling against. To upend history, you first have to know that history. Punk figures were openly influenced by long-past icons like Arthur Rimbaud (Richard Hell's *nom de punk* was inspired by one of his books) and Charles Dickens (punk impresario Malcolm McLaren drew from his work). Vivienne Westwood, the designer most associated with the punk movement, has an encyclopedic knowledge of tailoring and of art and fashion history and placed her designs, which she called "confrontation dressing," on a continuum with the Situationist art movement of the '50s and '60s, with its attention-getting "interventions." She may have sold torn-up T-shirts with Queen Elizabeth's face on them, but she was still incorporating a symbol of tradition and constancy. By defacing something, you inherently acknowledge its symbolic power. That's why Hebdige called punk's refusal "just the darker side of sets of regulations, just so much graffiti on a prison wall." It was done in the hope of a reaction. Even the punk DIY ethos originated from a traditional precedent—the idea of "make do and mend," which came from the name of a wartime pamphlet issued by the British government about ways for households to conserve clothing in an era of rationing. In a way, it was an extension of a long do-it-yourself tradition. Plus, like all subcultures, punk created an orthodoxy of its own. Only those who hewed to its rules were included, and posers, who weren't committing authentically enough to the bit, were scorned.

In the '90s, a fashion statement arose in tandem with the grunge music that was coming out of the Pacific Northwest. Flannel shirts, ripped jeans, and carelessly layered thermals went perfectly with keening choruses and scuzzy feedback. Soon, the look would show up on the runway. Marc Jacobs's famous spring 1993 collection for Perry Ellis, which resulted in his firing from the brand, was his high-end riff on the trend. This was in the heyday of supermodels, perfectly made-up and strutting in body-con ensembles, and here was Jacobs, putting Naomi Campbell and Christy Turlington in flannel shirts (made of silk) and waffle-weave thermal shirts (albeit in cashmere). They wore beanies and Doc Martens, their hair intentionally unkempt. Plenty of critics didn't know what to make of the collection. It received negative reviews from Suzy Menkes, then the fashion editor at the *International Herald Tribune*, who had

"Grunge is Ghastly" pins made up, and Cathy Horyn, then writing for the *Washington Post*, who said, "Grunge is anathema to fashion, and for a major Seventh Avenue fashion house to put out that kind of statement at that kind of price point is ridiculous." The audience found it baffling that this scruffy youth culture could be considered aspirational.

And it definitely pissed off the grunge establishment—Courtney Love has said that after Jacobs sent her and Kurt Cobain clothes from the collection, they burned them. Kathleen Hanna of Bikini Kill recalls her and her peers' reaction as, "So now some weird highfalutin fashion designer in New York is calling this grunge and you're going to go in and take over and say this is our fashion?" The way some grunge insiders framed it, it was not completely removed from what we would now call cultural appropriation: taking something that belongs to a specific culture and turning it into saleable product with no input coming from or profit going to the original inventors. (Call it subcultural appropriation.) Jacobs had somehow managed to put off both the Establishment fashion gatekeepers and the anti-Establishment kids he was trying to pay tribute to.

In a 2015 follow-up story for The Cut that I edited, Horyn thoughtfully walked back her comments on the grunge show, examining her own, and her peers', resistance to something that felt threateningly new. "More than twenty years on, I find myself questioning my own reaction to the show, the violet-scented peevishness of my tone," she wrote, adding, "I ignored, if I even considered, the charm and sweetness of the attitude—an attitude, by the way, which I happily embraced in my own brand of slob appeal." Recalling the collection that cost him the job but ultimately made his name, Jacobs told Horyn, "It went against everything that one could aspire to . . . You could say, 'I want to look like Cindy Crawford or have my hair cut like Linda Evangelista.' But you couldn't go into a shop and say, 'I want a child's Victorian dress that looks torn.' I think that's where the fear comes from."

It ultimately didn't hurt Jacobs's career—he went on, of course, to become famous and critically acclaimed. In 2018, long since vindicated, he reissued twenty-six looks from the "Grunge" collection under the name "Redux Grunge"—perfect timing, given that young musicians and actresses were beginning to turn to the grunge styles of the past as a way of pushing back against the Facetuned perfection of Instagram.

In some cases, subcultures haven't involved clothes in diametric opposition to the dominant paradigm, but rather taken the popular kids' clothes and put them in a new, subversive context. Look at the Lo Lifes, a group of Black and Latinx teens in Brooklyn in the '80s and '90s who reappropriated preppy clothing, particularly Polo Ralph Lauren (thus the "Lo"). They admired Lauren, with his Bronx origins, having built his company into a global brand. Sometimes they would "boost," or shoplift, coveted pieces. The Lo Lifes had taken a style culture—preppy—that was predicated on exclusion and reshaped it in their own image. As hip-hop journalist Bönz Malone wrote in his foreword to *Bury Me with the Lo On*, "Society told them they couldn't afford the American Dream, and they chose not to listen. They challenged classism by wearing Polo—taking something that wasn't meant for them and making it their own." The group has since spread to chapters of enthusiasts around the world, including Japan and Australia.

In recent decades, even subcultures themselves have been reappropriated, spawning new, ever-narrower categories. For example, Japanese teen culture saw the rise of groups like Gothic Lolitas or Visual Kei, which take some cues from goth and glam rock/metal, respectively. With time has come not just the splintering but the softening of subcultures: You can be a Hot Topic mall goth or a Coachella hippie, for example. As trends make the ever-shorter trip from teen subcultures to corporate fast fashion, they become, as Hebdige writes, "codified, made comprehensible, rendered at once public property and profitable merchandise." They have always been absorbed into the mainstream—the only difference now is that the process happens exponentially faster.

I think adolescents will always crave both standing out and asserting themselves while also needing to fit in somewhere. A subculture can function as a substitute family for teens who are getting ready to move away from their birth families, but years away from starting new ones of their own. That might explain why the "hipster" movement that began in the aughts and continues today extends into people in their twenties and thirties, as cultural factors like economic hardship continue to prolong youth and delay parenthood.

What will happen to style subcultures now that so much socializing happens on social media? Once, you had to see and be seen—whether at a coffeehouse in your beatnik attire, the hallowed halls of the mall in your best preppy look, or on the streets of Harajuku in your Gothic Lolita finest. All of this is changing now that social media has become the dominant method of self-expression, and what you reblog on Tumblr might be more important than what you wear. Even street style, the basis for so much fashion inspiration, is changing. *FRUiTS* magazine, which chronicled youth street style in Japan, closed down in 2017 after twenty years. Founder Shoichi Aoki said simply, "There were no more fashionable kids to photograph."

That may be true when it comes to the physical world, but fashionable kids are still thriving on the internet, and their influence goes far beyond it. There are VSCO girls, with their take on crunchy '90s eco-warrior style—Birkenstocks, scrunchies, ever-present Hydro Flask water bottles. While the archetype may look, to an outsider, like a variant on typical California-girl style, it also comes with a baked-in social consciousness. The VSCO girl's concern about climate change and reverence for nature has spilled outside the confines of the subculture and into fashion at large. Look at the rise of high-end eco-friendly design or the sudden chicness of the virtue-signaling water bottle. (Maggie Rogers carried a Chanel version to the Grammys.) The once-unfashionable crunchy-chick stereotype has been reborn, and is now something to aspire to.

Another subculture that freely intermingles past and present: e-girls and e-boys, whose style combines aspects of Japanese kawaii culture, goth, skater, and punk, all remixed in classic bricolage tradition and heavily mediated by internet culture. E-girls and e-boys are, writes Rebecca Jennings for Vox, "what would happen if you shot a teenager through the internet and they came out the other side." As with many current subcultures, they're not precious about hewing to the outdated idea of sticking to a single aesthetic. The resulting look is the fashion equivalent of having so many open tabs that your laptop starts overheating. Their hallmarks—neon hair studded with clips, makeup in Cinemascope hues, and punk-meets-anime fashion—are meant to radiate through a screen, as they broadcast from their bedrooms.

Perhaps the biggest difference between the subcultures of then and now is that instead of being tied to a region or a social class, these subcultures are linked to specific social media apps. Rather than being formed around cultural identification, like a shared genre of music, these in-groups are actually shaped by the corporate platforms they live on. E-girls and e-boys are particularly prevalent on TikTok; VSCO girls are literally named for the highly filtered photo-sharing app; and Instagram is home to "baddies" with heavily contoured makeup and well-defined brows. Whatever "the algorithm" of that specific app, it heavily influences the resulting aesthetic: Contoured faces turned to the light "do well" on Instagram, while the more natural, subdued look of the VSCO girl looks good in that filtered paradise. Your appearance needs to "perform" in the same way a stock or a viral article might. In a *New Yorker* story about the phenomenon of "Instagram face," Jia Tolentino wrote that some influencers are going so far as to get plastic surgery procedures to achieve the features the platform rewards: high cheekbones, a defined jawline, prominent lips. "I couldn't shake the feeling that technology is rewriting our bodies," she wrote, "to correspond to its own interests—rearranging our faces according to whatever increases engagement and likes." That statement might seem to assign too much power to technology, but at this point, it's hard to gauge how much of this is due to human tastes—what society deems attractive at the moment, what people "like," click on, watch, or linger over—how much to some unknowable urges on the part of the technology itself, and how much to the constant feedback loop between the two. They have become inextricable from one another, to the extent that we can no longer reliably say that our taste is our own, and not a machine's.

While the ways in which ever-shifting algorithms impact the culture can be worrisome, the access and participation they allow is, at least, encouraging. Teens in Brazil, Singapore, and Canada can all participate in a shared style culture even if they don't sit at the same physical lunch table. And while once, loyalty to a specific, exactingly defined in-group was everything, TikTok allows for a swifter adoption of style and more cross-pollination between worlds. Despite concern that, for millennials and Gen Z, documenting your many phases on social media arrests personal growth, the fly-by-night nature of many of these subcultures suggests that the kinds of overnight self-reinventions I once practiced are alive and well in this milieu. And new cultures flower constantly in its soil.

The commonality in all these subcultures—besides their online origins and motivations—is that they pose little to no risk to the monoculture. The barbaric yawp of the punks, who considered themselves not just outside of but in opposition to society, has turned into the carnival barker yell of the "content creator." Any form of online self-expression is now inherently monetizable, and the prospect of "selling out" that loomed large with the punk generation and grunge seems to have mostly disappeared. Now, participants are unabashedly doing this for profit, in public, which inevitably influences what they're making: The inclination is to be as broad and universal as possible. Snobbery is discouraged, sure, but so is peculiarity. The rarely challenging "content" they create is less a shot across the bow at society and more the components of a résumé for future gigs.

If you were a '70s-era punk, you were mostly influencing yourself and those around you who were cool enough to "get" it. Bands like the Velvet Underground didn't exist to sell millions of records, but to encourage their listeners to make music of their own. Brian Eno said that while the first Velvet Underground album moved a paltry thirty thousand copies in its first five years, "I think everyone who bought one of those thirty thousand copies started a band!" The titration of influence was measured not in likes or views but in its ability to push others to make new things.

For young creators, numbers are more important than cred. Their content makes money for corporations as well as, potentially, for themselves, so their selling out is baked in from the beginning. When everyone is grasping for capital, that's mostly seen as a good thing. Hippies weren't dressing to get noticed by Paris fashion designers, and the grunge world was horrified to see their looks reproduced on the runway. But now, subcultures have a monetary stake (if they're lucky) in seeing themselves ascend to monoculture. No wonder they're so eager to please.

And, in an age-old dynamic, the old Establishment wants a piece of the new Establishment. Members of TikTok "collab houses" are signed by Hollywood agents and pursued by reality-show producers. Inevitably, these teen cliques have moved into the corridors of high fashion, too: E-boy Noen Eubanks was chosen to star in a Celine campaign, and TikTokers have been seated front row at Prada and Dior shows. And therein lies the biggest shift: Punks may be on designers' mood boards today, but they would never have been invited to, or wanted to, sit in the front row. The most rebellious move you can make these days might be getting the Establishment to cut you a check.

CHAPTER THREE

The "French Girl" Industrial Complex

THE SAYING "THE grass is always greener on the other side" applies to oceans, too. At least, that's what you'd think given the collective American fascination with the mythical "French girl." You can find endless guides on how to eat breakfast, wash your hair, tie a scarf, and entertain like a French woman—a *young* French woman, since "girl" is always the noun of choice. A lot of this seems to pertain to looking effortless: wearing no-makeup makeup, styling hair to look unstyled, arranging outfits just so with the goal of looking haphazard. Goop even has an entire landing page devoted to the topic, recommending things like "the ultimate French-girl hairbrush."

The prototypical "French girl" referred to here seems to be a young, urban-dwelling woman with a cashmere budget, a woman who is almost always thin and white. Think about the stock images and profile subjects that illustrate these stories, and how rarely they depict women of color or plus-size women, despite the fact that these women also make up the population of France. You'll find more berets and baguettes in these images than you will people of color.

You might think that this obsession would end or ebb, and that we would move on to another nation and its mythical sylphs. And to some extent, we have: Look at the way we idolize the Scandinavian lifestyle or Korean beauty practices. But the "French girl" myth has a weird staying power. Like Marianne, the symbol of France since the 1700s, she is an undying marketing symbol.

The lionization of French women by the rest of the world, especially Americans, really took off with the rise of French film as an international export. Stars like Catherine Deneuve, Brigitte Bardot, Jane Birkin (English, not French, but regularly misinterpreted as such), Anna Karina (Danish, but also regularly misinterpreted as French) became household names, at least in the kinds of households that subscribed to *Cahiers du Cinéma*. At the time, they represented a new standard of beauty and were tied to a revolutionary, exciting moment in culture. They also stood for a kind of liberation for women, with Bardot even attracting the attention of noted feminist Simone de Beauvoir. When I first read de Beauvoir's 1959 *Esquire* essay "Brigitte Bardot and the Lolita Syndrome," I was in high school and found it confusing, because de Beauvoir makes Bardot sound so effortless and unconstructed. Vampy, with heavy eyeliner and a tightly hairsprayed beehive, she did not strike me as particularly liberated. But compared to the female standard at the time, Bardot read as natural and unaffected, which ran counter to the traditional, artificial femininity of '50s France. Her self-possession felt like a threat to the gender norms of the time. De Beauvoir notes that the actress was detested in France while being beloved outside it, saying, "B. B. now deserves to be considered an export product as important as Renault automobiles." (To give a sense of how much Bardot was disliked in France during her heyday, de Beauvoir cites the fact that a murder in the town of Angers was blamed on the perpetrators having seen *And God Created Woman*, her most famous star turn.)

To de Beauvoir, Bardot was an "ambiguous nymph" whose body was "almost androgynous," at least when glimpsed from the back. Her hair was that of "a negligent waif." "She goes about barefooted," she wrote. "She turns up her nose at elegant clothes, jewels, girdles, perfumes, make-up, at all artifice." De Beauvoir compares her to a child and a creature. If all of this reminds you of similar rhetoric around modern-day French It girls like Jeanne Damas, Charlotte Gainsbourg, and Camille Rowe, it should, because the way de Beauvoir described Bardot in 1959 is strikingly similar to the way these women are described in the press more than six decades later. The bottom line is: They're not calculating. They're not trying too hard. Their innocence is fetishized long into adulthood. Almost every aspect of this feels sexist—these women aren't a chore to be around, they don't overthink, and they don't have the tiresome qualities that adults do. At the same time, they know more than we do—about how to dress, eat, and live.

This supposed knowledge is doled out in guides to everything from parenting (*Bringing Up Bébé*) to beauty (*The French Beauty Solution*) to more generalist studies (*How to Be French*, which is presumably not a guide to applying for French citizenship). The urtext of this genre is probably *French Women Don't Get Fat*, in which author Mireille Guiliano offers diet tips that range from sensible to extreme: She advocates asking for *la moitié, s'il vous plaît* (a half portion, please) and going on a boiled-leek cleanse. Weirdly, she defines this as "eating for pleasure." Guiliano makes a lot of salient points about shopping locally and seasonally and taking pleasure in high-quality food, both of which are dependent on a certain level of disposable income. But ultimately, her approach is a mental game about eschewing pleasure: "the useful art of self-deception" must be employed by women to place mind over matter, or mind over croissant.

Helena Frith Powell, in her guide *All You Need to Be Impossibly French* (the adverb is revealing), includes similar counsel: "You need an iron will to resist any (edible) temptation that comes your way." This doesn't sound like the effortlessness that we ascribe to the French at all. And right there is the disconnect between French fashion and beauty culture and our experience of it. It's an infrastructure of rigid rules, many of them built on what looks to current-day eyes like disordered eating—a rigid social code that we misinterpret as effortless and free.

Around the release of *French Women Don't Get Fat*, Kate Taylor elucidated this in Slate:

> The French accept a level of government paternalism that would not go over easily here. The way that French families eat, or until recently ate, is actually a product of state intervention, as Greg Critser pointed out in a 2003 piece in the *New York Times*. At the beginning of the twentieth century, concern over France's high infant mortality rate led to a largely state-sponsored movement called puericulture. The movement's initial focus was on getting mothers to breastfeed; clinics were set up across the country, and the government required factories to have areas for nursing. But puericulture advocates also stressed that overfeeding infants was worse than underfeeding them. For older children, they advised regular mealtimes, modest portions, no seconds, and no snacks. Children's own appetites and preferences were to be ignored. This is

the tradition in which Guiliano was raised, and which she proposes to those of her readers who are parents. It is another interesting paradox: The French ability to take pleasure in food, and to choose food based on taste rather than dietary dogma, begins with a child's lack of choice, and a degree of parental and state authoritarianism.

Taylor identifies just one of the ways the supposed natural, free French lifestyle is shaped by government intervention. There is also the very real consideration that French people live healthier lifestyles because of said paternalism: the banning of GMO ingredients, the availability of fresh healthy food, government-mandated shorter work hours and ample vacation time, and, most crucially, access to universal health care. If we all worked less and had free health care, we'd probably be more beautiful and relaxed, too. But that is a less glamorous conversation that doesn't sell lipstick and boyfriend jeans.

And the "French girl" convention has sold plenty of both. Coasting on the phenomenon, brands like Sézane, Maje, and Sandro have made inroads into the US with their chic, somewhat-more-affordable-than-designer clothes. The clothes are sexy and youthful in a tasteful way, and benefit from their Parisian connotations. But the way the average French person dresses is a bit more understated. When I enrolled as a foreign student at L'École nationale supérieure des Arts Décoratifs (EnsAD), a French art school, I expected to find my peers in colorful eyeliner and miniskirts, but they mostly wore variations on the same black or navy outfits, like *Peanuts* characters reimagined by Yohji Yamamoto. Drawing attention to oneself in any way, especially sartorially, felt verboten, and the strictures around acceptable behavior felt oppressive—which is definitely not what you expect in art school.

Color and prints were considered tacky, and showing skin was still shocking—when I wore shorts on a hot day, people seemed perturbed, though that may have been because I hadn't been following a diet of boiled leeks immediately beforehand.

My classmates, who mostly hailed from the Parisian upper class, were following the tenets of French haut bourgeois style, which is built on the concept of *"bon chic, bon genre"* or BCBG ("good style, good class"). Thierry Mantoux's *BCBG: Le guide du bon chic bon genre* is the French equivalent of *The Official Preppy Handbook*, and it outlines a discreet, Right Bank aesthetic that is all about in-group adherence and not drawing undue attention to yourself. Simple, well-made, classic clothes are de rigueur, and anything else will brand you as an arriviste. Eliza Brooke wrote for Vox about the classism inherent in these style rules. "The lingering attachment to the eighteenth-century aristocracy still exerts social influence today, and it's not uncommon for parents to ask after the last names of their children's friends, to see if they come from so-called good families," she writes. "Indeed, many of our French Girl style icons have a *de* in their last names, indicating noble status, like the Chanel muses Caroline de Maigret and Inès de la Fressange. (Wherever you go, high fashion favors those who can afford it.) If the nouveaux riches dress in a gaudy manner and the upper crust exerts restraint, emulating the latter is an attempt, intentional or not, to tap into its privilege."

While we're obsessing about, and freely misinterpreting, the principles of French style, what are actual French people doing? Rather than reveling in their sheer Gallic supremacy, they're actually looking to *us*. Americans. Well, Brooklynites. The fascination goes both ways. And it turns out the French conception of "Brooklyn" may be as whitewashed and mistaken as our concept of the "French girl." We are two cultures looking at one another through one-way glass.

Adding "Brooklyn" to anything French is like adding "Paris" to anything in New York—an immediate injection of cred. There are Parisian establishments called Brooklyn Café, The Brooklyn Pizzeria, Le Brooklyn, and The Brklyn (bonus points for dropped consonants). The French streetwear label BWGH (Brooklyn We Go Hard) was named after a Jay-Z track and included a sweatshirt with the phrase BROOKLYN PARLE FRANÇAIS. The Parisian department store Le Bon Marché held a Brooklyn Rive Gauche (Left Bank) takeover, selling beanies and mason jars from the beloved borough. Of course, when French people look at Brooklyn, they're looking at it as myopically as Americans do Paris, emulating specific neighborhoods (Williamsburg, Park Slope) and ignoring both the borough's diversity and its working-class population. (White people are now in the minority in Brooklyn as a whole.)

The disconnect between what you expect from a culture and the reality you experience can be so extreme, there is actually a cluster of psychological and physical symptoms called Paris syndrome, a form of culture shock among visitors to the city. It can manifest itself in hallucinations, feelings of persecution, and even physical symptoms like dizziness and vomiting. It's affected many tourists on their first visits, after experiencing the filth, noise, and unfriendliness of the city—it is, after all, a city, like any other—that don't show up in films like *Amélie*.

Given the amount of critical thinking I have done about the "French girl," it's surprising that I fell so hard for her Danish equivalent. When Copenhagen Fashion Week began attracting more attention than ever, I was glued to the street-style images of cool Danish girls wearing, say, a puffy parka and neon dad sneakers. Danish labels like Ganni, Saks Potts, and Cecilie Bahnsen started gaining followings for their riotous, anarchic mixtures of color and print. It didn't matter that you really had to be a cool Danish girl to pull off the look—I was ready to try.

The Copenhagen craze is just part of our ongoing fascination with Scandinavia, with its modern design, its cuisine, and the Danish concept of *hygge* ("a quality of cosiness and comfortable conviviality that engenders a feeling of contentment or well-being," per the *Oxford English Dictionary*). Like France, it offers ample social benefits and a "better" lifestyle, the weather aside. And in the vein of the guides to becoming French, guides to becoming more *hygge* have been published in droves in the past few years. Books like *The Year of Living Danishly*, *Keep Calm & Hygge*, and *How to Hygge* advocate mulled wine, cashmere socks, and comfy blankets.

State-mandated coziness is all very well, but it can be as stifling as a shearling blanket. The Norwegian writer Karl Ove Knausgård has complained about the conformist, eccentricity-snuffing aspects of Scandinavian society. Growing up there, he recalled in *T* magazine, he experienced a kind of tall-poppy syndrome. "It didn't take much more than a slightly outlandish hat or a pair of unusual trousers before people told you off, laughed at you or, in the worst case, ignored you. 'He thinks he's special' was the worst thing anyone could say about you." In *Hygge: A Celebration of Simple Pleasures. Living the Danish Way*, Charlotte Abrahams asserts that in a *hygge* household, "There is no discussion of politics or anything controversial that makes you feel uptight." The writer Michael Booth called it "self-administered social gagging, characterized more by a self-satisfied sense of its own exclusivity than notions of shared conviviality." In fact, *hygge* imagery turns up in Danish far-right political ads, evoking the home, and the nation, as a closed circle without foreign interlopers.

Another country whose lifestyle has recently been exported to the rest of the world is South Korea, which is experiencing a *hallyu*, or wave of cultural exports, right now. The rise of Korean beauty, or K-beauty, along with the soft-power influence of Korean pop

(K-pop) stars on fashion and beauty, has been abetted by the Korean government's investment in cosmetic technology. The country helped popularize BB cream, cushion compacts, sheet masks, and essences, among other innovations that have quickly been adopted around the world. Brands like Glow Recipe and e-commerce sites Soko Glam and Peach & Lily promise the Korean ideal of poreless "glass skin," and you can now find Korean products at your local CVS or Ulta. Even twelve-step skincare routines have been normalized (done, of course, as "self-care," not for the nefarious purpose of looking good) in the service of skin as smooth as a BTS member's.

While Korea's supremacy in the beauty and skincare world remains unquestioned, it doesn't necessarily stem from a longtime beauty tradition in the country. In a New York Times op-ed titled "I Grew Up Around Korean Beauty Products. Americans, You've Been Had," Euny Hong questions the copy on many beauty sites referring to an ancient culture of beauty and skincare in the country. Hong explains that when she was living in Korea in the '80s and '90s, those products and twelve-step routines were nonexistent; beauty aficionados used products from France, America, and Japan. Now, Korea is undoubtedly a beauty-driven culture, though much like France, it's hard to generalize that everyone in the country adopts the same beauty routines. What is true is that the perfect skin and youthful appearance of many Korean people can be attributed as much to the widespread use of cosmetic surgery and Botox as it can to snail mucin. "If there are such things as 'Korean beauty secrets,'" Hong concludes, "they seem to amount to this: Put a lot of time, money and energy into your skin, and you'll probably see results." The "ancient tradition" of Korean beauty is really just an enticing marketing strategy—albeit one that has helped many people feel a little more beautiful.

At its best, looking to another country for inspiration about how to live a better life can be a force for genuine self-improvement, if a tad narcissistic. It's part of why we travel and seek out information about other cultures and ways of life. At its worst, it can reinforce the supposition that there is only one way to be a woman or to be fashionable, that no matter what you're doing—washing your hair, eating your breakfast, breathing—you're doing it wrong.

CHAPTER FOUR

Patagonia on Bedford Avenue

KAIA GERBER WALKS around New York City in a Carhartt jacket. Fashion Week attendees in Milan and Paris sport Patagonia fleeces, lovingly dubbed Patagucci, alongside their actual Gucci. And camouflage, cargo pants, and fatigues appear on countless runways—the same goes for sailor-style pants, leather Perfectos, and bomber jackets.

We don't think about it too often, but many of the garments we wear every day have their roots in military gear, workwear, and outdoor apparel. Having traveled far from their original realms, they are now the basis for so many fashion staples—the building blocks for our modern-day wardrobes, in fact. And the way they have been adapted into the fashion vernacular reveals plenty about our contemporary mores, especially when it comes to class, labor, and even our relationship with combat.

There are times when style lays bare a society's hidden obsessions. Think of the mid-aughts obsession with trucker hats and ironic "white trash" dressing among coastal elites, the woodsy, outdoorsy hipster trend of flannels and wolf T-shirts in upscale cities, and the ongoing obsession with workwear and outdoor brands as high fashion. I've long had a theory that just as a segment of society—like the rural farming population, for example—begins to wane, that's when we begin to fetishize it the most in fashion. Cue the hipsters and supermodels bundling up in Carhartt.

So many of our fashion essentials originated on the battle-field, though some of the items we're used to wearing every day might not even strike you as deriving from the military. Take the trench coat—yes, as in trench warfare. The trench evolved from the nineteenth-century Mackintosh waterproof coat, intended for out-door pursuits, into lighter-weight versions by Burberry and Aqua-scutum that were a bit more fashion-forward, but still functional. During World War I, the trench was adopted as a shorter, lighter, waterproof alternative to the standard heavy wool greatcoats worn on the front lines; its drab khaki color blended into the landscape. Reserved for officers, who bought them with their own money, trenches also became a status symbol—a class signifier on the battlefield.

After the war, the British government gave away its surplus to the rest of the population, and the trench coat began to filter into everyday life. Divorced from its sporting-goods and mil-itary context, it was now civilian wear, and it soon took on other connotations. It became the uniform of suave private detectives, epitomized by Humphrey Bogart playing Sam Spade in *The Maltese Falcon* and Philip Marlowe in *The Big Sleep*. It complemented both the bourgeois reserve of Catherine Deneuve in *Belle de jour* and the sleaze of your stereotypical flasher. It could even feel sinister: After the Columbine High School shooting in 1999, many high schools banned students from wearing trench coats, because the killers wore them and were (incorrectly) associated with a clique that called itself the Trenchcoat Mafia. Amending gun laws might have been a more pragmatic protective move, but such is the symbolic power of fashion that the coat stood in for some unknowable menace.

These days, a Burberry trench coat is a status item, though in a different way than its World War I—era cousins. Its military-inspired features, like epaulets, a gun flap on the right shoulder, and a D-ring belt meant to hold a sword, are now like vestigial organs, reflections more of style than of substance. The trench's familiarity has become something to disrupt: a canvas for designers to reinvent in countless ways. Viktor&Rolf, the Dutch design duo, has made ruffled versions, while Comme des Garçons designer Rei Kawakubo reimagined a Burberry trench in 2016, giving the jacket avant-garde new proportions that made it look almost like it had exploded. Some have even approached it the way a Dadaist artist might a ready-made, reworking the existing garment. For his fall 2000 "Midtown" collection, downtown deconstructionist Miguel Adrover showed an inside-out Burberry trench coat, a hand-me-down from a friend. He had ripped it up and made it into a dress that showed off the interior label and checked lining, perhaps a comment on the status markers inherent in this reserved-looking item.

Designers have brought the same ingenuity to those other army standbys, camo and fatigues. Yves Saint Laurent designed the Saharienne in 1968, inspired by the uniforms of the German expeditionary force operating in North Africa, where the designer grew up. Now we know the style colloquially as the safari jacket. For spring 1991, designer Franco Moschino showed an army-green suit labeled "Survival Suit," complete with pockets for the modern woman's "arsenal": lipstick, makeup brushes, compact, etcetera. And high-end versions of cargo pants continue to proliferate. In 2010, Balmain showed a $2,000 version with a Saran Wrap—skinny fit, worn with a T-shirt so shredded it resembled a spiderweb.

It didn't take long for fashion to metabolize these military styles as ready-to-wear, or to turn wartime motifs into a fashion statement. In 1919, only a year after the end of World War I, the Chelsea Arts Club in London held an event where attendees wore looks painted with "dazzle" camouflage, the almost-Cubist designs painted on warships to confuse the eye into misjudging their size. The tropes and motifs of war had already become fashion fodder for the glittering class.

Almost fifty years later, camouflage in its more familiar fabric form started to become a hallmark of antiwar movements. Vietnam War protestors favored it, and Jane Fonda wore an army surplus jacket to the FTA (Free the Army) tour, protesting the conflict. Soon, the style moved further into an apolitical, message-free realm. In the '80s, designer Stephen Sprouse made pieces in Day-Glo camo, inspired by Andy Warhol's reimagined camouflage. These neon versions of camo would continue into the '90s and early aughts, a variation for those completely unconcerned with blending in.

After 9/11, the battlefield motifs became more literal as the country plunged into its "forever wars." The aggressive fetishization of patriotism and American military strength went to, let's just say, some weird places. In Destiny's Child's 2002 video for "Survivor," the trio wears shredded, eroticized camo, their abs as armored as tanks. The same year, Britney Spears performed in low-rise army pants and a cropped vest covered with fake medals and insignia. The trend could have an ironic edge, coming as it did from people fairly removed from the front lines. Jeremy Scott designed an army helmet with Mickey Mouse ears, later telling *The New Yorker*, "It was poking fun at how childish and silly war is." Rihanna wore it in a music video in 2009, an ammo belt slung over her shoulder.

A few designers have used military tropes in more statement-making ways. Alexander McQueen's work was often concerned with violence and power, from his student collection "Jack the Ripper Stalks His Victims," inspired by the Victorian-era serial killer, to his controversial "Highland Rape" show for fall 1995, which took on English violence against Scotland. McQueen's fall 1996 show at Christ Church in London's East End, known as the "Dante" collection, was one of the few military-inspired collections to seriously grapple with the realities of war. In addition to camouflage and braided military overcoats, McQueen used photographer Don McCullin's images of the Vietnam War and the Somalian famine printed onto clothing. (McCullin refused permission for the photos to be used this way. McQueen went ahead anyway.) There were thorn bracelets, by the jeweler Shaun Leane, that evoked barbed wire. The show, McQueen told *Women's Wear Daily*, was about "war and peace through the years . . . I think religion has caused every war in the world, which is why I showed in a church."

Fashion critic Suzy Menkes's *New York Times* review of the 1996 season, where several designers showed military-inspired collections, noted that "wartime images tend to be absorbed into fashion when the clothing no longer serves its original function. Either practical things turn decorative—like the silver-ball buttons that were once designed as backup ammunition. Or in a postwar period, practical army gear is absorbed into civilian life, as with the blouson jacket or trench coat. . . . In a period when relatively few young people in Western societies do active military service, there is an esthetic attraction for trim clothes that are the antithesis of sloppy sportswear."

Her observation rings true today, when traditional warfare has changed—rather than a soldier in fatigues, it could be waged by a drone operator sitting in a dark room in jeans, or a hacker in sweatpants. And since coastal, upper-class people, the audience for much high-end fashion, are particularly out of touch with the military, this kind of dressing has become decontextualized.

In recent years, everyone from streetwear brands to high-fashion brands (including Marc Jacobs, Dior, and Chanel) has jumped on the military train to the point where it almost feels superfluous to point out. Some designers have, like McQueen, subverted it. Others have romanticized it, like Jacobs, who invented a rose-patterned camo for Louis Vuitton's spring 2001 show. As Jacobs has said, "Military clothes are part of the fashion vernacular now." They are now clichés to be enlivened and reimagined. They have arrived at the fashion equivalent of an event horizon.

A similar thing happened with the arrival of the "clout fleece." New York designer Sandy Liang's reimagining of the REI staple— this time in neon or leopard print, with contrasting pockets— became a downtown uniform, quickly copied by other brands. Liang's fleeces fit neatly into the "gorpcore" trend of city dwellers wearing upscale performance gear and hiking sandals. They appeal to people for whom the outdoors might not be a huge part of their lives, but who aspire to the cachet of being a person who spends a lot of time outdoors. It's a badge of fitness, wholesomeness, and *Walden*-style inner peace. The look is a marker of what the economist and sociologist Thorstein Veblen called "conspicuous leisure," which the upper classes tend to flaunt: the next best thing to Instagramming yourself from a scenic hike or vacation in nature. And with both leisure time and access to green space shrinking, time outdoors is increasingly the domain of the privileged. If you can't be a hiker, you might as well dress like one.

Outdoors-style vests have found purchase with the finance crowd, too. Given that trading floors tend to be slightly cold, a quilted designer vest became their standard-issue uniform. And post–financial crisis, the finance world has taken a page from Silicon Valley: Less wolves of Wall Street and more fleece-swaddled lambs, though the vests' company logos are still a reminder of status. On TV shows like *Succession* and *Billions*, the fleece is the uniform of the corporate raider; the Instagram account Midtown Uniform is devoted to spotted-in-the-wild photos of "Chads and Brads" in button-downs and vests. Vest-mania quickly expanded beyond finance to the power elite in general—serving as a kind of flak jacket for the Davos crowd. Jeff Bezos wore a quilted vest to a conference in Sun Valley in 2017. Apple CEO Tim Cook and Uber CEO Dara Khosrowshahi, among many others, have sported fleece versions.

Something about the vest feels counterintuitive as a uniform for the powerful. It seems like a way of seeking both physical and metaphorical insulation, a signal of some hidden vulnerability or self-protective instinct among the .01 percent. It's a uniform for a new era of finance, where many politicians and citizens are calling out plutocrats for their entitlement and said "plutes" feel exposed. And it's become one of several hyper-engineered outdoor garments that now feels synonymous with Everest-level privilege.

You certainly don't *need* a tricked-out fleece to scale the steppes of SoHo or the tundra of the Stock Exchange. You don't *need* a jacket originally designed for Antarctic scientists to walk a few blocks to Starbucks on a chilly day. But how many of our modern fashion choices have to do with needs, rather than wants? In a story for The Cut, Noreen Malone drew a comparison between the Iditarod-ready Canada Goose coats that were popping up as a fashion statement in New York and the adoption of military-grade Hummers and Land Rovers by people with much more pavement-bound lifestyles. The coat was, she wrote, "the latest item in an ever-evolving series of upscale signifiers." More than that, it was an attempt to hack discomfort, to stave off the elements by throwing cash at them, a grab at self-protection amid uncertainty. "[Its] real marketing genius," she wrote, "lies in making the wearer feel insulated against far more than just the cold."

Workwear is another potent source of so many of our fashion staples—and it also originated in a realm from which the elite have distanced themselves. Denim was worn by Italian sailors and, later, American cowboys and miners during the Gold Rush era. It was a tough fabric, meant for people who worked with their own callused hands. Starting in 1886, Levi's advertised its jeans with a label showing two horses pulling a pair of jeans in opposite directions. The jeans stayed intact, evoking their durability. (Levi's uses a variation of the same label today.)

Jeans had a mythic cowboy appeal, but they didn't become ready-to-wear until somewhat later on. In the '50s, stars like James Dean and Marlon Brando popularized them as a hardscrabble uniform for fellow rebels without a cause. (Brando also helped greenlight another workwear item—the T-shirt—for everyday wear when he wore one in *A Streetcar Named Desire*.) And unlike other, more distinctive pieces of Westernwear, like cowboy boots and snap shirts, jeans have been pretty effortlessly absorbed into the modern wardrobe. Except for a wedding, a funeral, a formal office setting, or a court date, you can probably get away with wearing jeans anywhere. They have gone from rebelwear to generic.

In the '80s, designers like Calvin Klein and Gloria Vanderbilt reimagined jeans as sexy, heavily branded must-have items. The rise of premium denim in the early aughts cemented jeans, which once telegraphed toughness and self-sufficiency, as a luxury good. Labels like 7 For All Mankind and J Brand commanded three-figure prices for styles with logos, whiskering, and other bells and whistles. Now, there are high-end labels devoted to intentionally ripped and intentionally paint-spattered styles. There is one that specializes in reselling reworked vintage Levi's—the workman's standard turned fashion holy grail. And the brand PRPS even introduced a pair of jeans made to look "muddy" in 2017. The item description lays it on thick: "heavily distressed medium-blue denim jeans in a comfortable straight-leg fit embody rugged, Americana workwear that's seen some hard-working action with a crackled, caked-on muddy coating that shows you're not afraid to get down and dirty." The style quickly drew Twitter mockery, with Reebok posting a (fake) "Authentic Sweat Shirt" with intentional stains to mock the idea of trying to lifehack hard work and authenticity. Mike Rowe, former host of the show *Dirty Jobs*, summed it up in a Facebook post: "Finally—a pair of jeans that look like they have been worn by someone with a dirty job . . . made for people who don't." He considered it "further proof that our country's war on work continues to rage in all corners of polite society." Just like that, something as seemingly insignificant as a pair of blue jeans had managed to tap into the red state/blue state divide.

Similarly, it doesn't seem like an accident that as fewer and fewer people are involved in farm work and manual labor—and as those jobs are being outsourced abroad or replaced by automation—workwear items like overalls and boilersuits have crested as status items. Their popularity may also have to do with a growing disinterest in body-conscious dressing post-#MeToo movement: Feminists had long pushed back against the hoary idea that what you were wearing when you were sexually harassed mattered at all. Still, fashion seemed to take on more protective, body-obscuring qualities in the wake of #MeToo allegations in every industry. It was almost as though the functional aspects of the garments were once again paramount, cloaking the wearer in the costume of labor to convey the message: I'm here to do a job, don't get any ideas. And their military-grade protectiveness felt like a tough cocoon for a wary generation of women.

Gwyneth Paltrow, Margot Robbie, and Dakota Johnson have worn upscale versions of coveralls. Paltrow's website, Goop, has sold a refined Stella McCartney version of the trend. However, while the boilersuit may no longer telegraph "working with your hands," that doesn't necessarily mean it's disconnected from labor entirely. The writer Olivia Stren connected the boilersuit to women's work in an *ELLE* story that I edited. For mothers like Stren who are trying to have (and do) it all, it's a functional garment that makes quite a bit of sense. "In an age held in thrall to ideals of multitasking and efficiency, where celebrities are papped running errands 'just like us,' the boilersuit—optimization on a hanger—is arguably the power suit du jour. It's the ultimate triumph of fashion-as-lifehack," she wrote. "It's a versatile workhorse, presumably ready to jump on a call, pick up a child from a playdate, head to yoga, and make grain-free granola." A boilersuit is now such common attire in downtown Manhattan and Brooklyn that when a photo of Felicity Huffman in her prison-issued coveralls was released, a Twitter wag joked "every girl in SoHo dresses like this now."

As with military motifs and outdoors clothing, workwear represents a reality many of its wearers have long since become disconnected from: farm work, factory jobs, and other working-class pursuits. To wear it is, on some level, to cosplay as someone who is "just like us" via a bourgeois version of a recognizable, generic, or generic-looking uniform item.

In *The Philosophy of Andy Warhol*, the artist writes:

> What's great about this country is that America started the tradition where the richest consumers buy essentially the same things as the poorest. You can be watching TV and see Coca-Cola, and you know that the President drinks Coke, Liz Taylor drinks Coke, and just think, you can drink Coke, too. A Coke is a Coke and no amount of money can get you a better Coke than the one the bum on the corner is drinking.

Much like Warhol's can of Coke, the generic nature of these clothes reinforces the lie that we're all the same—that a billionaire in a T-shirt and vest is no different than a farmer in roughly the same garments, Italian tailoring aside. At the same time, wearing these clothes outside of their original context is a way of throwing your separateness, your above-the-frayness, into high relief. No one is going to confuse Kaia Gerber or Hailey Bieber with a Cat operator. If anything, donning their Carhartt makes them look even more like supermodels.

CHAPTER FIVE

Caviar on a Potato Chip

Fashion loves what it calls a "high/low" moment: the elevation of something crass or lowbrow to runway status. A prime example of this came in 2014, when American designer Jeremy Scott took over the Italian house of Moschino with a junk food–themed debut collection. He showed gowns made to look like crumpled fast-food wrappers, a Golden Arches sweatshirt that read MOSCHINO: OVER 20 BILLION SERVED, even a Bud Light–inspired cape. Tongue planted firmly in cheek, he titled it "Fast Fashion."

Scott was playing up his Missouri country-boy bona fides and juxtaposing it with the big Italian fashion brand he'd landed at. The collection played with the archetypes of bourgeois fashion (ladylike suits that riffed on classic Chanel territory, but in the red and yellow of Mickey D's) while lampooning their stuffiness. It was instantly talked about—and seen everywhere, thanks to Scott's loyal stable of celebrity friends. But it also drew some critical ire. Writing for the *Financial Times*, Vanessa Friedman called it "a series of bad jokes," imagining the words of Scott's potential customers:

"What do you dream of?"

"Oh, I dream of wearing a party dress that makes fun of French fries!"

After that show, I went to Los Angeles to interview Scott for *ELLE*, asking him about the threatened reaction from some reviewers. "Maybe it's because people are realizing that [runway fashion] has gotten too stuffy and boring," he said. "It's ultimately a luxury in the real sense that you don't need it. We don't need another stitch of clothes. There are enough handbags in the world."

Scott's move was not as earthshaking if you dig a little deeper into fashion history, including the history of Moschino itself. Franco Moschino created clothes that looked like shopping bags, dressed Pat Cleveland in a jacket that resembled an airline flotation vest, embellished clothes with teddy bears, made gloves with "nail polish" on the fingertips, and went in for witty sayings (like a sequined VIP on a gown or WAIST OF MONEY along a jacket's beltline). Like Scott, he made irreverent "homages" to other designers, too. Moschino once told *GQ*: "Funny clothes have to be extremely well made because that is where you find the chic. It's easy to be funny with a T-shirt, but it's more clever with a mink coat. After all, if caviar was cheaper it would taste much less interesting."

That intersection of highbrow and lowbrow, the caviar and the potato chip, is where much of fashion lives, especially now. Diana Vreeland once wrote, "A little bad taste is like a nice splash of paprika. We all need a splash of bad taste—it's hearty, it's healthy, it's physical. I think we could use more of it. No taste is what I'm against." The peppering of a lowbrow motif into a collection can indeed add flavor and texture, keeping things from feeling dull. But it can also come across as condescending or, worse, offensive.

In fact, that is how some of fashion's biggest controversies have been born.

Look at Yves Saint Laurent, who showed a particularly polarizing collection in 1971. It was then called the "Libération" or "Quarante" (Forties) collection, but has become known as the Scandal collection, for reasons that will soon become clear. Saint Laurent's friend Paloma Picasso was a flea-market fiend long before vintage was considered cool. Inspired in part by her, the designer showed clothes inflected by another era—shoulder pads, brief hemlines, platform shoes, colorful furs, and heavy makeup.

No big deal, right? Designers take up "retro" inspirations all the time, right? Not in Paris in 1971. Even though more than twenty-five years had passed since the end of World War II, it was thought to be, as we might say now, "too soon" to dive back into wartime aesthetics. "He spared us nothing. His collection was a tour de force of bad taste," read one review in *The Guardian*. "Nothing could exceed the horror of this exercise in kitsch." The offense was twofold: The elevation of what were seen as thrift-store finds presented as couture was a threat to the closed world of Paris fashion, already buffeted by the winds of the counterculture. (Saint Laurent had shown a beatnik-themed collection for Dior in 1960 that was similarly treated.) There were also the political overtones—the 1940s looks called to mind the wartime occupation of France. Saint Laurent, who was brought up in Algeria and did not experience occupied France firsthand, was perhaps less cognizant of the way these references would be perceived. The gaudy styles and heavy makeup also evoked the looks of collaborationist women who slept with the occupiers—and were able to afford nicer clothes because they were not subject to rationing.

At times, fashion can dive into camp without condescension. In other cases, it feels like punching down. *Nostalgie de la boue* (literally, "nostalgia for mud," or as Tom Wolfe famously defined it, "indulg[ing] in the gauche thrill of taking on certain styles of the lower orders") plays into fashion's ongoing missteps.

Designer John Galliano and his trainer used to go for a run every morning along the Seine, where he saw homeless people sheltering under the bridges. To most Paris denizens, they went unnoticed, but not Galliano. However, instead of their plight, the designer registered what they were wearing. He later told the *New York Times*, "Some of these people are like impresarios, their coats worn over their shoulders and their hats worn at a certain angle. It's fantastic." Galliano incorporates extensive historical research into his collections, and, thinking of the people he saw by the Seine, he began looking into the history of the '30s Rag Balls, where members of high society swanned around in derelict-chic gowns by the House of Worth. His "Clochards" ("tramps") spring 2000 couture collection for Dior was the result of those inspirations, with models dressed in silk printed to look like newspaper or shredded or burned-looking clothing, accessorized with empty bottles and corks.

"I never wanted to make a spectacle of misery," Galliano claimed later. But groups like the Coalition for the Homeless raised the alarm, and some activists picketed the brand's store. He had his defenders, like *Women's Wear Daily*, whose reviewer wrote, "It wasn't offensive, perhaps because he shows such great affection and respect for his subjects, and even falls in love with them a little." The fracas around the show ensured that it entered the popular lexicon—to the point that it was later parodied in the movie *Zoolander*, where it reportedly became the basis for the "Derelicte" collection.

Looking at all this through contemporary eyes, it's hard to imagine this collection *not* getting its designer "canceled" today. But Galliano did make the point that part of the outcry came from the familiarity of the poverty he depicted—designers were often inspired by the developing world, but weren't called out for it, at least in those days. When it was closer to home—namely, on the banks of their own river—Parisians turned up their noses.

Galliano wasn't the only designer to dabble in the world of the demimonde. Designer Miguel Adrover once made a coat out of a mattress he found on the street, which had belonged to British actor and style icon Quentin Crisp. Crisp was Adrover's neighbor and had just passed away. The combination of humble, even abject, material and celebrity lineage was classic Adrover (you may remember his repurposed Burberry trench coat from the previous chapter). From what he told the Metropolitan Museum of Art, which has the coat in its Costume Institute collection now, it sounds like Adrover was, at least, engaging with the issue of homelessness in his design. "At the time the homeless had no [mattress] ticking, Giuliani kicked it out of the shelters," he told curators Andrew Bolton and Harold Koda, referring to the then-mayor of New York City's ban on homeless people sleeping on the streets. "I was trying to show the downtown [Crisp] represented. At the same time, I was trying to show how hard it can be for people who are sleeping in the street."

Another, less harmful way in which fashion borrows from low culture is the embrace of a soupçon of bad taste. Exactly what defines good and bad taste is hard to settle on, to the point where it's something philosophers have been grappling with for millennia. Plato and Aristotle engaged with questions of beauty and aesthetics, while Kant and Hume tried to cement the bounds of what constituted empirical beauty. The concept was tussled over by eighteenth-century philosophers like Anthony Ashley-Cooper and Francis Hutcheson, who advanced an argument for an innate standard of taste. But the idea as a more subjective quality took longer to come into vogue—sociologists have continued to debate whether it is an inherent quality or something that comes from our external environments.

The sociologist Georg Simmel believed in a trickle-down theory of taste—that it originates from the upper classes, the middle classes copy them, and then the upper classes have to come up with something else. He envisioned it as an ever-shifting roundelay. "The more nearly one set has approached another," he wrote, "the more frantic becomes the desire for imitation from below and the seeking for the new from above." There is certainly ample historical evidence to back that up. In the first half of the sixteenth century, the upper classes wore bright colors like red, and the middle classes tried to copy them, defying sumptuary laws that were meant to rein in extravagance in dress and other areas. James Laver, in *Costume and Fashion: A Concise History*, writes: "It is a curious comment on human aspiration that during the Peasants' Revolt in Germany, one of the demands of the insurgents was that they should be allowed to wear red like their betters." Toward the end of the eighteenth century, Marie Antoinette's hairstyle was endlessly copied by the common folk in the same way we copy Jennifer Aniston's now. If anything, the celebrity and influencer class might stand in for "the upper class" today.

Our modern understanding of this "trickle-down" theory of style influence comes from the famous "cerulean speech" Meryl Streep's imperious editor-in-chief character delivers in *The Devil Wears Prada*. When her assistant, played by Anne Hathaway, says she doesn't really see the difference between two similar-looking blue belts, Streep upbraids her:

> You think this has nothing to do with you. You go to
> your closet and you select, oh I don't know, that lumpy
> blue sweater, for instance, because you're trying to tell

the world that you take yourself too seriously to care about what you put on your back. But what you don't know is that that sweater is not just blue, it's not turquoise, it's not lapis, it's actually cerulean.

You're also blithely unaware of the fact that in 2002, Oscar de la Renta did a collection of cerulean gowns. And then I think it was Yves Saint Laurent, wasn't it, who showed cerulean military jackets? . . . And then cerulean quickly showed up in the collections of eight different designers. And then it filtered down through the department stores and then trickled on down into some tragic Casual Corner where you, no doubt, fished it out of some clearance bin. However, that blue represents millions of dollars and countless jobs, and it's sort of comical how you think that you've made a choice that exempts you from the fashion industry when, in fact, you're wearing a sweater that was selected for you by the people in this room.

The speech gets a few things right: Color trends do filter through fashion in a cyclical way, and certain colors can dominate a season. (For more on that, see the next chapter.) And fashion is more than just a random assortment of items (hey, look, the premise of this entire book!). But the "cerulean speech" is also predicated on an older model of fashion, where a few high-end designers dictated the season's styles to the masses—and we don't live in that world anymore. What Miranda Priestly doesn't acknowledge is that style can also trickle *up*.

In *The Theory of the Leisure Class*, Thorstein Veblen introduced the concept of "conspicuous consumption," or the practice of buying things, like designer clothes, that demonstrate one's wealth. There is also what author and academic Elizabeth Currid-Halkett recently identified, in her book *The Sum of Small Things*, as "inconspicuous consumption": things like private education, health care, and childcare, which bolster the upper classes but are less "visible" than a Birkin. Wealthy people in the Gilded Age, when Veblen was writing about status anxiety, had squadrons of servants; now they have French-speaking nannies, concierge doctors, and prep schools.

The French theorist Pierre Bourdieu's landmark work *Distinction* made the point that not all currency is conspicuous in the way, say, owning a McMansion or a yacht is now. Something he called "cultural capital" can be a form of currency. For example, attending a prestigious university or becoming a subscriber to the symphony can give you cultural capital, even if you do not possess actual capital—you're a broke grad student, say, or you spent your last paycheck on concert tickets. Here's a good way to wrap your head around the idea. Consider the two families in Bong Joon-Ho's movie *Parasite*: The working-class Kim family is able to scam the wealthy Parks into employing them without the Parks realizing they're all members of the same family. The Parks have tons of visible capital—their state-of-the-art modern home being the most obvious—but they lack cultural capital, which is why they are so impressed when the son and daughter of the Kims pretend to be a highly educated English tutor and an art therapist, respectively. The Parks hope the Kims can impart some of that cultural capital to their children, thereby enriching them.

A hyper-attuned fashion sense can be a kind of cultural capital as well. Logos and name brands aren't the only way to telegraph wealth. "Stealth wealth" is used to describe a kind of conspicuously inconspicuous consumption—like the minimalist, well-made clothes from Mary-Kate and Ashley Olsen's label The Row. Those not in the know may just see a gray turtleneck or a camel coat—but those who are will appreciate the refinement of those pieces. Shiv Roy's wardrobe on *Succession* has become the prime pop-culture example of stealth wealth. Her clothes—well-tailored high-waisted trousers and fitted turtlenecks—are by high-end brands like Armani and Ralph Lauren, but not easily identifiable in terms of their labels. They don't scream "luxury," but they definitely whisper it. On a less grand scale, wearing an item from Comme des Garçons Play, with its heart-with-eyes logo, is a sign of cultural capital and fashion insider-ness. It gives the wearer a connection to the ingenuity and avant-garde outlook of Rei Kawakubo, even though the item is relatively affordable and simple (a striped shirt, a Converse sneaker). The same goes for carrying a *New Yorker* tote bag. Even if back issues have been piling up on your coffee table for weeks, it shows you approve of the overall project.

This idea of fashion sense as cultural capital also explains the increased emphasis on craft in high-end fashion. In an age of mass production, the human touch is highly prized in so many realms of design precisely *because* it's become rarer—i.e., Emily Bode's meticulously quilted wares or rough-hewn pieces by the cult-favorite Japanese brand Visvim. Their exteriors may look homespun, but they also telegraph the labor contained within the clothes, which makes them more valuable.

Stealth wealth and rustic luxe aren't the only ways to express fashion superiority, though. Sometimes incorporating a little bad taste can be a way of indicating that you're cool and in on the joke— and so unconcerned about being perceived as tasteless, you're able to play with bad taste as a trope. With the advent of postmodernism, artists like Jeff Koons began incorporating the intentionally déclassé into their work with a wink, and the approach soon spilled over into fashion as well. For Chanel's spring 1995 show, Karl Lagerfeld put models in miniskirts, some so mini they revealed their underwear, and midriff-baring tops; they carried plastic Chanel shopping bags. It felt youthful and excessive while still adhering to house codes. The joke was that the revealing outfits still felt like the province of proper ladies. Lagerfeld's exuberant embrace of all things quotidian reached a peak with his fall 2014 "Supermarket" show, which opened with Cara Delevingne in an intentionally holey sweat suit walking through a *supermarché* set up in Paris's sprawling Grand Palais. Lagerfeld had once equated sweatpants with giving up, calling them "a sign of defeat"—now, he was giving in to a world where ultracasual attire and Whole Foods runs have become chic. The theme was also a way for Lagerfeld to delight in visual in-jokes: In the hardware section, for example, a Chanel chainsaw came with the house's signature chain link. Handbags were shrink-wrapped like something from the butcher department, with a sticker reading "100% Agneau," or lamb. The models wore tweed-accented dad sneakers and other forms of luxury schlepwear.

If I had to name a current designer who's embraced low culture with gusto, it would be Demna Gvasalia. The designer, who grew up in the Republic of Georgia, gravitates toward a kind of postmodern, post-Soviet aesthetic that celebrates all things supposedly déclassé. His first show for his design collective Vetements (French for "clothes") featured a mix of reimagined everyday wear (floor-sweeping, wide-legged gray sweatpants) and sexy glitz (slick thigh-high boots). Designer Gosha Rubchinskiy opened Vetements's spring 2016 show wearing a T-shirt with the logo of delivery service DHL. Its $300 price tag raised eyebrows in the fashion crowd—plus, what if someone mistook you for a delivery driver? In an interview with the fashion journal *Vestoj*, Gvasalia expresses admiration for the ambiguity contained in such a garment. "When I wear a sweatshirt with 'Monoprix' [the French supermarket] on it, what am I signalling? Am I saying it's cool to work at a super-market or am I making people ask themselves why I'm wearing a Monoprix logo, when I could be wearing one from Balenciaga? . . . Obviously everybody knows that I don't work at Monoprix, well everyone who knows me does anyway. If a stranger sees me in the street wearing my Monoprix jumper, they might think I really do work there and I quite like that."

In 2015, Gvasalia assumed the creative director position at Balenciaga, and his love of mingling high and low continued. He paid tribute to house founder Cristóbal Balenciaga's original silhouettes. But he also created BALENCIAGA T-shirts in a font that mimicked the Bernie Sanders logo, made a chunky dad sneaker called the Triple S an influential hit, and showed platform Crocs—a once-reviled shoe in fashion circles, now rendered cool thanks to Gvasalia's magic touch. In 2018, he even elevated tacky airport souvenir-shop items to must-have status by creating bags emblazoned with touristy landscapes of New York, London, Tokyo, and Hong Kong. Of course, the boundaries between high and low fashion are remarkably permeable, and the borrowing goes both ways, with low culture grasping at high fashion's status-inflating abilities.

The research bears out the fact that conspicuous consumption is more important to strivers than it is for those who are in the higher echelons of society. According to Currid-Halkett's book, the middle class now spends more on conspicuous consumption, relative to their income, than the upper classes. For what Currid-Halkett calls "the aspirational class," even small gestures like buying an heirloom tomato or carrying a status tote bag can be a way to signify they're keeping up with (or outdoing) the Joneses. The numbers break down along racial lines, too. A University of Chicago/Wharton study she cites found that Black and Latinx individuals spent more than white people in their same income and education bracket. "For minority groups with a history of being discriminated against," Currid-Halkett concludes, "conspicuous consumption becomes a means through which they can efficiently demonstrate their social and economic position before being pre-judged." Look at the legendary designer Daniel "Dapper Dan" Day. Beginning in the '80s, he had a store in Harlem where he sold his extravagant pieces, which "sampled" designer logos in the same way rappers were beginning to sample music. His customers were members of a growing aspirational class in the Black community, including Mike Tyson and Eric B. & Rakim. Rather than knockoffs, Day preferred to call his designs "knock-ups." And they served an important emotional function for his customers. In a time when luxury brands were not clamoring to dress Black celebrities, and were in some cases unwilling to do so, Day told GQ that his creations were "transformative" for the people he dressed. "I gave them a chance to see themselves on a higher level," he says.

The Austrian psychoanalyst Alfred Adler taught his patients a method called "acting as if," a way of inhabiting a new, more positive mindset. For many people in the aspirational class, fashion is a way of "acting as if," allowing them to assume the role of the privileged luxury customer. High fashion, though, can operate like the snobby sales associate in *Pretty Woman*, keeping out all pretenders. When British soap opera star Danniella Westbrook was seen on the street wearing a full Burberry check look, complete with matching baby stroller, in 2002, the fashion establishment jeered at what was seen as the ultimate example of trying too hard. *The Guardian* later called it "the ultimate symbol of nouveau rich [sic] naff." In a press release, Abercrombie & Fitch offered *Jersey Shore* star Mike "The Situation" Sorrentino a "substantial" amount of money (later reported to be $10,000) not to wear their clothing on the show. Similar efforts were afoot with his castmates—the writer and fashion commentator Simon Doonan claimed in a *New York Observer* column that high-end brands were giving the reality stars their competitors' luxury bags as a way to drive down their desirability.

"Acting as if" may be endorsed by power-posing enthusiasts, but it's not always a successful strategy when it comes to using fashion to feel good about oneself. A Harvard/UNC/Duke business school study found that "wearing counterfeit products makes individuals feel less authentic and increases their likelihood of both behaving dishonestly and judging others as unethical." In an experiment, those who wore fake branded sunglasses as opposed to the real McCoy were more likely to cheat on a test and also judged others' behavior as more unethical. "A product's lack of authenticity may cause its owners to feel less authentic themselves," the study's authors wrote, "despite their belief that the product will actually have positive benefits . . . these feelings then cause them to behave dishonestly and to view other people's behavior as more dishonest as well. In short, we suspect that feeling like a fraud makes people more likely to commit fraud."

Still, copycat fashion has always had a certain appeal. Once, department store copyists were sent to Paris to see the couture fashions with an eye to knocking them off for the average American consumer. Now, fast-fashion merchandisers do the same with clothes practically as soon as they appear on the runway—the only difference is that the cycle is much faster, and thus harder for customers to keep up with. And while Halston's collaboration with JCPenney in the '80s ended up hurting his high-end business, it's now commonplace for design houses like Versace and Rodarte to collaborate with H&M and Target. Masstige, the blend of mass and prestige, is now cool. It's been called the democratization of fashion, which is true in a sense—it's great that the work of talented designers is able to reach a larger audience, and that customers are able to buy into that dream at affordable prices.

Still, the overwhelming enthusiasm for masstige reminds me of the concept of "poptimism," usually applied to music criticism. Once, only "authentic," non-manufactured songs were considered worthy of critical discourse. Now, there's an enthusiasm for top 40 hits, which is a welcome turn of events, but sometimes overshoots the mark and becomes a blanket endorsement of anything popular. More fashion, even if it's more affordable and widely available, isn't always an unqualified win for democracy.

With the advent of these collections, there were more clothes than ever to be had, and more pressure to keep up with every new cycle. "High/low" became first a personal style directive, and then more of an order, for strivers. Millennial women, who entered the workforce during a recession, were advised to mimic a proper professional appearance by mixing fast-fashion items, often runway knockoffs, with "investment pieces" at a time when investments of all kinds felt precarious. The advice was less often given to men, due to the increased pressure on women to keep up with trends and the ever-moving target of what looked like "appropriate" attire for the office. You didn't want to be too provocative or too prim; you wanted to pass as older and more authoritative while still looking cool.

Fast fashion was a lifehack that would help you easily hurdle class boundaries, or at least that's how I saw it. My first job was at a fashion publication where my colleagues regularly wore Marni and Prada to work, and through a combination of fast-fashion approximations of the real thing and consignment versions of it, I was able to pass as one of them—never mind that I still lived with my parents, was paying off student debt, and was barely breaking even.

Luckily for me, I didn't need to pretend for too long. Fast fashion became normalized, and being able to carefully spot a chain bargain became as brag-worthy a skill as finding a great vintage score, a way to advertise you had champagne taste on a beer budget. The chains I'd once been embarrassed to say I shopped in got a glint of cool.

What we members of the millennial precariat either didn't realize or didn't choose to look into was the way the fast-fashion system was built on the backs of people who were underprivileged to a much larger degree than we were, whose working conditions and surrounding environment were negatively affected by the avalanche of new, trendy clothes being churned out to clinging-to-middle-class aspirants like me. (According to the nonprofit Remake, the fast-fashion workforce is made up of 80 percent young women ages 18–34, earning low wages.)

Resale sites and rental services have become more popular, politically correct ways for people like my past self to meet the ever-evolving standards of workplace dressing, and now, leisure dressing for Instagram. Rather than buy cheap clothes, you can buy expensive ones at a discount or borrow them for a week or two. The sense of fashion "imposter syndrome," however, does not entirely shift. And these solutions don't entirely remove the endless demand for more, more, more that threatens the stability of the brand's workforce, and that of our planet. So what is a broke millennial who loves fashion but has moral qualms supposed to do?

The recent push-pull between high and low culture—and the demand for high-end living at an affordable price—has led to a phenomenon that goes beyond fashion but has a lot of implications within it. In 2017, the writer Venkatesh Rao was eating at a fast-casual restaurant when a phrase popped into his head to describe the chain's atmosphere: "premium mediocre." He defined the concept in a blog post: "Premium mediocre is the finest bottle of wine at Olive Garden. Premium mediocre is cupcakes and froyo. Premium mediocre is 'truffle' oil on anything (no actual truffles are harmed in the making of 'truffle' oil), and extra-leg-room seats in Economy." A hallmark of anything premium mediocre is that it has a patina of exclusivity while still being relatively accessible. In fashion terms, that might mean a baseball cap with a designer logo on it, or inexpensive "luxury" cashmere. Rao calls the premium mediocre purchase "an inferior good in the guise of a Veblen good," the former being something customers usually trade up from when their income increases (like instant noodles) and the latter, named for you-know-who, something whose customer demand rises along with the price (like a luxury watch). It's something meant to be flaunted on Instagram, a way to show that you are part of a select few.

Premium mediocre "is ultimately a rational adaptive response to the challenge of scoring a middle-class life lottery ticket in the new economy," Rao wrote. ". . . [A]n economic and cultural rearguard action by young people launched into life from the old middle class, but not quite equipped to stay there, and trying to engineer a face-saving soft landing . . . somewhere."

The "Instagram versus reality" meme, which shows unrealistically perfect or luxurious images side by side with the less photogenic reality, is built on the tradeoffs of the premium mediocre lifestyle: Maybe you're carrying a Louis Vuitton weekender, but the flight is on Spirit Airlines. It's an encapsulation of the millennial condition: conveying the appearance of a luxury lifestyle while frantically cutting corners in secret.

What premiocre, as the writer Amanda Mull shortened it to in *The Atlantic*, ultimately boils down to is millennial instability and precarity. It seems to offer a chutes-and-ladders-like passageway into a new social class. With the gig economy, the scarcity of secure jobs, and economic uncertainty caused by the global financial crisis, the most millennials can do, writes Mull, is "playact modern success for as long as possible while hoping the real thing happens eventually." Premiocre items are "props for this Kabuki theater: things you buy because they're masquerading as more exceptional than they are." Just as you, yourself, might be.

PART II

The Top Layer

Fashion and the Wider World

CHAPTER SIX

Déjà Hue

Fashion is an industry so obsessed with chromatic exactitude that there's a constantly circulating anecdote about a designer who used to hand his assistant a light-beige Pantone chip to illustrate exactly how he liked his coffee. This doesn't even track as extreme behavior, given that color is such an all-consuming fixation among fashion people. Many of the fashion images we see are color-corrected to within an inch of their lives. Glossy printouts of models and celebrities are routinely dissected under interrogation-bright lighting for hours before a violet shadow is cautiously introduced.

Style is a business built on whim, emotion, and subjectivity—and nowhere is that quality more clear than in its palette. Colors can crest and wane, come to sum up a particular moment in time and then look hopelessly out of date. They can stand in for an entire worldview: The environmental movement's verdant green and Earth-from-space blue, punk's palette of Day-Glo neons, contemporary minimalism's muted grays and oats. They can come to be associated with a design house or a style icon, take on a political cast (see: red and blue states), evoke moods (feeling blue, seeing red, being green with envy, looking at the world through rose-colored glasses) or abstract qualities (purple prose, a blue movie). A specific hue can demarcate in-groups and out-groups by signaling loyalty to a sports team, a school, or a gang, or can, more troublingly, mark a group of people as Other (scarlet letters, yellow stars).

Color crazes balloon and burst like tulip-fever bubbles, seeping into design as a whole. Certain shades in fashion, interior design, and graphic design can come to stand in for and signify entire philosophies. (Think of the relentless pastel palette of ads for direct-to-consumer startups, which are far too cool to use aggressive, saturated brights.) In her landmark study *The Secret Lives of Color*, Kassia St. Clair explains how mauve, for example, was embraced by Empress Eugénie of France and Queen Victoria of England, the closest thing the nineteenth century had to influencers. Mauve seized Victorian-era London with such force that the humor magazine *Punch* said in 1859 that the city was "in the grip of the Mauve Measles." Its epidemic hold on the populace didn't last, though; soon, it was as out of fashion as it had once been coveted.

A specific shade can feel confined to a decade—avocado green in the '70s, hot pink in the '80s, turquoise in the '90s—and then come roaring back as a meta-retro statement. (The recent revival of avocado green in millennial design, for example, might reflect a return to '70s hippie/organic values. Or simply our apparent generational lust for avocado toast.) Rose gold, notably used by Peter Carl Fabergé for his luxurious gilded eggs in pre-revolution Russia, experienced a resurgence around 2015, most notably in the case of the iPhone 6S, which seemed to presage the rise of a specific feminized kind of luxury. A gold phone felt tacky, like a relic of the early aughts—but a rose gold phone felt pretty and status-bearing at the same time; like a Fabergé egg, it was a pure and beautifully pointless luxury object (no one *needs* a gilded phone just to call, text, and look at their social media feeds). It came at a similarly epochal, pre-revolutionary time, a fetish object perfect for a sailing-along economy and relative pre-2016 calm. (It was also, interestingly, catnip to men, who dubbed it "bros' gold" and snapped up iPhones in the color like baseball cards.)

It's astounding, when you think about it, that we've managed to find so many infinite variations of color. The color spectrum, like a musical scale, contains only a limited number of notes that we keep going back to, combining, chord-like. It's the closest thing that fashion has to a language. When the right notes are struck in unison, they can add up to a haunting chord made of individual refractions of light: a signature shade. St. Clair argues that colors "should be understood as subjective cultural creations: you could no more meaningfully secure a precise universal definition for all the known shades than you could plot the coordinates of a dream."

While Carl Jung was among those to recognize color as an important aspect of perception, the specialized field of color psychology is still relatively new. Angela Wright, one of the subject's pioneers, told the design podcast *It's Nice That* that "being a color psychologist did mean, for many years, being somewhere out there on the lunatic fringe, in the eyes of society." When she was growing up in England's Lake District, her family owned a hotel, and she observed the influence of color schemes on guests' behavior and preferences—how they would overwhelmingly prefer a room of a certain shade to an identical one painted a different hue. Wright came to believe, for example, that "too much yellow in the bedroom produced grumpy guests," because the color activates the emotions too much to allow for proper rest. She went on to create the influential Colour Affects System as a way to catalog these associations.

More subtle than a logo, a color works on us not with in-group appeal but as a blunt-force emotional statement. A favorite color used to be something you'd memorize about a crush as a kind of key to all their mythologies: "He likes BLUE!" Even a less exciting shade, like gray, can become synonymous with a personality. In the 1950s, Sloan Wilson's novel *The Man in the Gray Flannel Suit* came to define a certain kind of conformist, postwar business drone. It's a vision of neutrality, the Switzerland of colors, not nearly as decisive as white or black. And while it might seem that the office clones of Wilson's creation have nothing in common with the tech bros of today, it seems that little has changed, at least, when it comes to their power palette. In a 2016 Facebook post, Mark Zuckerberg wrote, "First day back after paternity leave. What should I wear?—feeling undecided." The accompanying photo showed a closet of gray T-shirts, a nod to Zuckerberg's unexciting uniform. His gray T-shirts evoke tech's obsession with eliminating decision fatigue and lifehacking away the friction of frivolous daily choices—why deliberate over V-necks versus crewnecks when you could be coding? They also call to mind that industry's dismissive attitude toward fashion and the male privilege inherent in not caring about it. (Though, reportedly, Zuck's shirts are special-ordered from the high-end Italian designer Brunello Cucinelli and cost between $300 and $400, so he may care about fashion a little more than he lets on.)

But most of us don't want to have a closet full of gray T-shirts. We're entranced by color—and when a designer strikes upon the right one, it can become emblematic of luxury: think of Hermès orange or Tiffany blue. When you unwrap that orange box or open that pale-blue bag, you feel special and important. There's a reason why there's a brisk secondhand business in luxury packaging, with empty shopping bags and boxes going for serious cash online. In the ultimate triumph of branding, the container has become just as important as the contents.

Color's link to luxury originally stems from its connections to royalty—for example, Dutch orange, the official color of William I of the Netherlands, or the various shades of red that were controlled by sumptuary laws, relegating the common classes to wearing brown. Henry VIII, not known for his flexibility in any realm, restricted expensive red dyes to higher castes of society; in thirteenth-century Spain, the color was reserved for monarchs. Nearly every civilization had some form of dress-based sumptuary laws, many of them centered around color and reserving brighter shades for higher-class citizens. Naturally, this only made certain colors more desirable and stirred up status anxiety around them. Michel de Montaigne devoted an essay to the topic, noting that the royal stamp made any item far more entrancing to the common people. "For to enact that none but princes shall eat turbot, shall wear velvet or gold lace, and interdict these things to the people," he wrote, "what is it but to bring them into a greater esteem, and to set every one more agog to eat and wear them?"

Purple is probably the color most associated with royalty. Julius Caesar wore togas in Tyrian purple, a plummy shade that he declared exclusive to him. In the later days of the Roman republic, trying to emulate the emperor's color palette was a crime punishable by death. Deep purple in classical Japan was considered *kin-jiki*, meaning forbidden, to those who were not royals or monks.

Color is no longer the province of the ultra-wealthy, because dyes are no longer so expensive. Now, anyone can wear bright colors, and perhaps there's been a concurrent reversal in their status: Fast-fashion stores are filled with bright, jangling neons, while high-end minimalist brands like The Row and Jil Sander eschew much color at all, instead opting for tamer, more neutral palettes. Minimalists brag about paring down their wardrobes to only the most monochrome, Zuckerbergian hues—a status move in itself. It's almost as if being moved emotionally by color feels like a productivity-sapping weakness to the ultra-successful. Better to remove one less variable from the mix.

Designers, of course, have long been entranced by color. Look at Elsa Schiaparelli, the pioneering Surrealist designer, who, in 1937, introduced the world to shocking pink, a hot shade that was genuinely shocking at a time when demure pale pinks dominated. The violent hue was startling, overt—femininity as warfare. It represented a new woman who was liberated and sexually brazen, the kind of woman that Schiaparelli wanted to dress. As legendary fashion editor Bettina Ballard wrote, "she changed the outline of fashion from soft to hard, from vague to definite."

"Shocking" went on to be the title of both Schiaparelli's perfume—the bottle mimicked Mae West's lazy-river curves—and her autobiography, forever associated with the designer and her fashion house. As for how shocking pink came to be, there are two conflicting origin stories. According to Meryle Secrest's biography of the designer, after the French jeweler and accessories designer Roger Jean-Pierre showed her designs for pink buttons, she selected the brightest one, saying, "We are going to call it Shocking Pink." Kassia St. Clair gives a different backstory: It girl Daisy Fellowes, once described as "a Molotov cocktail in a Mainbocher suit," was wearing a stunning bright-pink Cartier diamond during a meeting with Schiaparelli, inspiring the designer to put her own stamp on the color. Whatever the true origin of shocking pink, it changed the course of Schiaparelli's career. She called the color "life giving, like all the light and the birds and the fish in the world put together, a color of China and Peru but not of the West." She went on to work with Salvador Dalí on Surrealist designs that incorporated the hue, including a shoe-shaped hat with a shocking pink heel.

Like any trend, the color quickly caught on beyond its creator, with *Women's Wear Daily* breathlessly reporting, "Everywhere you go you are greeted with entire hats or hat trimmings in the daring, sometimes glaring, petunia pink shades which all started with Schiaparelli's Shocking." It became a form of bombshell plumage, the color of Marilyn Monroe's dress in *Gentlemen Prefer Blondes*, as she stood silhouetted against tuxedoed men. Anna Nicole Smith frequently wore it, including when she re-created that *Gentlemen Prefer Blondes* moment for a PETA ad, and Hollywood Barbie Angelyne sports the color so religiously she even has her signature pink Corvettes custom-painted to match her lipstick. The color has clung on even today—NARS makes a lipstick called Schiap, inspired by the bright color of a Schiaparelli powder box one of François Nars's friends picked up at a flea market. And Schiaparelli runway shows still prominently feature the shade.

Another fashion grande dame who will forever be associated with a color is the legendary fashion editor Diana Vreeland, who once declared, "I want my apartment to look like a garden: a garden in hell!" And indeed it did: Her Park Avenue living room, decorated by Billy Baldwin, was a fiery den of bright-red carpet, riotously printed red Fleurs de Mal fabric on the walls, bookshelves lined in red and chairs slipcovered with it, and her beloved red peonies everywhere. Even the door was painted red. Vreeland, who felt strongly about colors in general ("pink is the navy blue of India" was one famous dictum), lavished the color not just on her home but on herself. For her, it was a form of exaggeration: She favored rouge that extended out to her ears, scarlet lipstick, bloodred nails ("which some people objected to, but then some people object to absolutely everything," she wrote). "Red is the great clarifier—bright, cleansing, revealing. It makes all colors beautiful. I can't imagine being bored with it—it would be like becoming tired of the person you love." She spent her life in quest of the perfect shade: "I can never get painters to mix it for me. It's exactly as if I'd said, 'I want rococo with a spot of Gothic in it and a bit of Buddhist temple'—they have no idea what I'm talking about." She gave them a shortcut to the exact red she wanted: "copy the color of a child's cap in any Renaissance portrait."

Legendary Italian designer Valentino Garavani is also closely linked to the hue. He has explained his affection for red by calling it "a color that is not shy." Growing up, he went to see the opera *Carmen*, which made a formative impact on his famous eye. "The whole set was red—the flowers, the costumes—and I said to myself, 'I want to keep this color in my life.' Garavani's first couture show, which put him on the map internationally, took place at Florence's Pitti Palace in 1962. It included a series of bright-red dresses. Midway through his final couture show in 2008, the lights on the runway turned red. A bevy of models strode out in red gowns, remaining onstage as the designer took his final bow and cementing his association with the color forever. (The secret to the hue's punch: Valentino red contains a bit of orange.)

Red might as well be the official color of excess. Hyacinthe Rigaud's *Portrait of Louis XIV* shows the monarch sporting a luxurious ermine cape, silk stockings—and red-soled heels. In the era of the Sun King, they were status symbols. In *Dressed to Rule: Royal and Court Costume from Louis XIV to Elizabeth II*, Philip Mansel explains that red soles were "restricted to nobles with the right genealogical qualifications to be presented at court," and provided proof that the wearer was high-born enough not to dirty his or her soles. The modern equivalent of the royal red heels would be the red soles of Christian Louboutin shoes—though thankfully, while they're still steeped in luxury, you no longer have to possess a coat of arms in order to purchase them. The designer hit upon the idea when he was working on a prototype and saw an assistant painting her nails.

He seized the bright-red polish and painted the shoe's sole with it, creating a built-in, if relatively hidden, signifier of luxury.

Hermès's signature citrus orange had similarly happy-accident origins. During World War II, according to the house's website, "there was a shortage of cream-coloured cardboard boxes. The supplier resorted to what he had left. It happened to be orange." The rich hue has evolved slightly over the years. A collector could distinguish the boxes "by the depth of the shade, the grain, the logo, the band around the edges."

Tiffany blue came about a bit more intentionally. It was chosen by the house founder, Charles Lewis Tiffany, for the cover of the Blue Book advertising its jewelry in 1845. According to a history of the shade on the brand's website, "this distinctive color may have been chosen because of the popularity of the turquoise gemstone in nineteenth-century jewelry." By the 1880s, it began to be used on Tiffany's shopping bags, in its ads, and, perhaps most notably, on its boxes. The New York store even contains a Blue Box Cafe enrobed, from its walls to its booths, in the color.

But amid changeable style tides, some fashion people stick to the safety and security of monochromatic dressing. For example, the stereotypical "fashion nun" editor, penitent in all black, who's become as much of an archetype as the fashion victim decked out in this season's It items. The only person more associated with bright blue than artist Yves Klein (who patented International Klein Blue in 1960) is the late street-style photographer Bill Cunningham, who adopted bright-blue French workmen's jackets, originally worn by nineteenth-century laborers, as his uniform. He reportedly bought them at hardware stores for $20 apiece; he liked the way that the multiple pockets allowed him to carry rolls of film. The "bleu de travail," as it was called, evoked the American expression "blue collar," and suggested "I'm here to do a job," setting him apart from the street-style peacocks who milled around him, mugging for his camera. It fit in with Cunningham's insistence that he was not *of* this fashion world, but simply documenting it, and his staunch refusal to accept so much as a free glass of water while covering a gala. The color made him recognizable, but it also cloaked him in objectivity. The utilitarian chic of the garment has since brought the high-end "chore coat" into the fashion lexicon. Street-style stars now wear them as a fashion statement, and Vetements showed an oversized blue version on the runway for spring 2016. After Cunningham's death in 2016, photographers wore bright-blue ones in the photo pit at New York Fashion Week to pay tribute to their late colleague.

Blue is the color of consensus: Studies have found that it is the most agreed-upon favorite color in the world, perhaps because it evokes the widest range of associations. Blue has an appropriately ocean-like vastness that encompasses everything from staid, stable bureaucracy (the UN logo blue used by Balenciaga as a backdrop to its spring 2020 show) to intellectual, progressive women (bluestockings) to artistic agony (the blues, Picasso's blue period) to explicit content (comedians "working blue"). It simultaneously evokes democracy (the EU flag) and elitism (blue blood). William Gass devoted an entire monograph, *On Being Blue*, to the infinite connotations of the shade, calling it "the color of the mind in borrow of the body. It is the color consciousness becomes when caressed; it is the dark inside of sentences."

Even black, arguably a non-color, hits certain emotive notes. Long the symbol of mourning, it now connotes a kind of world-weary sophistication, an opting-out from fashion's vicissitudes. Coco Chanel took the color from the precincts of grief into the realm of the everyday. Her ingenious little black dress, which gave rise to many imitators, was the platonic garment that was appropriate for every occasion, simultaneously connoting chicness and disinterest in passing trends. Dressing in "basic black" may not be groundbreaking, but it's always a safe bet.

Black is perhaps the most fraught of the shades so far discussed: It can feel everyday and unobtrusive, or it can swing the opposite way, evoking death and the void. In the hands of avant-garde designers in particular, it reads as challenging and apocalyptic. When Japanese talents Yohji Yamamoto and Rei Kawakubo crash-landed at Paris Fashion Week in the early '80s, their deconstructed, tattered black designs were assailed with the ethnic slur-cum-review "Hiroshima's revenge." Kawakubo's models were deemed "nuclear bag ladies." Black felt radical at this point in time: In a decorative, flashy moment for fashion, their work landed like an avant-garde lead balloon, misunderstood by many. The writer Judith Thurman has compared Kawakubo's 1982 collection, "Destroy," full of oversize, intentionally holey garments, in terms of scandal fire-starting, to Stravinsky's *The Rite of Spring.*

Kawakubo and Yamamoto, who were at one point romantically involved, shared an affection for black. Kawakubo's black-clad coterie of fans was known as "the crows." Yamamoto once wrote a rhapsody on black, calling the color "modest and arrogant at the same time. Black is lazy and easy—but mysterious. It means that many things go together, yet it takes different aspects in many fabrics. You need black to have a silhouette. Black can swallow light, or make things look sharp. But above all, black says this: 'I don't bother you—don't bother me!' "

In the year 2000, Harvard's Graduate School of Design presented Kawakubo with its Excellence in Design Award, saying she "invented black." While she didn't literally invent it, Thurman argued later in *The New Yorker,* she did spur "the revival of black's cachet as the color of refusal." For Kawakubo, black existed in contrast to other favorite shades, including white and red, which she used to offset black in her collections for her label, Comme des Garçons—notably in 2005's "Broken Brides," 2012's "White Drama," 2015's "Blood and Roses," and 2015's "Ceremony of Separation." (Comme des Garçons has the best collection names in the business, no contest.)

When I interviewed curator Andrew Bolton for *New York* magazine on the occasion of the Comme des Garçons retrospective at the Met Costume Institute, he noted that the designer, though far from a traditionalist, is obsessed with rituals. "Sometimes, you're not quite sure whether they're birth, marriage, or death rituals," Bolton said. "She conflates the language of all three, but she definitely does revisit the idea of one's passage through life. I think she likes the idea of ceremony and ritual, the theatricality and performativity of rites of passage." Wedding whites, funerary blacks, and reds that feel alternately celebratory and anatomical show up constantly in her work. "Her three favorite colors are black, red, and gold," Bolton told me. "But white crops up all the time, and it makes sense because she likes very emphatic silhouettes. Monochromatic color, particularly white and black, emphasizes silhouette."

Theoretically, trademarked colors aside, no one *owns* a color. Sumptuary laws are, thankfully, a thing of the past, and now the entire chromatic scale seems like something that is available to all of us, like the sky. But that doesn't mean that some haven't tried to stake their claims. The tussle over Vantablack proves how contentious the ownership of a color can really be. In 2014, the company Surrey NanoSystems introduced a "blacker-than-black" shade by that name that absorbs 99.96 percent of visible light. A 3D object painted with this depth-defying hue appears as though all of its dimensions have collapsed. It is, as a member of Spinal Tap might say, "none more black."

Artist Anish Kapoor obtained the exclusive rights to the spray paint format of the color, Vantablack S-VIS, in 2016, prompting members of the art world to create #ShareTheBlack. No one was more incensed about this than fellow artist Stuart Semple. "I wanted to make a point about elitism and self-expression and the fact that everybody should be able to make art," he told Artnet of his decision to create The World's Pinkest Pink, and make it available to all except Kapoor. Those who bought the paint online were advised, "By adding this product to your cart you confirm that you are not Anish Kapoor, you are in no way affiliated to Anish Kapoor, you are not purchasing this item on behalf of Anish Kapoor or an associate of Anish Kapoor. To the best of your knowledge, information and belief this paint will not make its way into the hands of Anish Kapoor."

However, via his London gallery, Kapoor did manage to get his hands on Semple's pink—specifically, his middle finger, which he dipped in the paint for a defiant Instagram post. (The caption: "Up yours.") Semple's riposte was to come up with a series of ultra-black shades: BLACK, BLACK 2.0, and BLACK 3.0. He began selling them at his store, The Art Shop in London's Mayfair neighborhood, to any customers who wanted them, except Kapoor, whom he banned from the store. While this seems like a silly (and deeply British) feud, it does raise questions about the ownership of color. Can a specific shade really "belong" to anyone?

As we've seen, color is emotional, slippery, wholly subjective. It can mean completely different things across different cultures. (Russian, for example, has different words for darker and lighter blue; Danish, for light red and pink.) But if color has a regulatory body of sorts, it would be Pantone, an organization that describes itself as "the global authority for color communication and inspiration." Its mission might be summarized as trying to dam up and redirect the free-flowing river of color into something categorizable and cogent.

Pantone, which began as a printing company in the 1950s, began its work of systematizing the world of color in the '60s. The company began naming a Color of the Year in 2000, kicking off the new millennium with none other than Miranda Priestly's favorite shade, Cerulean. Since then the colors Pantone has selected for its annual honor have often encapsulated what society cares about in that moment: nostalgia, futurism, the natural world. Sometimes, they also unintentionally evoke loss. Living Coral, the color of 2019, came shortly after the news that half of the coral in the Great Barrier Reef had died off since 2016. Human awareness of climate change had never been higher. Nature was also seen as a refuge: "In reaction to the onslaught of digital technology and social media increasingly embedding into daily life, we are seeking authentic and immersive experiences that enable connection and intimacy," trumpeted a press release.

Similarly, Greenery, the color of 2017, played on the growing fetishization of nature, though this particular green hue felt slicker and more industrial than previous shades of avocado and grass. Reefs and trees may be finite, but color, at least, is a renewable resource.

World-historical events can also shape color trends. At the moment of the 2008 financial crisis, Laurie Pressman, vice president of the Pantone Color Institute, told Mental Floss, "All I could see in my head was a selling floor filled with grays and neutrals. Everybody was fearful about money—they weren't going to want to be spending it on bright color." The company responded to the coming austerity by creating new shades like Storm Front, a subdued gray, and Humus, a faint taupe. After the deaths of Prince and David Bowie, both associated with shades of purple, Pantone released 2018's Color of the Year, Ultra Violet, citing both musicians, as well as Jimi Hendrix, as loose touchstones for the shade.

It's particularly interesting to see how Cerulean, touted at the turn of the millennium, and Classic Blue, the color of 2020, bookended a two-decade period of particular societal tumult. The former is the color of the sky on a sunny day or a calm sea. It feels hopeful, the color of a pre-9/11, neoliberal world that was beginning to discover the possibilities of the internet. According to the company, it was meant to evoke "[this] paradoxical time in which we are heading toward an uncertain, yet exciting, future, and also looking back, trying to hold onto the security of the past. In this stressful, high-tech era, we will be searching for solace and Cerulean Blue produces the perfect calming effect." The statement noted that looking at blue has been proven to reduce blood pressure and slow the heart rate, and also cited the ecological significance of the color, adding that "water issues are emerging at the forefront of the public's consciousness. Exhausting our natural resources and polluting our environment, particularly our water supply, continues to be a concern, another reason for the popularity of blue for the future."

Classic Blue is more subdued, coming on the heels of the optimistic, late-morning hue that represented the dawn of a new millennium. Interviewed on NPR, obviously not a visual medium, Pressman was asked to describe Classic Blue to the listeners. She called it "the sky at dusk . . . a blue that speaks to the end of a day." According to Pantone, it's meant for "instilling calm, confidence, and connection." Sometimes, it was described in the language of a progressive political candidate delivering a stump speech: "We are living in a time that requires trust and faith. It is this kind of constancy and confidence that is expressed by Pantone 19–4052 Classic Blue, a solid and dependable blue hue we can always rely on," according to Leatrice Eiseman, executive director of the Pantone Color Institute. Waiting in the wings of this statement were all the unreliable elements of contemporary life that were, supposedly, causing us to seek refuge in this dusky shade.

Classic Blue also came with more fanfare than its light-blue ancestor. The company collaborated with brands to evoke the color's mystical appeal to each of the five senses, with items like a candle that smelled like sea salt, a velvety fabric representing the comfort of the hue, and even a three-minute-long instrumental track that, according to Pantone, "takes us to a place that is comforting and familiar." (I listened to it, and it sounded like Diplo's attempt to score the credits for a PBS documentary about the ocean.) The crepuscular shade had already made a dent in fashion, turning up on the runways of spring 2020 shows before the official announcement, from Balenciaga's bell-shaped ballgown in the hue to a slinky long-sleeved dress at Gucci. But while the crowd-pleasing color was undoubtedly in vogue, the announcement didn't meet with universal approbation. In an article for *Fast Company*, Evan Nicole Brown witheringly declared Classic Blue "the color equivalent of watching *Friends*"—bland and universally palatable. While Pantone had touted its anxiety-easing properties, the color, which hangs on the awnings of multinational banks and shows up in the background of software, felt too associated with corporations, technology, and work for it to be truly comforting. Brown wrote:

> To me, the hue calls to mind Facebook's logo and my Google Docs icon. A vivid blue reminder of data surveillance and the tireless demands of work in 2019 doesn't exactly soothe the soul . . . Then again, perhaps a corporate color is apropos, since Pantone's Color of the Year has always been about selling merchandise and dictating the palette companies use to encour-

age consumers to buy new clothes, furniture, and more stuff they don't need. In this way, Classic Blue is a depressingly cynical color to usher in the 2020s— passive, plain, and always for sale.

In twenty years, though, we might just be nostalgic for it.

CHAPTER SEVEN

Who Is She?

W HAT IS THIS quivering—pulsating—throbbing—beating—palpitating IT?" hyperventilated the Hollywood fan magazine *Photoplay* in 1926. "Undeniably IT is a product of this decade. Indeed, you might say IT is a product of this hour. But what is IT?"

The answer, at that point in time, boiled down to one woman: Clara Bow, who became associated enough with the word that fan letters addressed only to "Miss It, California" or "The It Girl" piled up at her doorstep. Bow wasn't the first "It girl," as a concept—in the nineteenth century, women like the actress Lillie Langtry and the opera singer Jenny Lind could qualify as such, since they fascinated the public and were heralded by the press. Still, Bow was the first to claim that specific title, thanks to her starring role in a 1927 screen adaptation of Elinor Glyn's novel *It* (not to be confused with the murderous-clown saga of the same name). Bow, a scrappy striver who made it from Brooklyn to Hollywood, was already a known quantity before *It* hit screens, but the film exponentially multiplied her star power. She—and the inheritors of the It girl mantle—would come to define a very specific slice of the fame pie:

the young women who split the difference between superstar and nobody.

Glyn defined It as a kind of sex appeal that defied mere looks or style. With It, she wrote, "You win all men if you are a woman—and all women if you are a man." Each era got the It girls it deserved: While Bow and her cohort in It-dom, actress Louise Brooks, had a louche flapper appeal, by the '40s and '50s the new icons were the Swans—a group of society women as perfectly groomed as their namesake—like Babe Paley and Slim Keith. Paley was the ultimate Lady Who Lunched, an unapproachable figure with carefully set hair and a designer wardrobe. Her friend Truman Capote famously said of her: "Mrs. P had only one fault: She was perfect. Otherwise, she was perfect." In contrast to Paley's WASPy East Coast vibe, Keith was a West Coast beauty who, with her sporty, menswear-inspired style, helped originate the sun-kissed, athletic "California Girl" archetype. (She also helped give birth to another It girl: She pointed out a young Lauren Bacall, on the cover of *Harper's Bazaar*, to her husband, director Howard Hawks; he cast her in a Keith-like role in *To Have and Have Not*.) Capote's roman à clef *Answered Prayers* nearly upended their reputations with its unflattering depictions of Paley's marriage and Keith's drinking, but thanks to their wealth and powerful husbands, both hung on to their It girl status.

The title doesn't typically confer much longevity on the honoree. Bow and Brooks had relatively short careers, especially when compared with successful actresses today. Bow's tenure in the spotlight was filled with relentless press speculation about her sexual exploits, which led the studio to cancel her contract. She "retired" at the age of twenty-eight, attempting suicide shortly afterward. The end of Brooks's acting career was more voluntary than Bow's—she hated Hollywood and turned down plenty of offers, perhaps finding that the roles she wanted weren't out there. She turned to on-and-off escort work after the dimming of her star wattage: "I found that the only well-paying career open to me, as an unsuccessful actress of thirty-six, was that of a call girl," she wrote in her autobiography, *Lulu in Hollywood.*

Unusually for the time, neither Brooks nor Bow had a career that was specifically linked to a man's—despite having Hollywood dalliances, both women operated as free agents, which didn't exactly help them thrive in the patriarchal studio system. They were also easily dismissed: Bow's appeal could be chalked up to charisma and charm, not talent. And Brooks's onscreen naturalism was so complete that some questioned whether she was really acting. Early on, the It girl was doomed to be called effortless even when she was actually making an effort.

With the advent of the '60s, the counterculture got its own It girls, notably "Youthquaker" Edie Sedgwick. The Youthquake, coined by Diana Vreeland, was the era's shift to mining youth culture for fashion and pop-culture inspiration. The decade saw teen-friendly brands Mary Quant (known for her Mod dresses and makeup) and Biba (Barbara Hulanicki's line of romantic, printed pieces) soar to popularity with their inexpensive designs. World War II–era hardship had helped create the rail-thin, youthful aesthetic Hulanicki described as "postwar babies who had been deprived of nourishing protein in childhood and grew up into beautiful skinny people. A designer's dream." She and Quant were there to clothe these stunted child-women in infantile Peter Pan collars and miniskirts, accessorized with big, innocent false lashes.

Sedgwick-as-It-girl marked a transitional moment between a culture fixated on the classical beauty of adult women like the Swans and one electrified by youth and rebellion. She was the perfect union of a swan and a hipster: a debutante whose veins ran pure blue, but who dove wholeheartedly into Andy Warhol's Factory scene. But despite her underground cred, the press she got mirrored that of her predecessors, in that it was entirely focused on her physical attributes. In 1965, *Vogue* described her as "twenty-two, white-haired with anthracite-black eyes and legs to swoon over." In the same year, *Life* proclaimed that she was "doing more for black tights than anybody since Hamlet." She inspired songs by Bob Dylan and the Velvet Underground, and continues to be a muse for current artists, including G-Eazy and Beach House, with the latter titling its song "Girl of the Year" after Sedgwick's informal moniker.

"Girl of the Year" (hereafter GOTY) is a more truthful appellation than "It girl" because it hints at the expiration date attached to the role. Sedgwick's time in the spotlight was like lightning—electric but brief. Behind the cool facade, she struggled with an eating disorder and a drug and alcohol dependency. Six years after the *Vogue* and *Life* headlines, she'd be dead, in California, of a barbiturate overdose.

If Sedgwick's short life, as chronicled in Jean Stein's unsparing oral history *Edie*, is the real-life epitome of the GOTY phenomenon, then the 1970 cult movie *Puzzle of a Downfall Child*, directed by fashion photographer Jerry Schatzberg, is its fictional apotheosis. Faye Dunaway plays Lou, a former GOTY—a model who has been summarily ejected from the fashion world after a string of drug problems and mental health issues. She goes from a red-lipped glamour kitten to a recluse hiding out in a beach house, wearing a beatnik's black turtleneck. Told in the achingly '70s format of audiotapes (Sedgwick was also obsessed with them, perhaps because they were a non-visual medium and a way to control her own narrative), the story is based on recordings Schatzberg made of the model Anne St. Marie. In the film, Aaron, a Schatzberg-like photographer and close friend of Lou's, is determined to make sense of her breakdown. Though, to his credit, Schatzberg's final product is much more empathetic toward its subject than what Aaron would probably have come up with. To a contemporary viewer,

Lou's deglamorized self looks aspirational for our stripped-down, "no-makeup makeup" era, but at the time it was a portrait of what happens when the camera retreats and the endorsement deals fade away—when the Girl of the Year approaches her inevitable sell-by date.

While the stars of today dole out skincare tips like candy, another class of retro icons clogs the mood boards of the internet—the Pinterest and Instagram feeds and the style blogs. Adorned with black-and-white glamour shots, these narratives, too, are goal-oriented service journalism lite, and vaguely SEO-driven. You can find out how to wear stripes like Jean Seberg, sport white eyeliner à la Sedgwick, or pull off a caftan with the élan of Talitha Getty. These women are differentiated by their stylistic quirks, but they're ultimately not all that different. They are almost all white and thin and well within the bounds of pretty much every standard of beauty that has been set since the beginning of the modern era. Those who aren't are usually known for some other pursuit—singers like Josephine Baker, movie stars like Dorothy Dandridge or Anna May Wong—but the crucial distinction is that they're not famous for simply being famous, the way Sedgwick was. Their beauty and style are contingent on their talent. Simply being decorative, sans résumé, seems to be a privilege reserved for white women, at least when it comes to this retro class of Pinterest stars. That's because while the contours of the It girl might change slightly, her novelty shouldn't be confused with newness. She is just a different iteration of an unchanging archetype, with looks that don't deviate far from the original and a personality that doesn't shatter the mold. See: Cara Delevingne channeling Edie Sedgwick with her wild-child-of-the-one-percent narrative, Emily Ratajkowski reincarnating Brigitte Bardot's sexpot smolder, or Alexa Chung emulating the British insouciance of Jane Birkin.

You might leave these online altars to the departed wondering why the "style icons" we worship are so often troubled and tragic figures whose pain is posthumously muted by their style. These style paeans rarely mention Seberg's suicide, Getty's overdose, and Sedgwick's drug addiction. (Stein's book is, of course, a correlative exception.) But if you want a pixie cut to bring to your stylist, an eye-makeup tutorial, or some ideas about how to work a caftan into your vacation wardrobe, they're your girls. (Always girls, rarely women.) And their very unknowability makes them a comforting antidote to the contemporary influencers who keep us drinking from a firehose of TMI. Sedgwick isn't exactly going to come back from the dead and start lecturing us about colonics.

Besides their alluring aura of mystery, it would stand to reason that there is some commonality that makes these women appealing as style icons. Surely some of it is that, like the party guest who arrives late and leaves early, she never lingers long enough to get boring. When Jay McInerney profiled the actress and '90s It girl Chloë Sevigny for *The New Yorker*, in what is perhaps the ur-It-girl-as-seen-by-fortysomething-man profile, a friend of hers told him, "She's smart enough to hold back, and that allows us all to project whatever we want to [onto her]. I could go on and on about Chloë, but actually I know very little about her." Sevigny, through her unorthodox acting choices and personal style, managed to break out of the box that stories like this placed her in. Perhaps being underestimated early on worked to her advantage, as she was able to parlay her GOTY blankness into a well-regarded film career, disappearing into roles like a Mormon housewife in *Big Love* and Lizzie Borden in *Lizzie*. "To me, the coolest thing is to keep something to yourself," she told *The New Yorker* in a sort of follow-up piece to McInerney's, "Chloë Sevigny at Forty."

Sevigny has been able to extend the parameters of It-dom, but she's an exception. More often, these women remain forever girlish, never fully realized, without weird and distasteful second acts, never boring us with context. They skirt our rejection, but on the other hand, they never get to be fully known. And when they try to escape the bounds of the role, the public doesn't react well. In the late aughts, the early days of her It-girl-dom, Alexa Chung had gone from a TV presenter and model to a kind of muse-for-hire, with her own namesake bag from Mulberry and a series of fashion collaborations with different brands. Still, "I don't want to be known for floating around and just going to parties," she said at the time. Yet her attempts at different careers—including author (of a book called, what else, *It*)—were resolutely overshadowed by her style and image. People didn't want Alexa the personality; they wanted the look. Chung is now primarily a designer, with an eponymous fashion line that heavily channels her own personal style. Like Victoria Beckham or Mary-Kate and Ashley Olsen, she traded in wider celebrity for a kind of fashion celebrity.

The It girl may be the only American archetype that doesn't usually get granted a second act. They become recluses (Brooks, Bardot), or they die, prettily. A particular cachet seems to attach itself to those gone too soon. Carolyn Bessette Kennedy's every minimalist look is dissected with reverence on Instagram, and there's a reason that Peter Weir's *Picnic at Hanging Rock* and Sofia Coppola's *The Virgin Suicides*, two of the movies most cited as "inspiration" in the fashion sphere, both concern girls disappeared by the maelstrom of adolescence. The source for the latter was Jeffrey Eugenides's novel written from the perspective of a group of neighborhood boys who are fascinated by, but barely know, the girls at its heart. It's not so different from McInerney's Sevigny opus. It girl stories are often narrated by distant, entranced men. Or look at Marie Antoinette, pre-Revolution: a perennial muse for the way she built a life around frivolous beauty, and the basis for another Coppola film. Had she gone on to a long, stable life, it's unlikely she'd be as celebrated.

These women's affects have flattened into aesthetics and self-help, as immediately identifiable, yet detail-free, as a turn-of-the-century silhouette drawing, the tragedies associated with them conveniently swept under the rug. The It girl is the master of externality, all joy and charm and no visible suffering.

But the pain, too, is part of it. Those who write about these women would have you think that style is innate, clinging like a classic string of pearls to our DNA strands—that Jane Birkin was just born knowing how to wear Breton shirts better than the rest of us. But style sometimes—often—develops as a defense mechanism. Look at Isabella Blow, who used her signature outré hats to offset lifelong melancholy (she compared them to antidepressants) and to distract from what she believed to be her own flaws. Or Big and Little Edie Beale, the mother-and-daughter duo in the documentary *Grey Gardens*, whose strange semaphore of style—skirts worn as capes, turbans deployed to disguise hair loss—was born of their squalor and isolation but has been lifted for countless designers' collections. Then there's Sedgwick, who said herself that her signature makeup look was less style experimentation and more facade, like a wall around a medieval moat. "I'd make a mask out of my face," she told Jean Stein, "because I didn't realize I was quite beautiful . . . I had to wear heavy black eyelashes like bat wings, and dark lines under my eyes, and cut all my hair off . . . strip it silver and blonde and all those little maneuvers I did out of things that were happening in my life that upset me."

Fashion is often referred to figuratively as "armor," but what if we thought of it as something more akin to a defensive adaptation, much like an armadillo's bony scales? Think of Frida Kahlo, who favored long, colorful skirts to distract from her amputated leg, the result of being disabled in a bus accident, and a lower body that had been withered by polio. Her shawls and blouses disguised the back brace that encased her body; her elaborate flower crowns drew the eye upward. She painted her corset with flora and fauna and adorned her prosthetic leg with colorful paint. The accident also caused her infertility—when a metal rail pierced her uterus—a personal source of anguish she nodded at by painting a fetus on her corset over her abdomen. She found ways to externalize each vulnerability and refused to hide, depicting herself in paintings and posing for images by art photographers of the time like Edward Weston. Her insistence on being seen was her way of fighting back against the invisibility of disability.

But the painful genesis of Kahlo's image is usually lost in endless talk about flower crowns, unibrows, and Coachella-themed Pinterest boards. She is now seen by many as a shorthand for colorful personal style and not much else. An exhibit at the Brooklyn Museum in 2019 showed the artist's work alongside her clothing and personal belongings. The title of that show was "Appearances Can Be Deceiving"; the version at the V&A in London was called "Making Her Self Up," both of which point to the centrality of Kahlo's appearance in her legacy. See also: the Brooklyn Museum's Georgia O'Keeffe retrospective, which included the painter's makeup compact and 2010s-Brooklyn-appropriate wardrobe. It's hard to imagine a Matisse retrospective including the artist's shaving mirror or work from Picasso's Blue Period standing cheek by jowl with a tube of his toothpaste. But these little totems, talismans, and tools of beautification are considered as central to Kahlo and O'Keeffe's identities as their actual output. Susana Martínez Vidal, author of *Frida Kahlo: Fashion as the Art of Being*, has called her a "selfie queen," who would today be "a real influencer . . . with a legion of followers."

And like a present-day influencer, she has had an impact on designers. The corset that encased Kahlo's spinal column was the inspiration for Madonna's *Blond Ambition* corset, designed by Jean Paul Gaultier, though its origins in Kahlo's pain and ill-health are little remembered. Occasionally, a designer has delved a little deeper, as Riccardo Tisci did for Givenchy's fall 2010 couture show, which drew on the artist's obsession with her own anatomy. Tisci embellished dresses with beaded skeletons and spinal columns, in tribute to the way Kahlo turned herself inside out for our gaze.

Recently, I noticed a cluster of designers referencing Princess Diana, which could have had to do with the anniversary of her death, the trend cycle returning to her late '80s/early '90s heyday, her story arc on *The Crown*, or the saga of Meghan Markle mimicking many aspects of Diana's story. Kristen Stewart played Princess Diana in the movie *Spencer*, only intensifying the craze. (Stewart seems to have carved out a niche for It girl roles: She's also portrayed Jean Seberg in a biopic.)

Diana was known for her Sloane Ranger style—think an elevated British version of preppy—but that didn't seem to translate to the present day. Instead, design polymath Virgil Abloh drew on Lady Di's sportier looks in a 2017 show for his brand Off-White, re-creating, for instance, the bike shorts she wore out on walks. (There was also a plastic version of a glass slipper, made with Jimmy Choo.) For British fast-fashion chain ASOS, nail artist Sharmadean Reid created clothing designs inspired by the late royal. Some, like the off-the-shoulder "revenge dress" modeled after the one Diana wore post-split with Prince Charles, were drawn from her wardrobe or felt like something she might have worn.

As the ultra-approachable Markle—who, in the reverse of the Gwyneth Paltrow trajectory, *began* as an aspiring It girl, blogger, and influencer—started her ascent, some were calling her a successor to Diana, the next "People's Princess." (It's worth noting that men, who presumably possess less symbolic value, are never asked to be a People's anything.) When Markle made her famous Megxit from the monarchy, her return to being a commoner made her, just like Diana, even more beloved. Both were touched with the fairy dust of royalty while still standing in stark contrast to the presumed stuffiness and elitism of the institution.

And it was Diana's supposed unaffectedness that people were praising. Abloh's lineup included a "Natural Woman" jacket, suggesting that Diana was an antidote to contemporary artificiality. You could call it the fashion equivalent of those "In a world of Kardashians, be a Diana" memes. But part of Diana's appeal to current-day designers—besides her trapped-in-amber youth and beauty, of course—is that lack of affect. The way that she was uncomfortable with being a model princess and used fashion to compensate—wearing an attention-getting dress as "revenge" against her royal ex, for example—makes her style feel more exciting than that of today's self-assured, stylist-having royals. Whether Diana's style was, in fact, a transmutation of her pain is up for debate. But like the other women in her cohort, her relatively short life and the tragic nature of her death make her an ideal canvas for a designer's imaginings.

You might think that in a no-filter age that proclaims everyone to be beautiful in their own way, we'd be done with It girls, especially the classic breed of It girl who doesn't really "do" anything. But in fact, as beauty standards for real women have become slightly more forgiving, and "realness" (or a certain brand of it) more prized, their digital-age iterations have become even more flattened, with desirable traits assembled like members of a prefab boy band. That's how you end up with the affectlessness of Lil Miquela, a CGI "influencer" whose popularity only increased after the reveal that she was an avatar; Shudu, a virtual model who is the "art project" of photographer Cameron James-Wilson; or Poppy, a real-life pop star who has made a blank, CGI-like affect her signature. While Lil Miquela—whose popularity shows no signs of deflating; she appeared kissing Bella Hadid in a Calvin Klein campaign—represents a departure from white Western beauty ideals, she's not much of a departure from the It girl playbook overall. Her ethnic ambiguity feels like an algorithm come to life, an attempt to represent everyone of every background while at the same time feeling completely idealized and remote. Her inner life is just as mysterious to us as her predecessors', her glancing interest in social justice the only update to the standard It girl playbook.

One might think the uncanny-valley quality of these avatars would dim their appeal. But the rise of the CGI influencer is a reminder that the It girl at her core has always been a kind of avatar of a woman: reduced to angles and contours and easily identifiable personality traits, her pain shaved down as if by a plastic surgeon. (Thus the dehumanizing pronoun "it.") As a culture, we claim to love complex women, but the complexity behind our favorite It girls' style signatures is mostly lost to history; their endurance over the past century seems like proof that we're not comfortable with processing female pain, or even female eccentricity.

Instead of a Warholian future where everyone gets to be famous for fifteen minutes, maybe we're headed for a world where fake people are at the pinnacle of fame. Perhaps the CGI creation is the ultimate endgame of the It girl phenomenon. Why engage with a real woman when a paper doll will do?

CHAPTER EIGHT

Why Can't I Be You?

M AYBE EVERYTHING CHANGED when we went from having friends to having followers. Social media, in its early years, was an extended version of your address book, a place for friends to write goofy, performative messages on your Wall, share their latest 2:00 a.m. insights, and tag you in unflattering photos. Then, when we weren't looking, it morphed into a gated community you were allowed peeks into via a kind of attenuated Robin Leach tour. "Friends" implied a kind of easy rapport; "followers" had cultish echoes. What made someone worthy of being followed? Did they have insights that couldn't be found elsewhere? Hypnotically good taste? A life so perfect that looking at it on a screen resembled staring into the sun?

Who knows the exact rationale, but social media as an ever-updating stock ticker of the good life has triumphed, with people eager to gain access to those they don't know. More than 38 million of them follow Kylie Jenner on Twitter. And a Kylie tweet has a lot of zeroes attached to it. When she announced she'd be selling Lip Kits (essentially, a Gen Z–friendly repackaging of lipstick), her website crashed, but not before she raked in millions in sales. Conversely, with the flick of a Twitter finger, she can also send a company into the red: Snapchat stock lost $1.3 billion after Jenner tweeted about her growing disinterest in using the app.

When you have an audience like Jenner does, one that could fill a stadium's worth of stadiums, a 280-character burst contains the volatility of uranium. So can a simple monochromatic tile. Jenner's sister Kendall, along with fellow models Emily Ratajkowski and Hailey Bieber, was able to drum up buzz for the ill-fated Fyre Festival just by posting an orange square on Instagram. The festival and its accompanying high-concept trailer promised the opportunity to hang out with movers and shakers like themselves—instead, attendees arrived to find looted tents, soggy mattresses, and zero Jenners.

These are extreme examples, but even those of us who have never bought a Lip Kit and couldn't be less interested in seeing Blink-182 perform in the Bahamas are still prone to being, well, influenced by influencers. Anyone who's gotten lost in the weeds of an It girl's medicine cabinet that looks like a French pharmacy on Into the Gloss, a budding actress's succulent-filled home on Coveteur, or a freelance writer's irreconcilably luxe beauty routine on A Cup of Jo has had the feeling. Namely, is a $70 camellia oil the only thing keeping me from being this kind of person?

The influencer, a vague term derived from an already nebulous verb, has supplanted the untouchable, unknowable movie star, the supermodel who only wakes up for $10,000 a day, and the It girl of the previous chapter, with her paper-doll approach to style. Ostensibly, she is more down-to-earth than any of these previous tropes. In fact, her entire appeal is that she is a better version of one of us. The antithesis of the polished celebrity who's at a remove from the common man, she seems like she could be your best friend—with an emphasis on "could." After all, you already know so much about her, between her Instagram and the plenitude of lifestyle websites that chronicle her fashion, decor, food, fitness, wellness, and beauty proclivities. With a little digging, you could come to know every corner of her apartment, how she's raising her children (even the ever-so-relatable screwups and tantrums), what she eats in a day, and, most importantly, the products that prop up the whole illusion. At your best, you might be inspired to overhaul your life for the better. At your worst, you might take another look at a dusty corner of your bedroom, or your zit cream in the medicine cabinet, or the books that have the audacity to not be organized by color, and wonder what's wrong with you.

When modern-day influencers emerged in fashion, they were bloggers, and consequently seen as outsiders, the New Journalists to magazines' and websites' staid Establishment. At a D&G show in 2009, the blogger Bryanboy and the street-style photographers Tommy Ton, Garance Doré, and Scott Schuman—all of whom maintained their own blogs—were seated front row with their laptops while bigger names languished in the second row. At the time, it was seen as an insurrection; now, it's hardly worth remarking on. Influencers and fashion editors sit side by side at shows; editors are expected to maintain a social media presence as part of their jobs, and some have gone on to become full-time influencers. Some individual influencers command more followers than major fashion media brands. YouTuber Emma Chamberlain and beauty vlogger Michelle Phan appear on the covers of print magazines that once exclusively depicted celebrities and models. Complaints about magazines Photoshopping subjects beyond all recognition have resulted in unfiltered, no-makeup shoots that replicate Instagram's supposed spontaneity, while many influencers' pages are Facetuned to a T. The lines between who's real, who's fake, who has authority and who doesn't have not just blurred: They have mostly ceased to matter.

The progression has been much the same in the broader world. At a certain point, everything began to converge: Celebrities started acting like influencers themselves, influencers became more and more like traditional celebrities, and everyday people mimicked influencers. Average Janes with follower counts in the double and triple digits began propping and posing their lives for the 'gram. Everyone could now be a content creator and, by the same token, anyone could now be a potential influencer, too. Influencers act like your friends; meanwhile, your friends are all, strangely, acting like influencers. We're in a digital Stepford where identities flatten and an overwhelming aesthetic multiplies: white borders; soft, inviting colors; no filter. You would think constant variety and innovation would triumph, but in fact, some of the most successful people on the platform are those who, like rigorous conceptual artists of the '70s, limit themselves to a few repeating elements: patterned floor/pedicured feet; cute girl/colorful wall.

Once, I only knew what my close friends' apartments looked like—now I see all my Instagram acquaintances' perfectly appointed spaces, plus a rotating cast of their friends, families, and significant others, the vacations they take, the seltzer brands they prefer, the never-dog-eared, bright-colored hardcover books they're reading. It seems there are so many new areas to succeed in, even self-care, a term that has strayed far from its origins in radical Black feminism, when Audre Lorde, writing in *A Burst of Light*, declared that "caring for myself is not self-indulgence, it is self-preservation, and that is an act of political warfare." Now, we're expected to care for ourselves photogenically, in the form of the perfect sheet-mask selfie or of a photo of feet emerging from a bubble bath. Evolutions or progressions that have no visual corollary go unreported.

Tavi Gevinson began her public life as a tween fashion blogger whose avant-garde proclivities gained her entrée into the fashion mainstream even as she, still a child from suburban Illinois, retained outsider status. It was a one-foot-in, one-foot-out situation, a new type of fashion fame still in its infancy. As with many bloggers, her next step was to become an influencer. In a *New York* magazine cover story about Instagram's effect on her psyche, Gevinson wrote about a private account she briefly maintained to share things like pictures with famous people in their homes, which rewarded "the part of myself that had learned to register experience as only fully realized once primed for public consumption." On her public account, where she commanded a much larger audience, she strived to seem more authentic, while recognizing the contradictions inherent therein. "My propensity to share, perform, and entertain has melded with a desire far more cynical," she wrote, "to be liked, quantifiably, for an idealized version of myself, at a rate not possible even ten years ago."

For Gevinson, like so many others, Instagram became an extension of work and was sometimes more monetizable than her day jobs; at one point, she writes, she was living rent-free in a Brooklyn apartment building in exchange for posting about said apartment. It might seem like a dream existence. But as her Instafame, predicated on her image, grew, she also developed a habit of compulsively picking at her face. "Of all the nervous habits to have, why claw at my greatest asset?" she asked herself. "One friend suggests it is a territorial response to publicness, a way of exercising control. Another thinks it is a subconscious rejection of the type of fame I have both relied on and resented."

The "influencer" may be a coinage of our times, but advertising has always hinged on envy and the desire for self-improvement. It's also been linked to lifestyle: This cigarette will liberate you, this perfume will make you irresistible, this car will take you to new places. In Edward Bernays's 1928 manual *Propaganda*, he writes that in order to sell pianos, for example, a clever marketer wouldn't tout the qualities of a specific piano, but instead try to normalize the idea of having a "music room" in your home. They might also call upon the circa-1928 equivalent of influencers to help things along by, say:

> . . . organizing an exhibition of period music rooms de-signed by well-known decorators who themselves exert an influence on the buying groups . . . Then, in order to create dramatic interest in the exhibit, he stages an event or ceremony. To this ceremony key people, per-sons known to influence the buying habits of the pub-lic, such as a famous violinist, a popular artist, and a society leader, are invited. These key people affect other groups, lifting the idea of the music room to a place in the public consciousness which it did not have before . . . The music room will be accepted because it has been made the thing. And the man or woman who has a music room, or has arranged a corner of the par-lor as a musical corner, will naturally think of buying a piano. It will come to him as his own idea.

Violinists and popular artists may no longer have much sway over our tastes, but Bernays knew a few things about selling, and his methods have persisted. A famous public relations man and the nephew of Sigmund Freud, he was part of the US Committee on Public Information during World War I, helping to "sell" the war to the American people much as he would push any other product. He came up with a campaign to sell cigarettes to women by calling them Torches of Freedom and getting young, feminist women to smoke during the Easter Parade to associate the activity with wom-en's empowerment. He popularized bananas for another client, the

United Fruit Company, by getting bananas into the hands of the right celebrities and placing them at the right hotels. (On the more extreme end, he used his propaganda tactics to help undermine a leftist regime in Guatemala that threatened the United Fruit Company's profits.) Much of his work has a direct through line to the seeding campaigns brands do with influencers today, as well as the association of buying something with a cause, like feminism. He didn't so much promote the product as conjure the need to buy it out of thin air. It was what the popular columnist of the era Walter Lippmann would have called "the manufacture of consent."

The only thing that has changed is the distance between the consenter and consentee. Once, we looked up to untouchable stars who felt as remote as gods on Olympus. The influencer model represents a shallower form of aspiration—not the trickle-down effect of a fan seeing Elizabeth Taylor in her white diamonds and purchasing a bottle of White Diamonds perfume, or buying a Chanel lipstick after clicking through a slideshow of its latest runway show, but coveting the leggings or yoga mat or crystal-infused water bottle that an Insta-star hawks online. It's a smaller mental leap to make, comparable to the tiny consumerist itch of seeing something your friend has and wanting that thing—and, maybe, the lifestyle that goes along with the thing, too.

Once upon a time, these kinds of endorsements remained siloed in their own niches, with high-end stars playing to the luxury market and mass figures targeting the rest of us. Now, with the overall flattening of the fashion and beauty industry, that's ancient history. Kim Kardashian can simultaneously be the face of the French luxury house Balmain and a social media shill of the diuretic confections of the Flat Tummy Co. In the same way, actual A-list actresses and supermodels have taken on the traits of influencers: Look at Gwyneth Paltrow, blogging about her trusty pancake recipe on Goop, or Reese Witherspoon walking us through the making of her daily smoothie. It's hard to believe that movie stars once sought privacy—there are very few now, most of whose fame predates social media, who maintain a Garbo-esque anonymity when not on the promotional grind. An avowed interest in privacy, in not presenting your life for public approval and affiliate links, now carries with it the shame of a bizarre hobby, like painting model figurines in your basement. If you're hiding, you must be hiding *something*.

Even social media "detoxes" are presented with the gloss of personal branding, complete with rambling explanations about the toxicity of the medium, and almost always followed by a quick return to it. (Which makes sense—when your livelihood depends on these platforms, quitting them is like quitting oxygen.) And when an influencer shatters the fourth wall of the iPhone screen to "get real" about depression or anxiety, or to show the "imperfect" reality behind the airbrushed pictures, she's rewarded with even more likes, more engagement, more selling. Nothing sells like authenticity, or at least a simulacrum of it.

Rather than keeping their beauty and fitness tips shrouded in mystery or doling them out occasionally in interviews, these public figures evince a new (if narrow) openness, and with it a new expectation: You, too, can achieve what they have. A perversion of the Protestant work ethic prevails. Nothing, except your own laziness and maybe a few thousand dollars, is keeping you from getting there yourself. Is it any wonder that in an increasingly stratified society, we would be drawn to anyone promising an easy fix, a way to leapfrog across the moat that separates the haves and the have-nots?

Trying to keep up with the Joneses isn't anything new, but the seductive and dangerous thing about these new platforms is the way they create a false likeness between the Joneses and ourselves, a kind of faux-democracy where we're all just a splurge away from equality. Previous generations knew they couldn't actually be

Elizabeth Taylor and Audrey Hepburn, even as they tried to emulate them. But now there are plenty of women who want to be just like these influencers. And their appeal is predicated on telling us just how easily we can make that happen. Paltrow told the *Financial Times* that "the true tenets of wellness—meditation, eating whole foods, drinking a lot of water, sleeping well, thinking good thoughts, trying to be optimistic—are all free." Theoretically, this is true, but what she said sidesteps some important caveats: All of these things are a matter of privilege. Clean drinking water isn't available in many parts of the country, organic produce is expensive and not readily available in less well-off areas, and it's hard to meditate, eat and sleep well, or think good thoughts when you're saddled with debt, struggling with pain while uninsured, or working an on-call job. Then again, would we really want to hear the realities of what it takes to achieve wellness on an A-list level—the personal trainer, the nutritionist, the private chef? Even if we intellectually know that it's not as easy as they make it look, the ease is so tempting—a form of personal development as entertainment.

Self-advancement through self-improvement has always been a particularly American impulse; in the New World, people hoped to feel less beholden to the strictures of a hierarchical society. This attitude was crystallized in the writings of Transcendentalist thinkers. Ralph Waldo Emerson devoted significant ink to the importance of self-reliance, or what we might now call "working on yourself." He encouraged his readers to "acquire habits of self-help." (He also famously declared that "imitation is suicide," which might be the anti-slogan for social media.) Henry David Thoreau advised a Spartan lifestyle, including only eating one meal a day. For the Transcendentalists, self-improvement was a matter of tough, lifelong spiritual or philosophical work; now, we're given a frictionless shortcut: Buy (always buy) these things and you, too, can live this way, and then demonstrate to others that you live this way.

There's an influencer for everyone, at this point. Paltrow's brand is one of voyeurism—her website, Goop, is a chronicle of Paltrow's favored potions and unguents, and a catalog, if you can stomach $90 for a one-month supply of vitamins (or £4,500 for a ticket to her Wellness Weekend). There's an element of internet-era lifehack culture at play here: Maybe, the thinking goes, we can loofah our way to some perfectly exfoliated state of Paltrow-ness. Goop clearly gets as many hate-reads, or at least irony-reads, as it does straightforward viewings—its divisiveness is part of the entertainment, and its creator seems, to her credit, aware of that.

By contrast, some celebrities have built their lifestyle empires on inclusion, or the appearance of it. If Paltrow was the popular girl who wears designer clothes and drives an expensive car to school, then Chrissy Teigen's irreverent Twitter presence and cookbooks full of sinfully indulgent foods made her the celebrity equivalent of the "cool girl" who drinks beer, eats junk food, and isn't afraid to rib her A-list friends. The antithesis of the polished celebrity who's at a remove, she seemed like she could be your best friend, which gave her a potent appeal, even to those jaded by marketing.

Paltrow's and Teigen's brands may not have much overlap, but they're running on parallel tracks: They (and their social media teams) took the language of female friendship and turned it into marketing copy. They want you to spill. On Twitter, Teigen asks her fans for dating horror stories; Paltrow's "Ask GP" column on Goop allows admirers to write in and ask her for advice on how to take a good makeup-free selfie (answer: Apply Goopglow Microderm Instant Glow Exfoliator, $125) or how to get Paltrow's wedding-day glow (answer: the Goop Glow Kit, now marked down to $185). These are often confided in the manner of a secret or tip, the way a friend might. There's a mimesis of the language of female friendship, but the friendly makeup saleswoman or the Avon lady has been replaced by your celebrity BFF.

Intra-influencer contretemps have raised questions about what it means to be the "right" kind of influencer. In a viral interview with Dan Frommer for *The New Consumer*, the food writer Alison Roman, whose photogenic recipes were made for Instagram, "came for," as they say, two other lifestyle influencers, Teigen and Marie Kondo. Roman critiqued them for creating mass-market product lines and, in her view, selling out. The fact that her jabs were directed at two Asian women resulted in Roman, who is white, being rightfully called out. (Teigen was later called out, too, for her own, unrelated bullying scandals.) But in critiquing these women, Roman also seemed to be prioritizing a kind of false hipster purity—yes, I'm trying to monetize my brand, but not millions-of-followers-Target-line monetize, *that* would be uncool. Yet Teigen and Roman are both, incontrovertibly, brands. The writer Steven Phillips-Horst crystallized this in *Interview* when he described the two as amalgamations of other brands. "Roman is a former Madewell girl turned Rachel Comey girl, who makes Mediterr-adjacent recipes for other Comey girls and their moms," he wrote. "Teigen is an Everlane girl in gifted Yeezys making Cheesecake Factory recipes for Uncommon James shoppers." In this milieu, the concept of "selling out" feels like a relic of a different, *Reality Bites* era, when people could still afford to turn up their noses at the monetization of anything. Now, so many of us are merrily unboxing, doing viral challenges, and tagging brands, whether we're being paid to or not. The concept of non-billable hours has fallen away, with the gig economy atomizing into our downtime as well. "We submit even our leisure for numerical evaluation via likes," writes Jenny Odell in *How to Do Nothing*, "constantly checking on its performance like one checks a stock, monitoring the ongoing development of our personal brand." Free time, she says, "becomes an economic resource that we can no longer justify spending on 'nothing.' "

Men have lifestyles, too, but lifestyle website-having seems to be a largely female proposition—a fact Stephen Colbert used as a jumping-off point for his fake "Covetton House" lifestyle brand. In his parody videos, he lounges barefoot on a couch in a field of cattails, and he even brought a surprisingly game Paltrow on to help shill a $900 loofah. Colbert's take on Goop is intentionally ridiculous, but his brand name's nod to "coveting" is not accidental—these companies are built on monetizing the jealousy that we feel seeing other people win at life, and our sense that acquiring the things they have will have some talisman-like effect on our own lives. And women, from birth, are under more pressure to appear and act perfect, so it makes sense that covetousness would be gendered. This is starting to change, however. Tom Brady has emerged as the prototypical male influencer, with his book *The TB12 Method* and his branded dietary supplements pushing wellness concepts watered down for his jock audience. While his advice may be dubious, at least Brady's status as a physical specimen and top athlete makes him a good advertisement for a healthy lifestyle. He's a living embodiment of the "this is what peak performance looks like" meme. Someone like the far-right radio host Alex Jones, who hawks supplements, would probably be on the other end of that spectrum, but his business isn't as divorced from the chichi wellness world as you might think. The supplements he sells are, as Molly Young pointed out in the *New York Times Magazine*, sometimes near-identical to those hawked by Amanda Chantal Bacon, the founder of Moon Juice. For example, "Super Female Vitality," sold by Jones's Infowars, has many ingredients in common with Moon Juice's varied Dusts (which include Sex, Spirit Brain, and Beauty). Both advertise a cocktail of gender essentialism, youth, and energy, via hard-to-swallow promises like "neuron velocity," just to completely different audiences.

The influencer at her most ideal promises a kind of redress. Health and wealth—the two tenets of the influencer—are unevenly, unfairly distributed, and sometimes seem coercible by magic. You can't buy your way to health, and health alone is dissatisfying without some monetary means. As someone who has only sporadically had either, and never at the same time, I've found myself taken in despite my better judgment. Influencers promise individual solutions to systemic problems: being unwell and uninsured, being tired from overwork, feeling depressed and anxious. Young writes that "what they sell is self-absorption as the ultimate luxury product."

Products are at the heart of this whole enterprise. Whether we're passively viewing or actively posting, we are both being sold to and selling ourselves, our data points harvested for advertising. The arrangement echoes a piece of 1973 video art by Richard Serra and Carlota Schoolman back in the era when trashing television rather than upholding it as the peak medium of our time was de rigueur. They called it "Television Delivers People," and it included the following scroll of text:

- Commercial television delivers 20 million people a minute.
- In commercial broadcasting the viewer pays for the privilege of having himself sold.
- It is the consumer who is consumed.
- You are the product of T.V.
- You are delivered to the advertiser who is the customer.
- He consumes you.
- The viewer is not responsible for programming.
- You are the end product.

And if you are the product, it makes sense that you must always keep improving, to become as "New and Improved!" as a bottle of ketchup with a streamlined new logo. If you want to have a presence on Instagram at all, even as a garden-variety non-famous person, you've probably considered sprucing up your space, upping the ante on your vacations, and drinking more photogenic lattes, because nothing happens in a vacuum anymore. We live in a constant state of self-consciousness, a panopticon we've opted into, where our consumer choices and our personal habits have never been more public or more symbolic. You go to a museum to look, to an audience of strangers, like you're the kind of person who enjoys going to museums. You buy things that an ideal version of you might own. The insidious part is that this process feels hardly distinguishable from having fun connecting and expressing yourself. In reality, you are simply being asked to succeed on more levels and work more to keep up with your avatar's unholy pace. The hedonic treadmill goes up to 11.

I don't want to discount here the way that social media platforms have been successfully used in a genuinely productive manner: to connect, to organize, and to give underrepresented voices the platform they deserve. Hashtag activism obviously has its downsides, but it is also true that entire movements, from #BlackLivesMatter to #MeToo, have coalesced around the internet's ability to erase geographical and parochial barriers; writers and comedians have emerged on Twitter—which, for all its landmines, has brought about a certain meritocracy of the funniest and sharpest, and has given people who didn't come up through traditional channels an audience. But celebrity culture and self-improvement culture are threads of the overall experience and are ones that seem to be fraying as I write, while activism only appears to grow stronger and more organized on these platforms. Influencers no longer seem like a scrappy underclass: If anything, they're an overclass many now want to topple. And, as always once we accustom ourselves to a new medium, some healthy questioning starts to set in. In the infancy of reality television, it felt like we were watching an unmediated live feed of human depravity—now, the *Bachelor* and *Real Housewives* franchises are gleefully dissected for the finely honed cultural products they are, mandoline-sliced by an editor's savvy hand. After our initial wonder—the horses are running directly off the screen toward us! These people are just *living their lives* in front of the camera!—the same phenomenon inevitably happened with social media. People hate-follow influencers' lives the way they might hate-watch a trashy TV show. Influencer-trolling accounts document the awkward behind-the-scenes antics of getting the perfect shot; on online forums like Blogsnark and GOMI (Get Off My Internets), their feeds and lives are dissected in threads longer than *Middlemarch*. But as far as the influencers are concerned, a hate-follow is still a follow. Engagement is engagement.

The influencer bubble hasn't yet burst, but it's starting to shudder. The difference between selling and simply connecting on social media seems increasingly academic. Now, a sponsored post seems as straightforward as a Super Bowl commercial to trained eyes—in the same way that we don't believe a soft-drink spokesperson is fired up with genuine passion for their beverage of choice, we've come to be more suspicious of professional influencers. This effect is already in evidence: Companies are pursuing "microinfluencers," people with small follower accounts, precisely because they seem more trustworthy. When A-listers are striving to seem as "normal" as possible, why not one-up them by hiring an actual, honest-to-God normal person? A story in *The Atlantic* revealed that regular people who aspire to be influencers are even posting *faux* sponsored content, which one young would-be influencer said would help build "street cred." There was an "Is nothing sacred?" outcry when the piece came out, a pushback against yet another boundary being hurdled, as though it's not the sponcon that bothers us, but the unlinking of the practice with fame.

As the gap widens between the micro- and macroinfluencers, though, the sameness seems to be coming to a halt. Events like the coronavirus pandemic and the Black Lives Matter protests against police killings of Black men and women began to fray the fabric of the influencer illusion. With many people stuck at home and unemployment at an all-time high, we had more time to focus on, for example, the quarantine dwellings of the famous and how much their modern homes looked like the house in *Parasite*. Influencers in The Wild, an Instagram account that tends toward *America's Funniest Home Videos*–style footage of people falling off embankments or getting wave-smashed in quest of the perfect shot, pivoted, as they say, to "topical." It had a truly unbelievable run of posts showing the ways influencers, or people who fancied themselves influencers, were using boarded-up stores, "Fuck the Police" graffiti, and even the protests themselves as the perfect "gritty" backdrop for their latest posts. A bright-pink wall or an Insta-friendly mural were once their catnip; now they were replaced by lines of police in riot gear. The need to seem socially conscious and aware, or simply to affiliate yourself with something that was happening, led to an influx of protest shots, even as organizers warned that showing other protesters' faces could put them in legal jeopardy. The need to seem down for the cause was actually, in this case, hurting the cause.

It seems that anything can be turned into lifestyle content. Sponsored weddings, pregnancy reveals, and births have all become ho-hum in Influencer World. In 2019, plans for a #spon proposal by fashion Instagrammer and Goop employee Marissa Fuchs went viral. It was unclear if the proposal was the last shibboleth of private life and true romance unsullied by commerce, or if it was the fact that a pitch deck had been created to attract potential advertisers (headers included "Journey to Marriage" and the text described Fuchs's "fans" as her "extended family"). I wasn't that scandalized by *l'affaire Fuchs*, finding it more comical than sacrilegious. A year later, a few more scales fell from my previously jaded eyes when I saw the way quarantine—a national lockdown spurred by a global pandemic—found its way into content. Perhaps I shouldn't have been surprised. Suddenly, there were carbon-copy recipes that seemingly everyone was making, that trended and waned—sourdough starter, banana bread. There were identical TikTok teens in identical tie-dye sweatsuits, in their identical McMansionettes, doing identical dances. When I was a teenager, being like everyone else was the least appealing concept imaginable. Now, a series of replicants unfolded on my screen, all dancing to the same bars of "Savage." J.Lo was doing it; my friends in their studio apartments were, too. We were all one.

The celebrities were going on Instagram Live, telling us we were all in this together, but already-stark socioeconomic and racial divides were only made more visible by the pandemic. Essential workers were required to risk their lives; the privileged could stay home and get anything they wanted delivered. As Amanda Hess wrote in a *New York Times* piece titled "Celebrity Culture Is Burning," "The famous are ambassadors of the meritocracy; they represent the American pursuit of wealth through talent, charm and hard work. But the dream of class mobility dissipates when society locks down, the economy stalls, the death count mounts and everyone's future is frozen inside their own crowded apartment or palatial mansion. The difference between the two has never been more obvious." The same tools that let us into influencers' lives, selectively, became liabilities. We became fixated on their surroundings, their pools and yards and walk-in closets. And on their tone-deaf—in some cases, literally—missteps. Gal Gadot confessed that six days (!) of quarantine "got me feeling philosophical," and enlisted celebrity friends for an off-key telethon-style singalong of "Imagine" benefiting . . . nothing.

Hess wrote that celebrities "are accustomed to receiving accolades for 'using their platforms' to 'raise awareness' in the service of bland initiatives for the public good." Suddenly, that kind of reflexive activism wasn't good enough, or opened one up to criticism. Many influencers began awkwardly folding activism into their presences, or adding an unsubstantiated "slash activist" to their bios, the way everyone once claimed to be a "slash DJ." People who had stood for a very vague set of things—"I'm a girl with a lot of plants," or "I have twelve very distinct abs"—were now being asked what they stood for and what they supported. A medium that rewarded shallowness did not necessarily produce the most thoughtful content creators, nor did it allow for the most articulate expressions of solidarity. A prime example is Blackout Tuesday, which grew out of a project by two Black music executives, Brianna Agyemang and Jamila Thomas, called hashtag #TheShowMustBePaused, with the goal of spurring reflection about how their industry could support the Black community. Users posted black squares to their feeds, sometimes with the hashtag #BlackLivesMatter, and these posts were called out as not just performative, but counter to the cause: They gummed up the works of a hashtag that was essential for passing along real-time information to protesters. Were the people posting allies? Bandwagoners? Disingenuous performers of activism? And what were they doing outside the borders of Instagram? On this inscrutable app that makes intent opaque, people looked for signs of bad faith. For example, Emma Watson, who had become an avatar of a certain brand of white feminism, was critiqued for posting the square with a thin white border to match the rest of her account's aesthetic. Posts about real issues were being memefied and prettified in order to gain traction in the fishbowl, to the understandable frustration of activists.

Technology was supposedly going to disrupt the old order. "The algorithm," technical and little-understood, was seemingly random and unconcerned with traditional notions of status. But it inevitably reflected society's inherent prejudices. TikTok, for example, used human moderators to determine who would rise to the top of the "For You" feed. In internal documents obtained by The Intercept, TikTok instructed moderators to de-prioritize those deemed unattractive or poor. Someone's net worth might not explicitly be visible in a short video, but the latter was controlled by, for example, hiding content where "the shooting environment is shabby and dilapidated." We thought we were getting a democracy; what has resulted is a feudal enclosure, less an agora and more a moated castle. When Tavi Gevinson visited the offices of Instagram, she learned that its algorithm "shows you more of what you already like," whether that's chunky animals or Memphis furniture and fiddle-leaf fig trees. Dissenting, challenging, or out-there content is harder to locate. That makes sense if what you want is to engage with adorable pets or aspirational design, but it's the antithesis of crate-digging, of discovery. The theoretical expansiveness of the internet feels like it would allow for endless unearthing; in practice, it feels more like a big-box store where only more of the same store-brand product is available.

Our growing suspicion of influencers mirrors our distrust of all institutions, from government to mass media to finance. They've gone from gatecrashers to gatekeepers. We first saw them as rebel freethinkers, then wise-but-fun gurus, and now pillars of the Establishment to be torn down, or at the very least questioned. The social contract between follower and followed, of "I pay attention to you, you entertain/enlighten/help me," has become more fraught. But the influencers still have power of a kind. In looking to them to "use their platform," we were acknowledging the importance of having one. In chastising them for not doing enough, we confirmed their power. After all, you wouldn't care enough to cancel someone who didn't matter.

CHAPTER NINE

Trial by Fashion

D URING A RECENT New York spring, one woman's fashion statements were all anyone was talking about. And she wasn't, for once, an actress, model, or Real Housewife—she was a scammer. She was Anna Sorokin, aka Anna Delvey, the "SoHo grifter" whose grand larceny case was then unfolding in the tabloids. Delvey stood accused of scamming $275,000 from businesses, banks, and individuals, including one of her close friends, while posing as a German heiress. Delvey's trial was one for our grow-your-own-microcelebrity era. It came complete with an Instagram account, @AnnaDelveyCourtLooks, that breathlessly chronicled her courtroom outfits, studded with fashion credits, the same way a fan account for a Hadid sister might. Delvey (I'll use her *nom de scam* throughout this chapter, to avoid confusion) was to be the subject of a Shonda Rhimes–helmed Netflix series and a potential Lena Dunham adaptation for HBO. She might have been confined to Rikers at the time, but in every way that counted in the media landscape, her stock had risen.

I've often encountered a strange kind of jealousy of scammers or those caught up in scams or other untoward situations. I think it has something to do with the fact that, in an environment where everyone has so few chits to bargain with, sometimes the only currency you have is the bizarre events that have happened to you or that you've set into motion. The crazier the source material you can harvest into fruitful IP, the better. The attention economy rewards a "wild ride" of a story that collars you with its virality. Apologies to John Updike, but no one wants to read about your gentle epiphany.

Some of these beliefs are borne out by Delvey's case: Even those tricked by her eventually reaped rewards. Neff Davis, the concierge she befriended at the hotel where she was crashing, became a consultant on Rhimes's adaptation of the story, while *Vanity Fair* editor Rachel Deloache Williams spun an article about her relationship with Delvey into a book, *My Friend Anna*; HBO purchased the rights to that book, with Dunham set to adapt. And in the perfect illustration of the half-lives of scammers, Delvey made a post-prison return to fame, complete with her own line of merch.

But it wasn't just Delvey who captivated us. From Theranos villainess Elizabeth Holmes to the Fyre Fest crew to the scheming strippers of the ripped-from-the-headlines film *Hustlers*, we are in a scammer renaissance. It may be a bad state of affairs for society, born out of extreme economic inequality and the fact that attention is now as monetizable as panned gold, but it's a rich, tappable vein for documentary filmmakers. And, especially when it comes to female grifters, fashion plays a big role in the con. These stories aren't just titillating. They raise fascinating questions about the way these women used fashion in service of their frauds, and whether style itself is, always, a kind of scam. And that's nowhere more evident than it is in court, where the guilty and innocent alike cannily use fashion to convince us of the veracity of their story.

The courtroom has always been a fertile theater for style as a statement. It's become the inverse of the red carpet: Instead of trying to use clothing to stand out and land on the best-dressed list, courtroom-style aspirants use it to blend in and create such a Puritan abnegation of style that they couldn't *possibly* be culpable. While lack of knowledge of style codes can be seen as evidence of guilt, *too* much knowledge about style can also imply guilt. It's a razor-thin line to walk, especially for women.

In her *Vanity Fair* article, DeLoache Williams, who ended up losing $62,000—more than her annual salary—to Delvey's deceptions, describes the combination of high-end signifiers—Celine sunglasses, Rimowa luggage, Gucci sandals, a Supreme hoodie—and regular-girl mufti—"black athleisure wear" and other ratty workout clothes—that Delvey wore to impersonate an heiress. "She embodied a lazy sort of luxury," DeLoache Williams writes. In *Garage* magazine, Rachel Tashjian made the counterintuitive case that Delvey's bad style—looking, in her words, like "a slob"—helped make the case that she was, in fact, the heiress she claimed to be, because actual rich people don't care how they look. "She didn't look like her outfit cost a million bucks—and that's why she looked like she *had* a million bucks," Tashjian observed. "It's the same logic that makes Mark Zuckerberg think he can afford—intellectually, and financially—to wear a hoodie to work."

But under the microscope, something was off about her style: a shadow simulacrum of wealth, hot brand names and trendy silhouettes run through Google Translate. It was as though Delvey saw, say, the Olsen twins nonchalantly wearing sweatpants with Gucci loafers and tried to crack the calculus of their indolent rich-girl style. On the one hand, she caught a truism about a certain kind of rich person, who can get away with a certain lack of obvious grooming or polish, though the messy hair is expertly tousled by Sally Hershberger and "this old thing" is Balenciaga. Instead, the way she dressed came across as gauche as ordering bottle service in a Meatpacking District club long past its prime. For the writer

Amanda Mull, Delvey's ultimate "tell" was her hair—which wasn't Sally Hershberger disheveled but Supercuts messy. In an article for The Outline, Mull wrote that Delvey's "enormous tangle of frizzy, poorly colored, untrimmed straw" didn't fit in with the pampered lifestyle of the typical wealthy woman, who has endless time to focus on the scrimshaw-like minutiae of personal grooming.

But appearances were important to Delvey. Ever mindful of the optics of the scandal, she reportedly wanted Jennifer Lawrence or Margot Robbie to play her in the screen adaptation of her life story. Perhaps to that end, the courtroom was where Phase Two of her fashion full-court press began. Delvey seemed to think of herself as a celebrity, and like a star attempting a mid-career reinvention or a post-divorce, revenge-body-abetted comeback, she needed a new look. In court, she wanted to wear "something that didn't scream 'inmate,' " according to the New York Post. When her lawyer presented her with an Ann Taylor dress, she wept. So she decided to avail herself of the services of celebrity stylist Anastasia Walker, who'd worked with the similarly embattled Courtney Love. Delvey didn't attempt to hide the machinery behind this sartorial transformation. Her attorney, Todd Spodek, told GQ in an email: "It is imperative that Anna dress appropriately for the trial. Anna's style was a driving force in her business, and life, and it is a part of who she is. I want the jury to see that side of her and enlisted a stylist to assist in slecting [sic] the appropriate outfits for trial."

Walker reinvented Delvey's SoHo-slob look, outfitting her in classic, neutral or black-and-white ensembles by Miu Miu and Victoria Beckham. She wore her own oversized Celine glasses and black choker. The resulting looks were prim with a hint of barely controlled chaos, like a fugitive's attempt to disguise herself in nine-to-five office attire. They played with extremes: light and dark, schemer and saint. On one more daring day, she wore snakeskin; on another, a lacy white dress, a garment that more often evokes a First Communion or a wedding than Baby's First Conviction. (@AnnaDelveyCourtLooks noted that she resembled a "true angel.") Sometimes the choices felt a little on the nose. Quipped Tashjian, now covering her trial style for *GQ*, "Only a guilty woman would think that wearing a white lace dress to the final day of your trial would make you look innocent." Whatever the reasoning, it didn't work: Delvey was sentenced to four to twelve years in prison.

"We were trying to broadcast that this was a woman who's ambitious and an entrepreneur," Spodek told the *New York Post*. "Making her look fashionable . . . was important because, from our position, she didn't trick anyone. [Her style] is what helped convince these people to want to help her out." He's right that Delvey's style was inherent to her appeal, but elides the way she used it as a form of trickery. If she could (semi) dress the part, she'd be allowed into the spaces—boutique hotels, private clubs—to which she craved access. And to those looking for a benefactor, she seemed good enough to be true.

The Anna Delvey courtroom look was popular enough that it gave rise to Halloween costumes that October. Artist Cynthia Talmadge created a piece, "Four Courtroom Outfits of Anna Delvey," that was installed at the Piccadilly Circus underground stop in London. The assemblage consisted of an old-fashioned changing screen, decorated with faux heraldry representing Delvey's high-end peccadilloes—American Express cards, a Henri Bendel shopping bag, hotel slippers (she famously skipped out on the bill after living at 11 Howard in SoHo)—evoking the old-money European background she traded on and faked. The link between fashion logos and the more old-fashioned status connoted in family coats of arms represented the way Delvey used fashion to try to create a faux blue-blooded lineage. Fashion could transform her from what she really was—a small-town Russian woman of humble parentage—into German solar-panel royalty. It was a *Sister Carrie*–

like narrative of immersing oneself in a city and swimming up to the surface as a new, shiny self.

Behind Talmadge's screen, pieces of Delvey's courtroom outfits are tossed up and disappear, a hysterical laundry cycle, in a kind of bizarro-world inverse of Cher Horowitz's computerized closet. According to a press release, these clothes, "presented in an infinite loop of 'hysterical' indecision, represent the closest we can get to her inner reality." Talmadge told the *Art Newspaper*, "People are obsessed with the case because it hits so close to home. . . . As young women we constantly battle with feelings of fraudulence. Anyone who is hustling in the creative industries can relate to her."

Most of us haven't perpetrated Delvey-level fraud, but the idea of subsuming one's small-town, unsophisticated self into a big-city identity is familiar to most of those who've moved to a major urban area from somewhere else. In her attorney's opening statement, he cited the song "New York, New York," with its refrain of "If I can make it there, I'll make it anywhere," and portrayed Delvey's narrative as that of the typical newcomer to the city. "Through her sheer ingenuity, she created the life that she wanted for herself," he said. "Anna was not content with being a spectator, but wanted to be a participant. Anna didn't wait for opportunities, Anna created opportunities. Now, we can all relate to that. There's a little bit of Anna in all of us." In his portrayal, she was a populist hero, *The Music Man*'s Professor Harold Hill in luxe athleisure. In reality, Delvey wasn't exactly Robin Hood, but she did mainly swindle banks, a private jet operator, and luxury hotels—hard targets for many people to sympathize with.

There may or may not be a little bit of Anna in all of us, but we've all known low-level charlatans: perhaps someone in our industry who pretends to have knowledge that they simply don't have and seems to get ahead not just despite but somehow because of that ignorance, or that Instagram personality whose appeal seems to be built on a foundation of shifting sands. Many of us have been that person ourselves—spending money we don't have on the "right" clothes while delaying that student loan or trying to make rent. Millennial culture encourages us to have a side hustle, as though it's a fun, incidentally monetizable hobby rather than a grim necessity. How many of us have used clothes the way Delvey did, amassing them like syllables of a foreign language, trying to cloak ourselves in unearned confidence and faking it until we make it? How many people who've supposedly pulled themselves up by their bootstraps are later revealed to have been propped up by parents or spouses the whole time? How many startups with charismatic founders have been artificially inflated by venture capital money only to collapse like a kiddie pool in the breeze?

When Elizabeth Holmes, the founder of Theranos, had her malfeasance exposed in print by *Wall Street Journal* reporter John Carreyrou, most of the discussion centered around the fake science her startup was shrouded in: Her much-touted Edison blood-testing machines didn't work and were feeding false health information to patients, something Holmes well knew. When her story migrated to HBO, where the documentary *The Inventor* used extensive footage of Holmes, the reactions were different. Twitter was ablaze with comments on her unruly hair, poorly applied eye makeup, and semi-buttoned blazer almost as much as it fixated on her artificially deep voice. Hindsight is twenty-twenty. We all think we wouldn't have been fooled by Holmes's too-good-to-be-true promises—that we would have picked up on some detail that alerted us to the scam. The reactions that were most interesting to me were those that delved into the gender dynamics of the question, implying that Holmes's lack of fashion and grooming savvy were somehow indicative of her larceny, and that fellow women would've instantly been in on the con. "It truly speaks volumes to how little powerful men know about women that so many of them were taken in by Elizabeth Holmes as this incredibly put-together, magnetic woman when her makeup and hair so blatantly screamed 'something is very wrong here,' " read one tweet; another echoed, "if women ran silicon valley she would have been sniffed out as a scammer immediately. her makeup and hair are like almost good but so bad, like uncanny valley type shit."

The tenor of the conversation went from "How could she fool us with that crazy blood machine?" to "How could she fool us with that eyeliner/hair/blazer?" It was as though Holmes's lack of mastery of what were presumed basic feminine tasks should have alerted us to her lack of mastery of her chosen profession. You can deplore what Holmes did and still find the reactions to her grooming uncomfortably sexist. Yes, some of the speculation exists because we don't have much to go on other than her appearance—Holmes has yet to open up via first-person confessional—but it feels untoward to conflate "being bad at fashion" with "being a bad person."

In Mull's piece for The Outline, she also examined Holmes's style and beauty cues and posited that they may have come from a more intentional place than previously acknowledged. She wrote:

> [The slightly off-base hair and makeup] seemed to acknowledge that she understood what was expected of her appearance as a relatively young woman, but she'd really rather focus on more cerebral matters. She couldn't let herself be ugly enough to turn men off or pretty enough to make them doubt her intelligence, so she appeared to color her hair but left the ends scraggly and dead as it grew. Her blonde highlights were always present, but that was part of the problem—you could see them and where they were painted on, and high-end hair color would have hidden in plain sight. Holmes also always wore the same makeup, and not

only was it always applied poorly, but specifically in such a way that you noticed its poor application. She created problems with her appearance that weren't really there—like the fuzzy hair of a bad blowout that could have been easily smoothed, or the slightly askew application of a neutral, easy-to-apply lipstick—and then she pointedly declined to solve them. Just look at her over there, being beautiful but serious.

Holmes bent to the overall "rules" of cisgender female appearance, but didn't follow them closely enough, in other words, to seem like "one of *those* women" to her audience of mainly male investors, venture capitalists, and tech reporters. Her look conveyed disdain for the detail work involved in beauty while still hewing to the overall project of "looking put-together."

What's strange is that much of Holmes's media appeal was originally built on her good looks and her fashion cred. The nascent girlboss culture needed a face, and Holmes was as good as any. As a thin, conventionally attractive white woman, Holmes was also given more leeway to look askew than women of color and plus-size women are usually afforded. She was the beneficiary of what I think of as female paratrooper syndrome—the way women who fit into our narrow standards of beauty are elevated by the media without much examination of what they stand for or whether they're worth immediately being given a pedestal. And this especially applies to women who've come up in male-dominated environments like business, the military, and tech. (The name comes from a throwaway line in *The Devil Wears Prada* where Miranda Priestly, discussing upcoming stories for the magazine, asks, "Is it impossible to find a lovely, slender, female paratrooper? Am I reaching for the stars here?")

Holmes was, for many, that paratrooper. She was embraced

by fashion magazines, and her fashion was central to her news magazine coverage, too. *The New Yorker* noted her Steve Jobs–like uniform of a black turtleneck and black pants. Henry Kissinger—hardly unassailable himself, and a board member of Theranos—called her "striking, somewhat ethereal" in his paean in *Time*. I'd challenge you to find a story that would describe Twitter CEO Jack Dorsey that way.

Holmes also inhabited a world, Silicon Valley, where normal style values were turned on their heads. Dropping out of Stanford, as she did, was considered far more impressive than graduating (after all, Mark Zuckerberg and Bill Gates are both Harvard dropouts). When disrupting every other industry is your stated goal, you're not likely to hew to every stylistic rule or nicety. Adopting something like Delvey's hasty collage of designer labels would not have worked in the male-dominated, frivolity-fearing Valley. Instead Holmes counted on clothing herself in the authoritative and sexless uniform of a famous, and, crucially, male tech titan. She told *Glamour* in 2015, echoing the decision fatigue and disdain for fashion of male founders like Zuckerberg: "It makes it easy because every day you put on the same thing and don't have to think about it—one less thing in your life. All my focus is on the work. I take it so seriously. I'm sure that translates into how I dress."

Like her affected baritone, her clothes were an attempt to project male authority. Her "ethereal" looks provided the contrast necessary to make her a press darling. And she was nearly Jobs-level savvy about the aesthetics behind her self-promotion, hiring famed documentarian Errol Morris to direct a Theranos commercial and photographer Martin Schoeller to shoot her portrait for the company website. (Enlisting Morris, who ferreted out the truth behind a false conviction in his documentary *The Thin Blue Line*, was a particularly inspired choice when it came to miming authenticity.) Holmes had transformed herself from a makeup-free brunette sporting thick glasses and favoring things like ugly Christmas sweaters into something iconic, if referential. Holmes, like Delvey, would become a popular Halloween costume.

And like Delvey, Holmes changed up her look for court hearings, exchanging her Jobs cosplay for nondescript suits and elaborately barrel-curled hair that resembled a teenage beauty pageant contestant's. From the way that was covered, you would think it was the denouement of *She's All That*. "Elizabeth Holmes Debuted Flowing, Beautifully Conditioned Waves," read one post. "Congrats to Elizabeth Holmes on her keratin treatment," tweeted political reporter Olivia Nuzzi. The hair felt softer, more feminine. Holmes's style evolution was straight out of the playbook of women on trial since the beginning of time—amp up the femininity and youth to channel innocence.

People, on many levels, dress to get what they want, and courtroom style is a theatrical, heightened way of doing so. Those who have less power in a system need to do more maneuvering to get power, and fashion is one way to do that. For women on trial, transforming their image through fashion has often been a necessity. Marie Antoinette doffed her pre-Revolutionary finery for a ragged black dress, which she wore for the entirety of her imprisonment and trial. This costume, with its hem dirtied from the prison floors, made her appear far from the decadent monarch the prosecution wanted to paint her as. (Though its color held more symbolism than just mourning—it was also considered at the time to signal support for the monarchy.) "Even as she faced execution, Marie Antoinette's will to control her image, to manage it through her clothing, had not left her," writes Caroline Weber in *Queen of Fashion: What Marie Antoinette Wore to the Revolution*. For her execution, she changed into a pure white dress and plum-colored high-heeled slippers.

She was traveling to the guillotine in an open carriage, with crowds watching her every move: If she was going to go out like this, she might as well go out in style.

These concerns might seem frivolous when life and death hang in the balance, but failure to read the room, when it came to fashion, could even be punishable by death. At one of Joan of Arc's trials, she promised to cease wearing "male clothing," and when she resumed doing so again in prison, she was executed.

Even in the liberated '60s, antiquated ideas about female image and innocence still predominated. Charles Manson was a master of what was then not yet called personal branding, and his acolytes followed suit. The Manson Family used fashion as a complement to their hippie personae—and as a shield for genuine sociopathy. In the guise of peace-and-loveniks, they wore nightgown-like, bohemian dresses and loose, flowing hair. Rhonda Garelick breaks down the paradox in a piece for The Cut: that "combination of youthful sweetness and shocking violence, war and peace, love-ins and murder." Manson, she writes, "understood the great power in yoking together opposites in this way. In fact, Manson weaponized style—its surface, as manifested in fashion or cultural trends, but also its structure, the way it reproduces itself via contagion or imitation." It helped the family float like hippie jetsam along the surface of the countercultural movement and allowed them entrée into wealthier bohemian worlds.

Manson Family member Linda Kasabian had a particular stake in appearing innocent, as she was testifying for the prosecution in exchange for immunity. Joan Didion writes about covering the Manson trial in The White Album. Didion, no stranger to the hypnotic power of fashion herself, picked out a dress for Kasabian at the I. Magnin Hi Shop in Beverly Hills, in what feels like a loose interpretation of journalistic ethics. Kasabian, who had been wearing a blue prison uniform, center-parted hair, and zero makeup when Didion first met her, wanted an emerald or gold dress that was "mini but not extremely mini," Didion recounts in the title essay of the collection. The Family's lawyer Vincent Bugliosi had deemed the long white shift Kasabian had planned to wear too long and formal.

And Kasabian's appearance did come in for some attention. At a press conference, she wore pigtails and a polka dot dress, appearing even younger than her twenty-one years. *New York Times* reports on the trial noted that she "appears demure in braided hair and a peasant-type dress" and that, in a "blue and red, peasant-type gown, [she] smiled from the stand." The evocation of an older time felt intentional—like much of hippie fashion, her look evoked the courtly values of medieval times and the ethereal femininity of the pre-Raphaelites, lending her some of the fragility of a Millais painting's heroine.

Dressing in the style of an era to reap the benefits of that era's gender politics has become a well-thumbed playbook, especially when it comes to courtroom attire. Winona Ryder, arrested in 2001 for shoplifting at a Beverly Hills Saks Fifth Avenue, went for a '50s and '60s gamine look in the courtroom. It was a 180 from her usual goth and grunge styling; Ryder looked pixieish, almost like she was going Method for a Jean Seberg biopic and not standing trial. She wore headbands, demure little twinsets, Peter Pan collars, and kitten-heeled Mary Janes in benzodiazepine yellow. "She may be a shoplifter," Robin Givhan admitted in the *Washington Post*, "but she has impeccable taste." The *Daily Press* wrote that "she appeared adorable, respectful and, at times, even helpless." Still, the looks had an edge—slightly sheer dresses and sweaters that revealed her bra and underwear. Her wardrobe wasn't all by Marc Jacobs, whose clothing she had shoplifted, but she was the perfect sweetly perverse Jacobs pinup. Her rotation of outfits might well have served as a template for Delvey's child-woman looks.

Ryder was convicted of felony grand theft and vandalism, though not burglary. She got off relatively easily with probation, community service, fines, and counseling. A non-white, non-famous woman would surely not have received such leniency, and Ryder's fashion, along with her race and status, added to the perception of her innocence. (In a strange and perfect coda to all this, she appeared in Marc Jacobs ads post-sentencing; clearly, there were no hard feelings between her and the designer.)

Accused of reckless driving and a DUI, respectively, Paris Hilton and Nicole Richie later took their marching orders from Ryder's demure courtroom looks: Hilton in a gray blazer and headband, far from the abbreviated club attire she had become known for, and Richie dressing like Audrey Hepburn at her peak—little black dress, chignon, oversized sunglasses—looking every bit the damsel in distress.

We've also seen the opposite of this approach: women transforming their look to evoke authority and being in charge, often as a way to conjure a power they don't really have. To give her grand jury testimony in the Bill Clinton impeachment case, Monica Lewinsky wore stodgy blue and gray suits, pearls, and big newscaster hair—markers of an authority and adulthood she didn't yet possess, but was trying to convey. She may have been a preyed-upon intern, but she was trying to dress like a Washington power player. Lindsay Lohan, usually seen in trendy clubwear, similarly transformed herself for the courtroom, though more successfully. She wore a sharp, fitted suit and a sleek white minidress, with the kind of cantilevered high heels endemic to the mid-aughts. If not fully repentant, she at least looked *in charge.* And serious-ish, in a way that suggested she didn't regularly stumble out of nightclubs. The only hint of rebellion was, famously, an accent nail emblazoned with a tiny Fuck U. "It had nothing to do w/court. it's an airbrush design from a stencil," she claimed on Twitter.

Those who flaunted it on the courtroom steps also came in for jeers. Martha Stewart got flak for wearing a mink stole and carrying an Hermès Birkin bag to her trial for securities fraud. The latter, noted Givhan in the *Washington Post*, was an item so coveted that its waiting list had its own waiting list. It was well beyond the reach of the average American. "Stewart's Birkin was a hand-stitched symbol of the underlying issues—the privileges of success—that have so agitated her detractors," wrote Givhan. *The Telegraph* called it a "haughty show of disdain" and said that Stewart was rumored to have hidden the It bag inside a larger, nondescript black bag on the advice of her lawyers. It didn't seem to matter that Stewart was a famous woman well known to be a multimillionaire, a person who, in other words, could well afford a top-of-the-line designer bag. In the theater of the court, she was supposed to act, and look, remorseful.

The closest current analogue to Stewart's unrepentantly luxe, look-at-me courtroom attire is probably Cardi B, who rotated a number of high-end pieces—including Birkins, furs, and a cleavage-baring suit bought at Barneys—for her courtroom appearances following an alleged assault on two bartenders. Her outrageous fashion statements got as much ink as the incident. Barneys seemed to enjoy the buzz, posting a picture of Cardi in the suit on Instagram and writing, "Can you be sued for looking this good? We'll let you be the judge of that." But not everyone was so thrilled. The bartenders' attorney Joseph Tacopina told the *New York Post* that "Cardi treats her trips to the courthouse like a runway show," suggesting a lack of seriousness on her part. "Here's a woman who got indicted by a grand jury with felony charges, and appears to only be concerned about what she's wearing. There's going to be a

'Come to Jesus' moment with her, because it's not consistent with someone who's taking this seriously."

Cardi reacted to Tacopina's comments in an Instagram video: "Where am I supposed to get my suits from bro?! H&M?!" Instead, she leaned in to the excess. Her video for "Press" dramatized the courtroom saga, with sign-waving fans waiting outside the court as though they were outside a concert, while the rapper strutted by in designer ensembles. The video served as a meta-narrative about the reactions to Cardi's courtroom fashion.

In her Instagram video, she also said, "If I was a man, it would not bother you." Cardi has a point. There's a reason that all the examples I've covered are women. Men in similar high-profile cases, like Bernie Madoff and Billy McFarland, rarely face the same scrutiny for their fashion, grooming, and overall looks. (I had to Google image search Madoff just to remember how he dressed; meanwhile, I clearly remembered that his wife, Ruth, faced scrutiny for carrying a Birkin bag out and about after her husband's conviction.) Our reactions to women's courtroom style mirror our reactions to women in general: Too much excess and egotism is evidence of guilt. To appear truly innocent, you need to cloak yourself in the modern-day equivalent of a hair shirt.

Even if you're not in the position of defending yourself, there's still an emphasis on dressing to be believed. In her memoir *Know My Name*, Chanel Miller writes about Googling "women's court clothes" before going to testify against her rapist, trying to find the right clothes at Kohl's. For her, those were earth-toned sweaters. She finally settled on a "soft, quiet" one, "the color of old milk." She looked, she writes, "like someone who would lend you a pencil." In an essay for the *New York Times* titled "How I Learned to Look Believable," Eva Hagberg writes about what she wore to testify against her former graduate school adviser in a sexual harassment case. Hagberg's account underscores the very real choices even

non-famous women face when it comes to how they present themselves in the courtroom. "I wanted to look good," she writes. "I also
wanted to look credible." She details the inherent contradictions
involved in all the roles she needed to play, simultaneously, in the
course of the process. "I have needed to be ready, at every moment,
to be seen as both a poverty-stricken graduate student and a reliable
adult. As an accuser, I need to be a news-team-ready correspon-
dent and someone who certainly wasn't doing this for the lime-
light." She came to favor black turtlenecks and hair worn up.

Hagberg's looks didn't just have to help her fit into the various narratives around her trial—they also needed to wipe out any
potential negative projections, which is a lot to ask of a blazer and
pants. "I didn't want to look like what I imagined a victim looks
like," she writes. "I didn't want to look so downtrodden that I would
look obsessed with being a victim, as it was suggested. I didn't want
to look so feminine and girlish that I wouldn't be taken seriously;
I'd seen the way young-looking women are treated. And yet, I didn't
want to look too aggressive, too much like a 'rabble-rouser' with an
'agenda.' " The correct image was one of "hapless powerlessness."
And, of course, "You always want to stay 'just plausibly sexy enough
to look like you could have been harassed but 100 percent weren't
asking for it.' "

In situations like these, the onus is unfairly on survivors like
Miller and Hagberg to do the work to look credible, to stave off
the "wrong" perceptions—even though they did not invite this
spotlight or these events. For a less image-savvy person, or someone with fewer means, the calculus is even more challenging. Justice may be blind, but juries are not.

PART III

High Heels

Dressing Up for
the Patriarchy

CHAPTER TEN

Gaze of Our Lives

THE FOLLOWING THINGS have all, at one point or another, been cited as examples of the female gaze: the films of director Anna Biller, the *Twilight* series, Lana del Rey's music, the writing of Chris Kraus, the mythological character Medusa, and a commercial for Kraft Zesty Italian Dressing that features a sexy man.

We all know what the "male gaze" is—we've either done it, been subject to it, or maybe even both. The phrase was coined by the film critic Laura Mulvey in her 1975 essay "Visual Pleasure and Narrative Cinema" to describe the strict binary she perceived in Hollywood cinema between those who looked and those who were looked at. She summed the distinction up starkly as "active/male, passive/ female." For Mulvey, Hollywood movies were a sanctioned form of voyeurism. In the classic instance of the male gaze in cinema, the camera lingers over the female body, slashing it into tranches and offering it up to the viewer. Some form of it shows up in the work of everyone from Alfred Hitchcock to Michael Bay. Film—like all other forms of visual media—inculcates us into the gaze. When I watch Jimmy Stewart's ballerina neighbor through his zoom lens in *Rear Window*, or see Megan Fox arcing her torso over a car in *Transformers*, I'm encouraged either to see them the way a straight male would, or to identify with them and what Mulvey calls their "to-be-looked-at-ness." For Mulvey, the pleasure of looking and the pleasure of being looked at are the twin indulgences of moviegoing.

Of course, the male gaze dominated visual culture long before the first films flickered into existence. The art critic John Berger summed up this tradition in the BBC show *Ways of Seeing*: "Men dream of women. Women dream of themselves being dreamt of. Men look at women. Women watch themselves being looked at." A prime example of the male gaze in art is Édouard Manet's *Olympia*, where the painter shows a courtesan posing nude in odalisque style, consciously updating Titian's portrait of a lounging Venus. The painting caused outrage at the time, but not for its prurient subject matter. It was Manet's starkness and realism, this elevation of a *demimondaine* to a goddess, that upset critics. This imagery felt more like a documentary depiction than an elevation of its subject, but the overall project was still the same as Titian's. The poses are not active, but passive, and they can easily be mapped onto the standard style of selfies today. So many of us contort ourselves into Olympia-like odalisques on Instagram, where art-history tropes still reign supreme: the doe-eyed nude, the landscape, the lush still life of a piled-high plate of food. The modes of depiction have changed so little even as the depicters and the platforms have changed.

Of the typical woman, Berger wrote that "from earliest childhood she is taught and persuaded to survey herself continually. She has to survey everything she is and everything she does, because how she appears to others—and particularly how she appears to men—is of crucial importance for what is normally thought of as the success of her life." For anyone who's had the experience of living in a female body, these words resonate eerily. The male gaze catches and

latches onto us. We internalize it even when it's not there; it's a corset pinching us at all times, and it's a struggle not to see ourselves
through its prism.

Beginning in the late '80s, over a decade after Mulvey published
her essay on the male gaze, the phrase the "female gaze" began to
be bandied about. But the latter is more of a slippery concept. Is
it simply the inverse of the male gaze, the lens of objectification
turned back onto men, or onto other women? Is it a wholesale rejection of the male gaze? Or is it something completely outside that
conception? And what does that look like? Is it the stark, desexu-
alized documentary viewpoint of a Dorothea Lange picture? The
Vaseline-lensed soft focus of a Sofia Coppola film or a Petra Collins
photo shoot? The cheesecakey reverse objectification of a movie
like *Magic Mike* (which, as it happens, was made by a man—Steven
Soderbergh)? As the film scholar Caetlin Benson-Allott has put it,
the female gaze "has been haphazardly defined more often by what
it is not than by what it is." After all, if something can encompass all
these definitions, isn't this a sign that it is meaningless?

The "female gaze" strikes me as the twenty-first century's biggest aesthetic con, breathlessly reported on and rarely credibly defined. On further reflection, I'm not entirely sure it exists at all. We
live under patriarchy and thus we are all inclined to see ourselves
through the male gaze or view others through it. If everything we
have seen has been mediated by the male gaze, can we ever really
subvert it fully?

The works I have seen touted as examples of the "female gaze"
when it comes to visual art have mostly been either a soft-core version of the same old objectifying or self-objectifying tropes, or a
formless triumph of style over substance. This kind of art hasn't
progressed that far beyond Lacan's mirror stage, the moment
when a child recognizes herself in her own reflection. "Selfie feminism" found its apogee in, what else, self-portraiture. There is,

of course, a certain power in self-depiction, in showing and celebrating yourself, saying "I exist." (As Susan Sontag writes in *On Photography*, "photographs furnish evidence." A selfie is the "pics or it didn't happen" principle, but for your own personhood.) The mid-2010s peak of this movement was rife with artists who, in the mode of Cindy Sherman, reinvented themselves and played a cast of characters. Look at the Argentinian artist Amalia Ulman's 2014 series *Excellences and Perfections*. A Banksy-like prank on gullible social media users, the series shows Ulman engaging in a form of performance-art-via-selfie, letting her followers track her through a typical LA influencer reinvention. She pretended to go through an extreme makeover, including a breast augmentation and extreme dieting. Ulman was hailed as a Cindy Sherman for the smartphone age; *The Telegraph* asked, "Is this the first Instagram masterpiece?" But she was also a slim, young, white-passing blond woman taking selfies that often looked identical to something Emily Ratajkowski or Kim Kardashian might post.

These artists—and these celebrities, too—were hailed for turning the gaze on themselves. And there is surely some power in negotiating the terms of your own objectification, of being your own Titian or Manet. It's something that recent technology has made more possible: It has never been easier or cheaper to capture, edit, and infinitely reproduce one's own image. Wealthy people used to have their portraits painted to guarantee immortality; now you can live forever with just a few taps. There's no need for access to a darkroom, expensive oil paints, or specialized training in art. The smartphone has professionalized us all, and to be immortalized, you no longer have to pose for a (historically male) painter or photographer and hope that his vision of you doesn't conflict too much with your own.

But if you're living in a slim, white, cisgender, conventionally attractive body, is that self-representation really that radical, or are you just playing into the dominant archetype? Uncritically celebrating these people, in these bodies, for simply existing doesn't feel that revolutionary. And this genre of art feels like it's playing both sides of the fence. If you get critiqued, you have a built-in escape hatch: the defense that this viewer either hates women, or is a self-hating woman, or has been poisoned by the male gaze. The maker can claim to be revolutionizing the way we look at women, then retreat into the pretexts that have both protected and imprisoned women. They've harnessed choice feminism as a justification that, to paraphrase an *Onion* headline, all women are empowered by anything an individual woman does.

Kim Kardashian published a book with the high-end imprint Rizzoli in 2015 called *Kim Kardashian West: Selfish*. Its nearly five hundred pages were stuffed with selfies, like one of those "I took a selfie every day for a year" viral videos spread across three decades. Her story is one of technology as well as celebrity: She begins with analog mirror shots on a film camera and progresses through several generations of smartphones over the course of the narrative. The artist is present, everywhere from the makeup chair to the driver's seat, stopped at a red light. The title was a clever bit of self-mockery; Kardashian, anticipating her critics, has jokingly referred to herself as a "girl with no talent." Like her California progenitor Angelyne, who put up billboards of herself all over Los Angeles, or her former employer, the famous-for-being-famous Paris Hilton, she was compelled to broadcast her image without the involvement of others. She, herself, became the work of art in the age of mechanical reproduction. Still, the is-it-art-or-is-it-narcissism question prevailed.

The model and influencer Emily Ratajkowski is another social media entrepreneur who has harnessed the power of selfies, in this case with a stated feminist intent. Ratajkowski has supported leftist causes: She campaigned for Bernie Sanders and was arrested protesting the nomination of Brett Kavanaugh. But when it comes to selfies, her feminist project feels less clear. In an interview with *Glamour UK*, she cited Mulvey's coinage: "I want women to understand their own sexuality outside of a patriarchal male gaze." Ratajkowski also supported the #FreeTheNipple movement, started by filmmaker and actress Lina Esco, which was meant to give women the right to go topless in public the way men do and not have it be seen in a sexual way. The hashtag soon garnered significant celebrity endorsement. Well-intentioned as it was, the movement was the kind of front-facing-camera activism that drew celebrity feminists eager to glom on to a "sexy" issue, oblivious to the solipsism of tearing down the scourge of hypersexualization by . . . posting a sexy selfie. In the attention economy, the selfie reigned supreme regardless of context, as with Ratajkowski's use of a nude self-portrait to raise awareness about an Alabama abortion ban or the many influencers who have captioned a thirst trap "Are you registered to vote?"

Circa 2015, writing about either of these women in a gushingly laudatory way seemed to be practically a requirement among the culturati. *The Telegraph* called Kardashian and her sisters "the true heirs to the Brontës," and deemed her a "feminist artist." The Pulitzer Prize–winning art critic Jerry Saltz compared *Selfish* to *My Struggle* ("that's Karl Ove Knausgård's epic, not Hitler's"). Slate's Laura Bennett deemed the book "an insane project, a document of mind-blowing vanity and deranged perseverance. It's also riveting. I can't recommend it enough." Kardashian and Ratajkowski might not be portraying themselves in a manner that was wildly different than a *Playboy* photographer's, but they had seized the means of production, proclaimed these Marxists in Aeron office chairs. They were their own Irving Penns and their own Gutenbergs at the same time. I don't fault either of them for vanity: If I looked like either of these women, I'd probably never leave my mirrored selfie lair. But I don't want to overstate their contribution to toppling patriarchy. It's subversive in the same way that robbing a bank subverts capitalism, in a small, non-paradigm-shattering way.

Ratajkowski's commitment to depicting herself makes more sense in light of "Buying Myself Back," an essay she wrote for *New York* magazine examining the use of her image by others. She recalled, as a young model, being sexually assaulted by a photographer who took nude photos of her that he then used without her consent in a gallery exhibit and book—a kind of double assault. The essay zoomed out to talk about other violations: the artist Richard Prince using one of her nude selfies as part of his New Portraits series, and a gallerist she knew buying one of those works so he could sit on his couch under her naked self-portrait. Instagram, she writes, had "felt like the only place where I could control how I present myself to the world, a shrine to my autonomy." But even that realm was not immune to reappropriation. As Ratajkowski earned more power, in the form of income, she was able to buy herself back in some ways but not in others: to own physical representations of these artworks, but not to exercise ownership over how they were seen. In this context, her selfies feel more like a political project than I'd previously believed. In a profession where one gives up so much control and has so little say over the final product, it makes sense to attempt to win back that control and turn the gaze on yourself.

Still, as with Ulman, the question remains: What if a woman who didn't fit these beauty standards embarked on such an epic project of self-representation? Navel-gazing is itself a privilege, and the ways in which these images disrupt the dominant beauty narrative is limited at best. The standard range of "imperfections" allowable in a single image is usually a pick-one buffet: body hair, stretch marks, or cellulite can appear as long as the rest of the image appears "perfect." Social media platforms may allow for a kind of democracy in that they allow everyone to depict themselves and disseminate those images, but they do not afford everyone equal attention.

The proverbial algorithm reinforces these norms—whether it's a social media platform or a streaming service, it serves up more of what you've already liked as opposed to unearthing new, surprising imagery and ideas that might challenge you. Especially when it comes to someone like Kardashian, who has notoriously appropriated many elements of Black culture, it begs the question: Would a Black woman be so critically lauded by highbrow publications for embarking on the same project?

My guess is no, as similar projects by Black women have received far less critical adulation than she enjoyed. As Aria Dean writes in *The New Inquiry*, "So long as the feminist politic with the most traction enjoys this uncomplicated relationship to visibility, it will only sink further into aestheticization and depoliticization. As long as its framework is derived primarily from its racist, classist, capitalist 'lean-in' equality-core (#freethenipple) predecessor, we—specifically Black women, but also perhaps all of us here whose bodies and selves are failed by a second-wave capitalist, classist, racist, cissexist, ableist feminism—do ourselves a disservice by considering it in the least bit viable." She adds: "Making one's subjectivity visible, or affirming one's existence through a selfie has yet to 'demolish the gaze.' . . . [C]atapulting our selves into circulation as image-fragments no longer makes for a resistance or revolution." She advocates, instead, "using tools like the selfie in ways that refuse, refute, and redirect, saying 'NOPE' to dominant ideologies, and 'bye' to a basic-bitch politic of visibility."

Among the Black artists who've tried to reframe and confront the gaze are Carrie Mae Weems and Adrian Piper. When Weems was teaching at Hampshire College in the late '80s and early '90s, she would assign her students to make a portrait and a self-portrait, with

Mulvey's essay in mind. She found that male self-portraits tended to be "deeply frontal," she recalled in a Lenny Letter interview with Kimberly Drew. "Women always photographed themselves turned to the side and slightly obscured," she said. "Their faces were never quite open and flat to the camera. They were always hidden behind hair, hidden behind objects, hidden behind things. It's sort of a vulnerability of revealing the self." That kind of disparity still exists today, with shyness, angling, hiding, and refusal to confront the reflection dominating many women's selfies. That can be read as artistic license—manipulating the image for the desired result—or as a reaction to a social imperative that encourages insecurity.

The original conversation around the gaze, Weems said, "very much excluded the black female body. It was just not a part of the discussion." Weems began her *Kitchen Table* series as an explicit corrective to that. "I realized at a certain moment that I could not count on white men to construct images of myself that I would find appealing or useful or meaningful or complex." So she had to do it herself. The resulting images show Weems in private moments at her kitchen table, the kind of domestic interludes that, before the selfie, would go largely unrecorded; in one of the most affecting, she and a young girl look at themselves in mirrors while applying makeup. They are on separate, but parallel, tracks of self-definition. As she told *W* magazine, "I use my body as a landscape to explore the complex realities of the lives of women." In another work, a riff on *Snow White*, she shows a Black woman looking into a mirror, with a witchlike character looking back at her, and the caption: "Looking Into The Mirror, The Black Woman Asked, 'Mirror, Mirror On The Wall, Who's The Finest Of Them All?' The Mirror Says, 'Snow White, You Black Bitch, And Don't You Forget It!!!' " Weems shows how omnipresent whiteness and Eurocentric beauty standards are even in the simple act of self-examination.

Piper explored her identity as a mixed-race woman through

performance art that included depictions of herself. Her *Self-Portrait as Nice White Lady* shows the artist posing in a turtleneck, with a level-eyed, unimpressed gaze. Behind her is a cartoon thought bubble declaring "Whut choo lookin at, mofo." Her *Mythic Being* series shows the artist disguised as a man, drawing attention to the ways in which she as a woman was circumscribed. When playing this character, she writes, "I swagger, stride, lope, lower my eyebrows, raise my shoulders, sit with my legs wide apart on the subway." In "becoming" this male character, she cast off the requirements of conforming to the gaze.

When it comes to fashion, the idea of the female gaze is even more amorphous. Women who dress completely for themselves are truly rare—most of us have an audience in mind, whether that is men, other women, or some permutation of both. Generally speaking, though, another woman is more likely to be attuned to the vagaries of fashion, to appreciate the footnotes behind your outfit, to start a dialogue with you because of a "conversation piece" you're wearing. Fashion is a playing field where women compete but also intersect, a locus of the intra-female fascination that builds up between women.

You might even say that women no longer need to dress for men, that we've evolved past that historical moment. It's certainly true that as women carve out more power and independence, fashion tends to follow. In the wake of the #MeToo movement, fashion has become more covered up, with "ugly-cool" styles adamantly designed *not* to appeal to straight men and instead focused on the comfort of the wearer: to wit, the hipster housedresses of Batsheva, the loose jumpsuits and wide-legged pants of Rachel Comey. Some female designers have reimagined fashion in a more female-friendly, comfort-oriented image, though those standards can be, in some ways, just as restrictive as the previous ones. What does it mean to dress for yourself, and can we ever really toss aside the preconceptions of others and our desire to appeal to them?

While fashion is thought of as a female-dominated industry, for the majority of its history men have primarily designed the clothes that women wear and dictated fashion trends from atop an ivory atelier. A kind of male gaze has been inherent in styles from the hobble skirt to the bandage dress—would someone who had to walk in them have designed either of those garments? Now that trends are less top-down and more self-generated, that's starting to change: a woman who's been living in No.6 clogs and Birkenstocks may convert to a kitten heel, but she probably won't adopt towering stilettos just because someone tells her they're back in style this season.

As female designers have become more prevalent, there is a tendency to affix the "female gaze" label to their work. But are female designers really more tuned in to what women want? Not necessarily. The gender essentialism of that statement doesn't sit well with me, not to mention that there are plenty of female designers who don't seem to know what a woman is shaped like. The idea that female designers are simply designing for *themselves*, unable to imagine beyond that sphere, feels too pat and limiting.

Still, there is a cohort of women designers who have either pushed back against the male gaze, using fashion almost as a form of violent satire, or made women's clothing more practical and livable. Comme des Garçons' Rei Kawakubo sits in the first category. She and Phoebe Philo, formerly of Chloé and Celine, seem to be the two living designers most credited with the "female gaze" approach. Kawakubo subverted the idea of the female body with her spring 1997 "Body Meets Dress, Dress Meets Body" collection, which became colloquially known as the Lumps and Bumps collection. It incorporated padding beneath the surface of innocent-looking dresses that, rather than molding the body into some "ideal" shape, rendered it surreal: hunched backs, globular hips, exaggerated derrières. To some critics, it was grotesque, evoking disfigurement and disease. Some fashion magazines elected to shoot the clothes with the padding removed. But for Kawakubo, it was a way of reinventing the relationship between the wearer and the worn. "I realized that the clothes could be the body and the body could be the clothes," the designer has said. Kawakubo has also used her collections to explore rituals, both social and biological, that are unique to women's lives. While couture shows traditionally end with *la mariée*, the beautifully attired bride who closes out the proceedings, Kawakubo has used her shows to confront topics that aren't usually a subject for fashion. Her 2014 "Blood and Roses" collection included white garments that looked soaked in blood, evoking menstruation, childbirth, and death. "Broken Bride" (2005) explored weddings, but in a different light than the triumphant couture-show endpoint. "There are many kinds of marriages," the show notes declared. "Typically, marriage is associated with being 'tied up' and is conservative; this collection is anti-conservative, allows one to be free, and shows what marriage can be like." Many of the models wore loose, wide-legged pants and other non-constricting takes on nuptial wear; they were accessorized with trailing, Miss Havisham—like antique veils and flat shoes rather than the fussy trappings of the typical bride.

Philo, meanwhile, was working in the tradition of someone like Claire McCardell, the twentieth-century American designer whose practical designs popularized the idea of sportswear, the classic American genre of ready-to-wear that was freeing and down-to-earth. When she was at Celine, Philo designed clothes that didn't seem to have men in mind at all. It was fashion that passed the Bechdel test, the pop-culture benchmark created by cartoonist Alison Bechdel that requires that at least two female characters speak to one another about something other than a man. Her acolytes called themselves Philophiles and dwelled in a kind of *Herland* utopia where fuzzy flat "Fur-kenstocks" and oversized blanket coats were the norm. Realism is not often a quality praised in fashion, but for Philo it was a selling point. Sofia Coppola told *T* magazine that she liked Philo's aesthetic precisely because "it's not based on some weird idea of what a woman should be." Philo's idea of a pinup was Joan Didion, who appeared in her 2015 Celine ads sporting oversized sunglasses. The Philo woman looked rich and serious, like she owned a gallery, but merely as a hobby. Her stripped-down seriousness was a serene antidote to the early aughts' decadence and logomania. Philo's woman didn't need to show off her body—in fact, doing so would have seemed déclassé. But her clothing quietly showed off status and whispered about the wearer's class ranking. Was this another unattainable female ideal?

Whenever a "real" or "natural" woman is evoked, there is some kind of critique of the "artificial" woman lurking right behind it. This kind of "anti-fashion fashion" has something in common with "no-makeup makeup," which is, after all, still makeup, just in the form of "your lips, but better" lipstick and tinted moisturizer. Bim Adewunmi, writing about the no-makeup makeup trend for BuzzFeed News, said that "effortlessness has become the greatest commodity a woman can own." The bare-faced crusade, she wrote, was "not a bellwether for a worldwide movement; it's a display of gentle superiority." It transforms trying to look good, especially with a male audience in mind, into an unserious project. Which doesn't mean that beauty is abandoned; it's just transformed into something serious, bordering on academic. Skincare becomes science. Fashion becomes a cerebral exercise. Being and looking "low maintenance" is seen as a virtue that distinguishes you from lesser, shallower women even as you invest just as much time and energy into your appearance as they do. In a critical examination of what she called "the skincare con" in The Outline, Krithika Varagur classed the pursuit of perfect skin as "the thinking woman's quest." Doctor-fronted or medical-looking skincare lines have become faddish, as though they are a prescription for beauty issued to a dutiful patient. It's become fashionable to say that you enjoy skincare merely as a research-heavy hobby or as a private ritual, which certainly seems possible, but if its pursuit had no visible results, would so many people still be so committed to it? It's not so much that skincare is a rejection of makeup (and along with it, a host of patriarchal beauty standards), but that perfect skin makes the rejection of makeup *possible*.

And the quest for perfection has only become more quixotic, the hurdles higher and higher. "Beauty work" is a Sisyphean exercise. We have to erase pores, achieve glass-like texture, look HD-ready at any given moment. "Perfect skin," writes Varagur, "is unattainable because it doesn't exist. The idea that we should both have it and want it is a waste of our time and money. Especially for women, who are disproportionately taxed by both the ideal of perfect skin and its material pursuit." Worse, the quality of our skin comes to reflect on our inherent goodness. "Within the current paradigm, a blemish seems like a referendum on who you are as a person." The philosopher Heather Widdows has argued that beauty has now become an ethical ideal, and that failure to comply is seen as a moral failing. Compounding that is the fact that as technology improves, we now see ourselves through what she calls a "technical gaze" that surveils us even more cruelly than the human eye would, inventing ever-more ways to find fault, whether it's HD cameras or zoom lenses.

The binary between the male and female gazes is also problematic because it divides the two into stereotypical extremes, just as Mulvey's inert conception of men as active and women as passive does. The female gaze, in this conception, has a false purity. It does not pollute or cheapen; it does not objectify. The difference between a lingerie ad that openly objectifies women and an ad for a sustainable, body-positive, direct-to-consumer brand that mysteriously empowers them is a slim one that often boils down to styling and aesthetic niceties. The female gaze is employed here as a marketing tool to give tradition the semblance of upheaval, to make the same things that once felt objectifying magically shape-shift into something empowering. When a brand wants to signal seriousness, it tends toward black-and-white photography, stripped-down backgrounds, an absence of obvious retouching, an array of exceptionally beautiful models in a wider range of ages and body types. The scholar Paula Marantz Cohen has even posited that the female gaze could be "another means of manipulating women into dependence on a consumer culture," with its focus on the acquisition of clothes and accessories rather than bodies.

Similarly, when fashion wants to convey worthiness, it turns to press releases about the use of the "female gaze" in the process. Perhaps a female photographer will be touted, or an over-sixty woman, usually white, possessing an acceptable number of wrinkles to be considered to be aging gracefully but not enough to tip over into decrepitude, will be featured. We're rewarded for arresting the entropy of aging, so long as we don't visibly "cheat." The writer Heather Havrilesky tweeted that "aging gracefully" is "an inherently sexist concept that we only measure in women, like there's some special, *right* way to carelessly stay gorgeous as you get older." Much like the mandate for effortless beauty, "the message is, as with all lady things, don't try too hard or you're pathetic."

The stripped-down aesthetic has, itself, become a convention, with ironclad rules of its own. It's less a flight from the status quo and more a new kind of status quo. Magazines now often run purportedly makeup-free, un-airbrushed photo shoots as if to preempt complaints about the unreality of fashion imagery. Meanwhile, as I mentioned in chapter 8, retouching has never thrived more among individuals, who Facetune their own images into oblivion. The call for images that are "real" and unretouched has been made many times, with some even seeking to make the practice of retouching illegal, but as Hannah Giorgis pointed out in *The Atlantic*, airbrushing is just the tip of the Facetuned iceberg. It "functions as a symptom of a larger social ill," she wrote. "The dangers of navigating the world (and the mirror) in an othered body—a body read as black or queer or trans or fat or disabled, for example—extends far beyond the blight of photo-editing tools. Naming this reality, though, is far less sexy. . . . Any trends toward 'natural' aesthetics have tended to idealize the kinds of people who can afford to look flawless without much manipulation. Think dewy-faced Glossier models or 'makeup-free' Alicia Keys." Giorgis cites the disability activist Mia Mingus, who has spoken about the way women like herself—queer, disabled, of color—"have struggled long and hard to claim a place and be seen as women against the loud static noise of white-womanhood." For them, being seen is the powerful project that Kardashian and Ratajkowski purport their self-depiction to be. By showing themselves, they are, says Mingus, "refusing to let able-bodied femmes dictate what femme gets to be and demanding accountability to ableist notions of gender, beauty, sexuality and desire that supposedly represent 'all of us.' "

For her, the goal is "moving beyond a politic of desirability to loving the ugly. . . . We all run from the ugly. And the farther we run from it, the more we stigmatize it and the more power we give beauty. Our communities are obsessed with being beautiful and gorgeous and hot. What would it mean if we were ugly?" Against a tepid backdrop of feminist lingerie and fourth-wave foundation, what Mingus is talking about is truly revolutionary. In a world where there are tangible rewards—attention, money, love, job opportunities, followers—for being pretty, and harsh penalties for not being so, the quest for beauty is hard to renounce. How possible is it to detach from an entire system, like an astronaut unmoored from a space station, and swim in the void of self-rule? These are challenging questions, and selfies alone won't solve them.

Rather than living under the tyranny of a single male gaze or dueling male and female gazes, it's probably more accurate to say that we live amid various intersecting gazes, which cross one another like beams in a laser light show. Agnès Godard, the cinematographer of *Beau Travail*, told Vulture, for a series on the female gaze, that she felt the term itself was too stark. "I would rather consider the wide range of cinematography's variations and nuances as the richness of a human being's sensitivity, subjectivity—not necessarily split into two worlds: man and woman. Why should it be two different languages?"

This is in line with many of Mulvey's critics, who have suggested a plurality of gazes. Thinkers like bell hooks have pushed back on the white supremacy inherent in the original conception of the male gaze. In her essay "The Oppositional Gaze: Black Female Spectators," hooks notes that slave owners punished slaves for looking directly at them and that Black men like Emmett Till were lynched for simply looking at white women. She draws on these examples to talk about the power of the gaze and who wields it. Not only are Black women marginalized onscreen (hooks was writing in the early '90s but her statement still applies today), they are excluded from the gaze as well. "Are we really to imagine that feminist theorists writing only about images of white women . . . do not 'see' the whiteness of the image?" she writes.

There was another figure in Manet's *Olympia*, a Black maid who is waiting on the portrait's subject, standing partially obscured in the background. The artist Lorraine O'Grady has written about this tradition in European portraits of including Black female servants as peripheral characters. In her essay "Olympia's Maid," O'Grady writes: "the 'femininity' of the white female body is ensured by assigning the not-white to a chaos safely removed from sight. Thus only the white body remains as the object of a voyeuristic, fetishizing male gaze." Manet's portrayal keeps this character relegated to the shadows, while the white courtesan is the protagonist.

More than a century and a half later, even some supposedly progressive cultural products made with the female gaze in mind turn out to be racially myopic in the same way. The television shows *I Love Dick* and *Glow*, praised for their depiction of female agency, "introduce characters of color only in supporting roles that contest but never destabilize the white protagonists' racial solipsism," as Benson-Allott has noted. Or they fetishize the people they purport to empower. The film *Blue Is the Warmest Color*, which follows a tumultuous relationship between two women, was initially touted as a film seen through the female gaze, though it was directed by a straight man, Abdellatif Kechiche. The film won the Palme d'Or at Cannes and initially received acclaim for its candid portrayal of lesbian love and sex. Then the backlash began. Julie Maroh, who wrote the graphic novel on which the film was based, complained about the exclusion of lesbians from the making of the film. Crew members accused the director of creating an atmosphere of bullying on set. Lead actresses Léa Seydoux and Adèle Exarchopoulos were quoted calling the filming experience "horrible" and exploitative. Both said they would not work with Kechiche again. These outcries caused those who had once praised the film's verité depictions to look more critically at the film. (In 2018, the director was accused of sexual assault by an unnamed woman, leading to a further reexamination of his work.)

A different take on similar subject matter is *Portrait of a Lady on Fire*, Céline Sciamma's film about a late-eighteenth-century artist, Marianne, hired to paint a recalcitrant subject, Héloïse. The two fall in love, though it's doomed from the start, as Héloïse is betrothed to a man. Threaded into the story is the tale of Orpheus and Eurydice, a myth that makes clear the potency of looking, for which death is the ultimate penalty. The film is full of gazes: the refracting of images in mirrors, the framing and slicing of the body, the attempt to reconcile reality and what appears on an easel. Sciamma makes the challenge of depicting anything at all evident in these shards of vision as Marianne's brush attempts to draw her subject's image out of brown canvas like a divining rod. It's one of the best filmic portrayals I've seen of the kind of mental editing an artist has to do. The artfully fragmented body reminded me of the photography of Francesca Woodman, a prodigy who took self-portraits that splintered her own, often nude, torso, showing her body arrested in motion. Female artists have been relegated to the domestic sphere, to depicting themselves and the women around them, for so long, and Woodman's bodies in motion show the frustration at being so circumscribed—pinned, like a trophy moth, in place. At one point, Marianne mentions that she's not permitted to paint male nudes. Héloïse asks if it's a question of modesty, and she responds: "It's mostly to prevent us from doing great art." The idea of a woman looking critically at a man and deciding how to depict him would give women too much power.

For most of *Portrait of a Lady on Fire*'s run time, the gaze stands in for the touch. The few male characters have little screen time, and all of the action takes place between women. The movie triangulates the gaze: The two leads look at one another and Sciamma's camera revels in looking at their shared gaze. The contrast with *Blue Is the Warmest Color* was pointed out by some critics, who cited the fact that Kechiche is a heterosexual man while Sciamma is an out lesbian, leading to the movies' reputations as the Good and Bad lesbian art films. But Sciamma dismissed the comparison, telling

IndieWire, "We do not live up to the exciting nature of this moment if we start reducing everything to questions of 'good or not good; moral or immoral; voyeur or not voyeur,' that's not the point. The key is to understand what animates such images, and what they seek to impart. . . . [We should] avoid base judgments and have the courage to question the gaze—our own, and that of the director. But that requires some effort from the spectator."

What may finally unseat the gaze is creators finally giving us something new to look at. A movie like Sciamma's, by a female writer-director and starring two women, is still a rarity, and even rarer in American cinema. But as the pool of people who depict and are shown, and whose vision receives attention, gets bigger, these distinctions may slip away. We may never fully free ourselves from the capital-G gaze, but perhaps we can all remake our relationship with it.

CHAPTER ELEVEN

The Revolution Will Be Spandex-Clad

THE ONLY PIECE of fashion advice my father has ever given me is: Never wear anything you couldn't run from an assailant in. As pessimistic as that counsel may be, he has a point. So many of the hallmarks of women's fashion, from high heels to pencil skirts, in addition to being uncomfortable, slow us down and even endanger us. Women's clothes have been far more formally legislated than men's over the years, and even now there's still something unsettling to some people about a woman dressing for comfort and ease. Advances in women's rights, and the way those rights are still curtailed, particularly when it comes to bodily autonomy and reproductive freedom, can be mapped onto similar patterns in fashion. In a society that still seeks to control women's bodies, including through what they wear, being comfortable and unencumbered can be, in a very real way, revolutionary. But the progress toward "dressing for ourselves" has not been a straight line, a triumphant story that ends with total liberation. It has been a constant push-pull between taking into account our own needs and adjusting for society's, a tug-of-war between freedom and fitting in. As loungewear becomes acceptable in more and more precincts (a push intensified by the COVID-19 pandemic, which made comfort the overarching priority for so many), the movement for self-determination in fashion gets at a very real duality: Who we are versus who we want to be seen as. Do we want to be comfortable for ourselves or uncomfortable in the pursuit of attracting or impressing others? How much are we willing to restrict our own mobility and freedom for aesthetic gains? Do we want to use clothes to reshape, or show off, our bodies? Or do we want to eschew all of that in the name of reveling in ourselves as we are? This isn't as simple as saying that a woman in five-inch heels and a bandage dress must hate herself and one in a roomy sweatsuit must be more self-actualized; it varies with the person and even with the day. But the fact remains that there are advantages to be gained by fitting in with the way others prefer you to look.

All of these threads have come together in one of the most hot-button fashion debates of this moment. Recently, everyone from school administrators to TV anchors to an angry mom or two has been waging war against a common enemy: leggings. The fight over a few feet of harmless spandex might seem silly, but it is an extension of a long-standing practice: to regulate female bodies, especially those that do not conform to the norm in some way. The policing begins early, in the form of school dress codes that expose a gender double standard. A Cape Cod high school banned leggings and yoga pants (unless worn with a long top) for girls in 2015. The principal said the rule was about "employability" and preparing students for the working world. Senior class president Seana Aiolupotea said, "We're not wearing them to get attention from people, we're wearing them because they're comfortable." That same year, students began using the #IfAnythingSchoolTaughtMe to share stories of dress code policing: "shorts and spaghetti tank tops are so inappropriate and distracting to boys," "my shoulders are too risky to be seen at school," "[the] girls [sic] dress code is way more complicated than the guys [sic] dress code." Middle schoolers in Evanston, Illinois, spoke out against a leggings ban that deemed the look "too distracting for boys." Students at a high school in Montclair, New Jersey, protested the gender bias inherent in their school's dress code. "Shoulders are so hot—said no one ever," read one protest sign. Similar stories abound—of prom dresses being flagged as inappropriate, teenagers being told they need to wear bras, and students made to wear a "shame suit" as punishment for violating the dress code. Supposedly, a dress code is to keep students focused on schoolwork and their learning from being disrupted; in practice, the outsize punishments end up disrupting their learning far more.

During the coronavirus pandemic, when one might think that virtual learning would rewrite these kinds of rules, schools began introducing Zoom dress codes for students. One charter school in Brooklyn created a remote-learning dress code that banned items like headscarves and do-rags from its virtual classrooms. When photos of maskless students packed into hallways, like one in Dallas, Georgia, went viral, many schools threw up their hands and said they couldn't regulate masks, and students were quick to respond that they seemed to have no trouble regulating girls' clothes.

School dress codes often target female students, LGBTQ students, and people of color (as with the rules around Black hairstyles or the banning of hijabs and do-rags mentioned above). They body-shame plus-size students for wearing items like leggings that straight-size students wouldn't be penalized for. In 2017, a high school principal in South Carolina made national headlines after telling students they couldn't wear leggings unless they were a size zero or two. Lest this seem like a case of American puritanism run amok, a New Zealand school principal cited a rule about skirt length that would "keep our girls safe, stop boys from getting ideas and create a good work environment for male staff," framing the boys and *the male staff* as the victims and the girls as perpetrators.

These kinds of dress codes usually come into effect during a time—middle school and high school—where the experience of being female is comparable to seeing your body as a grenade that may go off anytime. And leggings appear to be a particularly loaded garment, tapping into all of our complexes about female bodies, freedom, and power all at once. They're simultaneously overly casual and overly sexually charged, a double bind in binding form. They are seen as both too masculine, in their comfort and utility, and too feminine, in their tightness and their revelation of the female form. In 2017, United Airlines banned two teenage girls in leggings from boarding a flight. (The airline later cited the fact that they were part of the "pass travelers" program for relatives of airline employees, which has a stricter dress code.) A child on the same flight pulled a dress on over her leggings in order to be let on board. Fellow passenger Shannon Watts, whose tweets about the incident went viral, told the *New York Times* that the restrictions didn't extend to men. That child's dad was wearing above-the-knee shorts and "there was no issue with that."

Women in leggings are both sexualized and then punished for the sin of "making" others sexualize them. A 2015 *Fox & Friends* segment asked a male panel to weigh in on women wearing leggings as pants. The host asked one of the "esteemed panel of fathers" if he was "comfortable with the women in your life parading in public in leggings." They then judged three women who walked out wearing them based on whether their outfit was appropriate enough. One was told, "Obviously her physique, God bless you, you've worked out, you've earned that. And there are appropriate places to wear that. But I wouldn't wear that to church on Sunday." (The woman countered that she felt comfortable in the outfit.) NowThis News called the segment "head-scratchingly creepy." This anti-leggings stance isn't only perpetuated by men, of course. A letter to Notre Dame's student newspaper in 2019 read, "I'm just a Catholic mother of four sons with a problem that only girls can solve: leggings." The letter writer recalled seeing a group of young women at Mass wearing leggings that she said looked "painted on." A culture that allows garments like these, she wrote, "makes it hard on Catholic mothers to teach their sons that women are someone's daughters and sisters." The onus here is on women: mothers to teach the sons, the women to not wear things that might provoke the sons, and by the way, said women only count as chattel ("someone's daughters and sisters").

Leggings seem to be the spandex lightning rod of modern garments, electrifying our debates about comfort, freedom, masculinity, body-shaming, the male gaze, objectification, and, apparently, the endangered souls of our large adult sons. If there's a past analogue to leggings, it's probably the bloomer. Bloomers, which originated in the mid-nineteenth century, were loose pants worn under dresses. Their namesake was the feminist Amelia Jenks Bloomer, though she didn't invent the style, nor was she the first to wear it (that distinction goes to suffragist Elizabeth Cady Stanton's cousin Elizabeth Smith Miller). Still, after writing about them in her women's newspaper, *The Lily*, Bloomer became so associated with the garment that it took on her surname.

The clothes women wore at the time were literally a danger to their well-being: the constricted silhouettes of whalebone corsets and stays made it hard to move or breathe properly, and in extreme cases harmed organs or punctured lungs. Heavy petticoats reinforced with straw or horsehair, typically weighing ten to twelve pounds, slowed their wearers down, and floor-length skirts gathered dirt or, for those who worked, got stuck in the machinery of factory assembly lines. The prevailing styles intentionally trapped women and restricted them to the sphere of the home—the more you followed trends, the more high-class you were, because you didn't need to work or move freely, and in fact had servants to help you put on these cumbersome clothes. Women were, as the academic Janet Murray has put it, walking "billboards of their fathers' or husbands' wealth." They were possessions to be shown off, not individuals with agency. Thorstein Veblen called them examples of "vicarious consumption." In "The Economic Theory of Woman's Dress," he wrote that fashion was a way for privileged women to flaunt their leisure, "to demonstrate to all observers, and to compel observation of the fact, that the wearer is manifestly incapable of doing anything that is of any use. The modern civilized woman's dress attempts this demonstration of habitual idleness, and succeeds measurably."

The advent of bloomers upended this understanding of women as inert chattel. "Reform dress," consisting of a knee-length dress over pantaloons gathered at the ankles, began popping up as a form of protest. Bloomer wrote about the new, corset-free style in *The Lily*. "We care not for the frowns of over fastidious gentlemen," she wrote of those who had adopted the costume. Finally, a woman could be "the free, healthy being God made her instead of the corseted, crippled, dragged-down creature her slavery to clothes has made her." After she included an image of herself wearing the style in the paper, she was inundated with hundreds of letters from women eager to cast off their traditional dress and requesting patterns so they could DIY the look. "Bloomerism," as it was called, became a bona fide movement, a fight for freedom in dress that was foregrounded by an overall push for progressivism. The fashion historian Anne Hollander has written that "clothes are social phenomena; changes in dress are social changes." The nineteenth-century movements for social freedoms, namely women's rights and the abolition of slavery, surely contributed to the drive for freedom in dress. Women were becoming more educated, and more were going to college. Progressive doctors and health reformers advocated for rational dress alongside causes like birth control, exercise, vegetarian diets, and the "water cure," an early version of hydrotherapy. There was an anti-fashion cast to their philosophies that contained a hidden sexism of its own—implying that caring about style was silly and frivolous.

Still, bloomers became a bona fide trend. Their silhouette drew on the trouser styles worn by women in the Middle East, thus why they were sometimes called "Turkish trousers." While unremarkable in many parts of the world, the look felt truly revolutionary to Western eyes. The idea being, free your body and so much else will follow. Some suffragists chose to call it "the freedom dress" for this reason. The Black poet and abolitionist Charlotte Grimké donned the outfit to climb a cherry tree. She wrote in her diary that she "obtained some fine fruit, and felt for the first time 'monarch of all I surveyed.'" Not only did it free women like Grimké for independent physical activity, the costume also took on a social aspect, with women attending "bloomer balls" where everyone wore them. It also represented a uniquely American take on fashion, freeing women from the top-down rule of the French designers who determined the trends, summed up in one reformer's "Declaration of Independence from the Despotism of Parisian Fashion."

Men didn't exactly react calmly to the rise of the movement. In fact, bloomers made them . . . really emotional. Cartoonist John Leech published multiple anti-bloomer cartoons in the humor magazine *Punch*, including ones that showed a woman on one knee proposing to a man, women smoking in a bar while waited on by a man (referred to in the caption as "one of the 'inferior animals'"), and women forming a police force. A cartoon by an unknown artist from 1851 shows the traditional household structures upended: A woman is lounging and smoking while her husband mends his coat. The implication was that women, in dressing more like men, would begin taking on men's roles in society as well—emasculating them. The *New York Times* spelled out these fears of gender collapse in an 1851 editorial: "there is an obvious tendency to encroach upon masculine manners, manifested even in trifles, which cannot be too severely rebuked or too speedily repressed." At the same time, since bloomers displayed the wearer's legs, they were also considered too sexualized and provocative—the same contradictions that cluster around leggings today.

At its height, Bloomerism began to take on a life of its own that threatened to eclipse the freedoms the first-wave feminists were fighting for. "We all felt that the dress was drawing attention from what we thought of far greater importance—the question of woman's right to better education, to a wider field of employment, to better remuneration for her labor, and to the ballot for the protection of her rights," Bloomer wrote. Susan B. Anthony said that when she wore the costume to speak, "the attention of my audiences was fixed on my clothes instead of my words." Eventually, even boosters like Bloomer and Elizabeth Cady Stanton cast off the bloomer costume, as lighter hoop skirts, which didn't require heavy petticoats to pad out the silhouette, came into fashion. (Bloomer also found that her beloved reform dress didn't stand up to the skirt-lifting winds of Iowa, where she then lived.) Even Miller, the bloomer pioneer, wrote that after seven years of reform dress, "I quite 'fell from grace' and found myself again in the bonds of the old swaddling clothes—a victim to my love of beauty."

The next wave of dress reform gathered steam around another new craze, the bicycle, which literalized female independence, allowing women to take on greater freedom and mobility, not to mention becoming stronger in a world where "frail" was still synonymous with "attractive." Susan B. Anthony said bicycling "has done more to emancipate women than anything else in the world." "Rational dress" was designed with the sport in mind and consisted of a short skirt worn over loose pants. Cyclists also wore divided skirts, a split-leg style that kept long skirts from getting caught in the spokes. They were controversial: In France, where a law banned women in trousers unless "the woman is holding a bicycle handlebar or the reins of a horse," women were arrested for wearing them. As women became more involved in other sports, too, athletic costumes became a way to give women more freedom and movement. The "New Woman" who emerged at this time was a descendant of the Bloomer—but even more independent and active than her predecessor.

A few high-fashion designers even got on board. Paul Poiret designed jupe-culottes. Coco Chanel, a fan of trousers in her own wardrobe, started putting them in her collections. In 1931, Elsa Schiaparelli designed a divided skirt for her "Pour Le Sport" collection (the proto-athleisure of the time). The tennis player Lili de Alvarez wore it at Wimbledon and received death threats. The *Daily Mail* wrote that de Alvarez "should be soundly beaten" for her choice of costume.

Pants, were, of course, the next frontier in Western dress. Amelia Earhart became known for wearing them, and when she started her own clothing line in the 1930s, it included plenty of trousers. (The line was inspired by a conversation Earhart had with fellow comfort advocate Schiaparelli.) In 1939, a woman in pants first appeared in *Vogue* in a nonathletic context, and trousers were worn by Hollywood stars like Katharine Hepburn and Marlene Dietrich both onscreen and off. During World War II, ordinary women adopted pants as they took on more traditionally male jobs, which helped to normalize the garment as genderless everyday wear.

By the '60s, androgyny became commonplace on the runway.

In 1966, Yves Saint Laurent introduced *le smoking*, an evening tuxedo for women that was controversial at the time but was quickly taken up by Catherine Deneuve and Bianca Jagger, who wore a white version to her wedding. In the '80s, as more and more women entered the business world in positions of power, padded shoulders and power suits were de rigueur. But even though leggings seem to be today's major battleground, women in pants are still controversial in some circles. Female British Airways flight attendants only won the right to wear them in 2016. Their union celebrated the fact that "Female cabin crew [members] no longer have to shiver in the cold, wet and snow of wintery climates." Some evangelical communities still ban them to this day. And more liberal domains, like Hollywood, aren't immune from these rules. While we now see more women choosing pants, suits, and jumpsuits on the red carpet, the gown remains the standard. When a woman does wear a suit to a Hollywood event, it constitutes a statement. When Lady Gaga wore an oversized Marc Jacobs suit to *ELLE*'s Women in Hollywood event in 2018, she said, "As a woman who was conditioned at a very young age to listen to what men told me to do, I decided today I wanted to take the power back. Today I wear the pants."

Whether it's the red carpet or the C-suite, women's professional dress codes are much more regulated than men's. Office temperatures are notoriously set low to favor suit-wearing men, while women shiver in their cubicles. Women have to wear a wider variety of clothes that are more subject to trends and end up having to spend more money on professional clothes. And there are far more rules to follow. In some cases, even clothing that's not visible to the eye is policed: As recently as 2019, union leaders critiqued British Airways for supposedly dictating what color bra flight attendants could wear under their uniforms. (The airline denies this occurred.)

Women's clothes also don't have some of the practical touches that men's do, most notably pockets. Pockets on women's clothes still tend to be decorative, not functional—either pointlessly stitched closed or too shallow to carry anything, which keeps women carrying purses. "Pocket equality," as the writer Tracy Moore has called it, may not seem like a big deal, but it is, on a small scale, political. The same questions of mobility, financial power, and independence that came up when women adopted bloomers or bicycle costumes are echoed in the pocket debate. A lack of pockets exerts a kind of "pink tax" for women, requiring you to spend additional money on a handbag. While both sexes once carried bags, the seventeenth century brought a division that still persists today—men had pockets sewn into their clothing, while women used detachable pockets that were hidden under their vast skirts. Post–French Revolution, as silhouettes slimmed down, secreting them away was near-impossible. The clunky exterior pocket was replaced by a reticule, or small purse, that removed the privacy of the tucked-in pocket and barely held anything of significance. It might seem like a small detail, but it shattered the financial independence, privacy, and self-determination that pockets had afforded women.

Feminists and reformers in the nineteenth and early twentieth century continued to push for pockets. Standing with your hands in your pockets was considered a masculine pose, and many emancipation-minded women proudly posed that way. Suffragette suits were made with pockets. It wasn't until 1974, with the passage of the Equal Credit Opportunity Act, that American women finally won the right to have their own checking accounts without a man cosigning for them. As Chelsea G. Summers wrote in a Vox piece on the politics of pockets, the fears around them pointed to larger fears about concealment and power. "It's not merely that women will strut with their hands in their pockets . . . it's that women's pockets could carry something secret, something private, or something deadly."

Now that phones have gotten larger, it's harder than ever for a woman to walk around unencumbered, since most women's clothes still either don't have pockets or have pockets too small to fit a current-model smartphone and wallet. The mobility that our various attempts at rational dress have promised is unattainable without access to pockets.

And then there are high heels. Ironically, they were once the province of men, originally worn by tenth-century Persian soldiers (they kept their feet in the stirrups). It wasn't until the 1700s that they became coded as feminine. Now, they sit weirdly at the junction of sexy and professional. Many women find them painful to wear, they slow down the stride, and they can have adverse health effects like strained tendons, weakened ankles, and back pain—not so different from the corsets and petticoats our ancestors once struggled in. British actress and activist Nicola Thorp was working as a temp and started a gig as a receptionist at Pricewaterhouse-Coopers in 2015. Thorp showed up for her first day in a pantsuit and black flats. The company insisted she change into a dress, much like a student asked to change into a more "appropriate" outfit for class. Then she was told there was a high-heel policy for women, and that if she did not go buy a pair right away, she'd be fired. Thorp started a petition against this gendered aspect of work dress codes and gained enough signatures (more than 152,000) that her case went all the way to Parliament. After collecting testimony from doctors and from high-heel-wearing women themselves, the government eventually issued a report concluding that existing law already prohibited employers from requiring high heels, but that the law was not well enforced. No further action was taken. Thorp has called the move a "cop-out." But while her campaign may not have been a legal victory, it was taken up on social media, and many employers relaxed their dress code rules as a result.

A similar thing happened in 2019, when female office workers in Japan mounted a campaign against the widespread requirement that women wear high heels in offices, part of a series of stringent dress requirements in the country (some companies bar public-facing female employees from wearing glasses, or require women to wear makeup and pantyhose). The high-heel conversation took off when Yumi Ishikawa, a model, actress, and temp worker, tweeted "Why do we have to work while hurting our feet? Whereas men can wear flat shoes." Tens of thousands shared her post, fomenting a movement that became known by Ishikawa's coinage hashtag #KuToo, a play on both the #MeToo movement and on the Japanese words for "shoe" and "pain." Ishikawa submitted a petition to the labor ministry calling for a law against the requirement. The country's health and labor minister, Takumi Nemoto, responded by telling a legislative committee that requiring high heels "is socially accepted as something that falls within the realm of being occupationally necessary and appropriate." In other words, this is what we've always done—the rationale for so many sexist dress codes over the years.

Sexist attitudes toward fashion aren't just uncomfortable, discriminatory, and a drain on women's time and energy. They can also be used to cast doubt on victims of sexual assault. "What were you wearing?" is still a question frequently asked of rape survivors. A 2019 exhibit of the same name included re-creations of what survivors had worn during their assault, including everything from sweats and a baseball cap to a sari to an Army uniform. In a 1989 sexual assault and kidnapping case cited in the journal *Law & Inequality*, jurors acquitted a man of the crimes after saying that the alleged victim's clothing suggested she was "advertising for sex" and "she was obviously dressed for a good time." Even though it's clear that clothing has no bearing on sexual assault, the idea that women are "asking for it" based on what they choose to wear unfortunately persists. As recently as 1999, an Italian court ruled that a woman wearing jeans couldn't have been raped (because the pants were too hard for another person to remove). With this kind of victim-blaming, the onus falls upon women to change their behavior—to dress differently, in a way that supposedly won't "provoke" men. While men can, of course, also be victims of sexual assault, their clothing is not put on trial.

In recent years, comfort has become chic even on the runway, with modern heirs to Paul Poiret and Coco Chanel proliferating. Designers are now celebrated for creating with comfort and practicality in mind. Celine's scarf-print culottes, designed by Phoebe Philo for her "Resort" 2013 collection, had echoes of their 1910s predecessors, and the style trickled down to mass fashion. Victoria Beckham swapped Adidas Stan Smith sneakers for her usual towering heels to take her runway bow in 2016. Birkenstock has collaborated with high-end brands from Valentino to Proenza Schouler, making the crunchy, soft-footbed sandal the height of fashion. And the increasing gender neutrality of fashion allows people to adopt the clothes that suit them and feel comfortable, regardless of how they identify. Bloomerism and rational dress turned out to be ephemeral movements linked to a moment in time. But culottes, pants, and comfortable shoes seem, thankfully, here to stay.

Fashion was already headed in this direction—increased comfort, expanded self-expression—before the pandemic, but the work-from-home mandate for students and white-collar workers only stomped on the gas pedal. Suddenly, people began questioning what aspects of fashion and beauty they were engaging in "for themselves" and which ones really existed only for the consumption of others. A full face of makeup or itchy black control-top tights suddenly felt less like a fact of daily existence and more like another form of low-grade torture. The myriad ways women have tried to free themselves through fashion and pursue self-definition, from bloomers to spandex, had led us to this moment of truth: When the question "What would you wear if no one was watching?" was put to the test, the answer was rarely "Anything that pinches, itches, or leaves marks when taken off."

But the concept of "dressing for yourself" is, ultimately, a vexed one. Can fashion really exist in a vacuum, or does it depend on a reaction? The pandemic was probably the best test case for this idea: When it put white-collar work clothes on ice, it freed us from certain strictures, but it also took away the social aspect of style—the admiring glance from a stranger, the new acquaintance who starts a conversation with you about your necklace, even the affronted stares when you intentionally wear something weird or ugly as a kind of sartorial middle finger. Without this element, fashion is the proverbial tree falling in the forest; even the progressive women who attended bloomer balls were, in their own way, looking for camaraderie through clothing. Style is self-expression, but it's also a way to communicate. And something is lost when there's no one on the other end of the conversation.

CHAPTER TWELVE

Politics and Fashion

We Can't Win

Recently, I watched something I never thought I'd see in my lifetime: a YouTube makeup tutorial done by a sitting congresswoman. On my laptop screen, Alexandria Ocasio-Cortez (AOC) was filling in her brows and applying her signature bright-red Stila liquid lipstick in the shade "Beso," all while talking briskly about the "pink tax" and how women are judged on their appearance in the workplace. With a flick of a brush, she was not only getting herself HDTV-ready. She was dismantling a system that relies on opacity—unpacking the beauty work that goes unacknowledged behind the scenes of her profession, where candidates both male and female rarely cop to getting Botox or buying designer clothes.

AOC often shares these behind-the-curtain moments on her Instagram stories, where she also breaks down the nuts and bolts of the political process for her followers. It's all there: The Rent the

Runway wardrobe, the press-on nails, the trusty stay-all-day lip-stick. She even proudly showed off the worn-through shoes she wore to knock on doors while campaigning. They were a visual shorthand for the unglamorous hard work that goes into a campaign.

That kind of forthrightness is extremely unusual in a politician—even a leftist, millennial one. And it may well be a tactical advance against people who have called the congresswoman's authenticity into question. The Washington establishment—both Republican and Democratic—was threatened by this young woman of color, with her regular-person backstory and progressive politics, and reacted by trying to cross-examine her credentials. Some of this credibility battle was fought on fashion grounds. Early in AOC's first term in office, reporter Eddie Scarry tweeted, "[A] Hill staffer sent me this pic of Ocasio-Cortez they took just now. I'll tell you something: that jacket and coat don't look like a girl who strug-gles," inferring a great deal from her outfit. It was a strange kind of backhanded compliment wrapped in condescension: She looks too put-together, too good, for her humble origins to be believable. But if Ocasio-Cortez roamed the halls of Congress looking like a slob, she'd never hear the end of it, either. The congresswoman pretty much said so herself in a tweet responding to Scarry's: "If I walked into Congress wearing a sack, they would laugh & take a picture of my backside. If I walk in with my best sale-rack clothes, they laugh & take a picture of my backside." Later, she added, "The reason journos . . . can't help but obsess about my clothes, rent, or mischaracterize respectful convos as 'fights' is bc as I've said, women like me aren't supposed to run for office—or win." When Ocasio-Cortez posed for *Interview* magazine in a $3,500 outfit (bor-rowed for the shoot, as most clothes worn by magazine subjects are), she was critiqued by conservative commentator Charlie Kirk as "someone who pretends to be a champion of the people." And she also caught flak for getting a $300 haircut, with the *Washington Times* calling out the supposed hypocrisy of the "self-declared socialist" spending three figures at the salon. Ocasio-Cortez's example proves that when it comes to women and self-presentation in politics, it doesn't matter whether you put in effort or don't. You're doomed either way. Effort will be taken as shallowness and superficiality, and maybe even undercut your platform, while lack of effort will be seen as laziness.

Since the days of the Founding Fathers, American politicians have always been required to project both perfection and humility. Writing about that time, the historian R. B. Bernstein has said, "It was best to conduct oneself in as plain, simple, and republican a manner as possible; ostentation was a sign of leanings to aristocracy or even to monarchy." In its attempts to distance itself from European forms of government, American politics has always at least pretended to a degree of egalitarianism.

As politicians have increasingly become celebrities, they remain public servants, and that line has become much harder to walk without it turning into a plank. We love ogling celebrities in their borrowed couture gowns at premieres, and then seeing them dressed down, looking "just like us!" on a coffee run. But politicians have to split the difference between these two modes. When such a large percentage of them come from the upper classes, that's sometimes hard to do convincingly. Which is where fashion, in its purest form—as costume—comes in. That pesky concept of "likeability"—the eternal question of "Would you want to get a beer with this person?" as though the main duty of an elected official is to be a wingman—creeps in. Likeability is not quite the same thing as authenticity, but it might attend authenticity's family reunion. And fashion is one way to communicate it, or feign it.

Even for men, fashion statements have been a political asset or a liability, depending on the context. There were the earth tones image consultants pushed on Al Gore so he would seem more like an "alpha male." Or George W. Bush's Wranglers-and-belt-buckles cowboy cosplay, meant to distract from his prep school and Yale background and amp up his populist bona fides. Or the folksy denim-on-denim looks that took Ronald Reagan from pampered Hollywood star to supposed man of the people. The "Washington outsider" posture has been affected by people on both sides of the aisle. Politicians roll up their sleeves to telegraph that they're mavericks straight out of *Mr. Smith Goes to Washington* who will get things done around here for a change. John F. Kennedy was considered refreshing because he didn't wear a hat, a fact that earned him the nickname Hatless Jack. But he was more high maintenance than he seemed, wearing makeup to the 1960 presidential debate against Richard Nixon, who went au naturel. Kennedy's instincts about the role television would play in his eventual victory were sharp. His foundation-assisted youthfulness beating out Tricky Dick's five o'clock shadow, Kennedy was considered the victor by those who watched on TV, while Nixon was thought to be the winner by radio listeners, driving home the importance of visual media in shaping our perceptions.

Candidates have even used military fashion to tout their masculinity and suggest an affiliation with the troops. In 1988, when Massachusetts Governor Michael Dukakis ran against World War II hero George H. W. Bush, he was eager to prove his military mettle. (Even though he didn't really have any; the Associated Press summed up his service with the headline "Dukakis' Military Service Uneventful, Say What Few Records Exist After Fire.") Bush joked, "He thinks that a naval exercise is something you find in Jane Fonda's workout book." Dukakis attempted to counter this perception with an awkward photo op that became notorious, where he drove a tank wearing a helmet that looked cartoonishly big on him. His speech about investing in traditional military technology was swallowed whole by the resulting image, which made him look weak and out of his depth. Bush ended up using the footage to his own advantage in an attack ad.

The junior George Bush had a less impressive war record—during the Vietnam War, he famously avoided combat by, like many privileged Texas scions, joining the Texas Air National Guard—but that didn't stop him from leaning into the warrior image. He famously wore a flight suit to land on the USS *Abraham Lincoln* aircraft carrier to give his "Mission Accomplished" speech. (There was speculation that he had padded the crotch of the suit.) Both the suit and the speech were a master class in image over substance: a person with no real military credentials borrowing the uniform for cred, while closing the book on a mission that had in no way been accomplished. But if there was a stars-and-stripes banner behind him declaring so, who could say for sure?

Less successful at this style-as-propaganda charade was Jared Kushner. When visiting Iraq, he put on a flak jacket—helpfully labeled with his name, kid's lunchbox style—over his preppy navy blazer and oxford shirt. The overall effect was as though Holden Caulfield had been conscripted. Twitter had a field day with captions: "Preparing to storm Martha's Vineyard," "When you have war at 7 but a croquet game at 8," "If Wes Anderson made a war movie." The man who was supposed to broker peace in the Middle East was an out-of-touch, overprivileged schoolboy; Jimmy Fallon wore the jacket to do an impression of him on *Saturday Night Live*. Whether it was an attempt to use fashion tactically or not, simply putting on a piece of military gear without changing the rest of his outfit only reinforced Kushner's spoiled-playboy image.

Still, while male political figures are sometimes critiqued for

what they wear, or for spending too much on fashion and beauty—
John Edwards's $400 haircut is one notable example—the onus
falls largely on women, who still make up the minority of elected
officials, to strike the balance between red carpet and just-us-
folks that contemporary politics requires. And when they don't do
so, they get called out—as Ocasio-Cortez has over and over.

First ladies, who are not elected officials, tend to have a bit
more leeway with their sartorial choices, from Jackie Kennedy's
Oleg Cassini sheaths to Nancy Reagan's Adolfo suits. Michelle
Obama was both praised and critiqued for her fashion choices:
She brought deserved attention to young talents like Jason Wu,
but drew ire for things like not wearing an American designer to a
Chinese state dinner (instead, she wore Alexander McQueen) and
sporting expensive Lanvin sneakers to volunteer at a food bank.
Reactions to Melania Trump's fashion were even more polarized.
Style Kremlinologists claimed to see hints of insurrection in
her attire: a pussybow blouse in reference to her husband's "grab
them by the pussy" remarks, a Gucci dress when the brand had
recently staged a show with a pro-choice message. But these seem
like dubious connections at best. Then there were the ill-matched
combinations of fashion and venue: the tone-deaf echoes of colo-
nialism in the pith helmet she wore in Kenya and the impractical
stilettos she wore when going to visit victims of Hurricane Harvey.
And finally, her most egregious misstep, wearing a jacket emblazoned with the phrase "I really don't care. Do U?" while visiting
migrant children who had been separated from their families by
her husband's administration. The outcry around the jacket was
a reminder that in the absence of substance, there is just style to
remark on. The jacket was fed right into the hopper of the "Is she
complicit?" debate. Her spokeswoman was then able to deflect with
the classic dismissal of anything fashion-related: "It's a jacket.
There was no hidden message." In this sense, the inert, easily de-

niable quality of fashion was the perfect venue for whatever message she was trying to send.

At least first ladies' style statements aren't weighted with the pressure of their being public servants elected to represent our country. For female politicians, the scrutiny is magnified. And the rules are draconian. "Politics is hell in general," Margaret Atwood said in a BBC conversation with classicist Mary Beard, "but I think it's probably double hell for women because not only do you have to have a position, you have to have a hairstyle." We accept, even encourage, a little glamour in our first ladies, but female politicians don't get the same breaks. A few years ago, Yale Law School hosted a Women's Campaign School that included a two-hour session called "Dress to Win." In 2016, the Barbara Lee Family Foundation released a study titled *Politics Is Personal: Keys to Likeability and Electability for Women*, which surveyed voters in seven focus groups. They concluded that likeability was "non-negotiable" for female candidates in a way that it wasn't for men, but that the quality was also hard to define. Meaning that those seeking to be likeable really had their work cut out for them. (Also, if you feel vindicated for constantly worrying whether or not people like you, you're not alone. Clearly, it matters more if you're a woman.)

So how is female likeability communicated via fashion? Not through the cowboy stylings of someone like Reagan or Bush, which would read as over-the-top. (Representative Frederica Wilson of Florida, who favors Western wear, was called a "buffoon" and a "clown in a cowboy hat" after she criticized Trump.) The focus groups told the researchers that "if they were giving advice to a woman candidate, they would make sure her wardrobe, makeup, and appearance are impeccable." To strike the balance between perfection and seeming uppity and high-maintenance is the stuff six-figure consultant salaries are made of.

The rules have always been harsher for female politicians. In

1969, Representative Charlotte Reid became the first woman to wear pants—a bell-bottom pantsuit, no less—on the House floor. One congressman walked over to tell her, "I was told there was a lady here in trousers, so I had to come over and see for myself." The Senate took even longer to catch up. "Doorkeepers" would monitor everyone's outfits before they went out onto the Senate floor, and women in pants were often forced to change into dresses before making appearances. Most frustratingly, male senators were allowed to sport casualwear, like khakis, during weekend sessions, but women still had to wear dresses or skirts and pantyhose. It took a flood of new female senators being elected to change those stubborn double standards. In 1993, Senator Carol Moseley-Braun showed up to her first day of work in a pantsuit; she was unaware the Senate frowned upon pants. That same year, Senator Barbara Mikulski decided she wanted to wear pants to work on a snowy day. "I just really wanted to be comfortable. I'm most comfortable wearing slacks," she told Vice, looking back on the day. Mikulski was able to get the higher-ups to confirm that the Senate rules didn't explicitly ban pants. She and another senator, Nancy Kassebaum, chose a weekend to show up in pants and encouraged female Senate staffers to follow suit (no pun intended). Mikulski later called it a "seismographic event," and it paved the way for political women in pantsuits, including the politician most associated with the look, Hillary Clinton. (She would become the first and only first lady to pose for her official portrait wearing pants.)

Early on, women in this sphere faced the kind of sexist, body-shaming nonsense that would result in an AOC clapback today. Moseley-Braun recalled in a Vox story that when she was a senator in the '90s, "*Women's Wear Daily* had me on its cover—actually a picture of my butt, and it said, 'this is what a Chanel sweater set should not look like.' " Until recently, the House of Representatives banned people, including reporters, for wearing sleeveless tops, a policy that tends to target women more than men, since sleeveless business attire is pretty much nonexistent for men. Though there is no written dress code for the House, in 2017, then–House Speaker Paul Ryan took to the microphone to reiterate that "Members should wear appropriate business attire." The right to bear arms is, it seems, more protected than the right to bare arms. (After an outcry, Ryan agreed to modernize the dress code, allowing for sleeveless dresses and open-toed shoes to be worn.)

Fashion that conflicts with a candidate's image can erode the message they're trying to convey. It's why Bernie Sanders often brags that he has never worn a tuxedo (though he did once get critiqued for wearing a Burton jacket whose price tag was nearly $700. In his defense, Vermont is cold!). When Sarah Palin, a humble "hockey mom" from Alaska, became John McCain's running mate, the Republican National Committee spent $150,000 on clothes for her and her family from Neiman Marcus and Saks Fifth Avenue. One Republican consultant told the *New York Times* that what became known as Wardrobegate "undercuts Palin's whole image as a hockey mom, a 'one-of-us' kind of candidate." Her advisers quickly distanced Palin from the shopping spree, saying that she hadn't been directly involved. When Elisabeth Hasselbeck, a conservative host on *The View*, defended Palin, her cohost Joy Behar snapped back: "I don't think Joe the Plumber wears Manolo Blahniks," referring to the populist oracle who was then making campaign appearances with McCain.

But fashion can also be, as a talking head would say, "on message," enhancing whatever image a candidate is trying to put out there. Like the rust-red Max Mara overcoat Nancy Pelosi wore as she emerged triumphantly from a meeting with President Trump about the looming government shutdown. The coat proved so popular that the brand reissued it. Less lauded was Pelosi's and Senator Chuck Schumer's adoption of kente cloth stoles, a traditional

Ghanaian garment, as they introduced the George Floyd Justice in Policing Act in response to the killing of Floyd and other Black Americans by police officers. "The announcement did not warrant such a visual stunt," wrote Doreen St. Félix in *The New Yorker*, "but the Democratic Party, the party of optics and gesture, apparently could not resist. . . . [I]ntent on conveying solidarity with their constituents, [they] only made themselves models of obtuseness." What they wore only contributed to the perception of centrist liberals co-opting causes only when it is politically convenient for them to do so, not far off from, as St. Félix cited, a Democratic mayor commissioning a Black Lives Matter mural without effecting any real change.

One of the politicians most criticized for her fashion, and someone for whom fashion also became a proxy for other critiques, is—who else?—Hillary Clinton. She adopted her signature pantsuits because she "thought it would be good to do what male politicians do and wear more or less the same thing every day," Clinton wrote in *What Happened*. Male politicians' similar fashion tactics went unnoticed, or they were praised for doing the same thing; President Obama's penchant for wearing only gray or blue suits was praised by *Fast Company* as one of his "productivity secrets." The only time Obama faced real fashion scrutiny was when he once dared to wear a summer-weight tan suit that was seen as too casual for the occasion, discussing the military's response to ISIS in Syria. Meanwhile, when Fed chair nominee Janet Yellen wore the same outfit for two public events a month apart, the press called her out. Clinton, too, suffered from this double standard. She could not seem to escape attention drawn to her fashion, either positive or negative. Her pantsuits were constantly commented on, whether mocked or celebrated, their rainbow hues becoming a trusty meme.

Before the pantsuits, there were the headbands. In the '90s,

Clinton favored the style. *USA Today* called her headbands "head-strong" and quoted a hairstylist who said that Clinton, then in her forties, was too old to wear such an accessory. When she abandoned them and began changing her hairstyle and fashion, her critics saw this flip-flopping as the equivalent of John Kerry's windsurfing—behavior unrelated to any political ideology, but something that could be used to paint her as indecisive and not to be trusted. If you think I'm exaggerating, one reporter called it "discomforting for the national sense of identity. . . . After all, you wouldn't want the Statue of Liberty changing her hemline every other week." Clinton was expected to be an unchanging, ever-reliable icon in the same way a literal statue was.

When she became a candidate, for Senate and then for the high-est office in the land, the jeers only intensified. After the press fix-ated on her hair accessories even after she'd served as secretary of state, she joked about calling her book *The Scrunchie Chronicles: 112 Countries and It's Still All about My Hair.* Her authenticity was ques-tioned in the same way AOC's is now, with Trump (yes, Trump . . .) claiming that his opponent wore a wig. Again, the inference that she's untrustworthy was drawn from her appearance. "Her hair's fake" was steps away from "Naturally, she must have orchestrated Benghazi."

But when Clinton did attempt to go high fashion, she was also critiqued for that. She wore a Giorgio Armani jacket that retailed for $12,495 to give a speech about income inequality. On the one hand, that combination of price tag and speech topic is a real unforced error. On the other hand, Clinton is a wealthy woman. Should she be pretending not to be? Trump favors four-figure Bri-oni suits himself. It became a truism that it was sexist to remark at all on what Clinton was wearing, but I don't think completely ignoring the visual statements of our public figures makes sense. It's more about weighing them equally, and it's hard to imagine a woman who flaunted her wealth in the same way Trump does reaching higher office.

Even those who *did* support Clinton often reduced her to her hair, pantsuits, and other visual attributes. Especially when it came to the fashion industry. When Clinton ran for president in 2016, I wrote a piece observing the fact that I saw, in my admittedly fashion-centric feed, many posts extolling '70s, hippie-esque Hillary or chic '90s Hillary in a shoulder-exposing Donna Karan blouse, but few images of what she currently looked and dressed like. Even her social media team seemed to be taking this tack, posting throwbacks to Clinton's Beijing speech, a shot of her standing in front of the Clinton/Gore campaign plane, and one of her and Bill eating breakfast just captioned "1979." A 1999 shot posted pre-debate showed her leaning against a wall, wearing sunglasses and a sweater tied, devil-may-care style, around her shoulders. It was captioned: "Let's do this. #DebateNight."

The discomfort with what the nearly seventy-year-old, comfortably unchic, monochrome pantsuit-clad Democratic nominee actually, currently looked like, and the need to sum her up in some kind of fashion statement, reflected the high standards we still hold female politicians, and indeed most women in public life, to when it comes to fashion wish fulfillment. Fashion-related Clinton memes multiplied, from a Death Row Records homage to an Instagram account, Hillary Street Style, which matched up her looks with celebrities'. Nineties Hillary starred on a T-shirt worn by Rihanna, and her campaign's merch included a yellow T-shirt with what looked to be a Wellesley-era black-and-white photo of the candidate. There was (perhaps unconscious) ageism at play in the fact that present-day imagery of Clinton was rarely celebrated in the same way. This insanity reached its zenith when the women's lifestyle site Hello Giggles ran a listicle of "10 throwback Hillary Clinton photos that will make you melt." I regret to inform you that one of them was . . . Clinton sitting in the Situation Room with the president and his national security team receiving word on the Osama bin Laden raid. (It seems to have since been removed from the article.)

Clinton, I wrote then, "doesn't need to be fierce, or slay, or be a style icon to lead." But part of the problem is that political culture has increasingly replicated celebrity culture. An entire news cycle could be built around Clinton "clapping back" at her opponent (who was, himself, a celebrity). Even Supreme Court justices have stans now, as Amanda Hess wrote in her piece on Ruth Bader Ginsburg's most ardent online admirers, who nicknamed her "the Notorious RBG." This wave of adulation led her to be perceived as the most liberal figure on the bench, but as Hess points out, that is actually Sonia Sotomayor: Ginsburg sided with the fossil-fuel industry and against asylum seekers. But within her cadre of fans, these less rosy realities didn't matter. Instead, they scanned the signals she wore around her neck, including her crocheted "majority opinion" collar and her "dissent" bib necklace, interpreting them as cryptograms to decode her decisions. (When your work uniform is a black robe, your accessories are one way to semaphore your true intentions.)

We now live in a world, Hess wrote, where people "consume their own politics as if they were kitschy pop-culture artifacts." The fact that Clinton and Ginsburg and Elizabeth Warren might as well have subsections on Etsy devoted to them at this point is not something worth celebrating. That is only the case because female political figures are either decried or held up as pixieish Pixar heroines. They don't live in the popular imagination as lawmakers with questionable votes and skeletons in their closet. Instead they remain flawless faves, especially online, where Kamala Harris has followers called the K-Hive, who take after the Beyhive in their fierce defense of their queen. This approach contributes to an inability on the part of anyone, even progressives, even progressive women, to analyze these women for who they really are, a process rendered especially tricky because sexist (and racist, in the case of Harris and AOC) critiques of all the above women continue to be a very real issue. But idolization isn't the counterstrike. Decrying real critiques as sexism doesn't serve anybody.

Nevertheless, the continual outcry that it's sexist or shallow to pay attention to what female politicians wear persists. As with the #AskHerMore movement, which encouraged red-carpet reporters to steer clear of "What are you wearing?"-type questions, any discussion of style becomes anathema, A *Forbes* article bemoaned the "presidential fashion police." Prior to the 2020 election, the *New York Times* published a defense of its political fashion coverage explaining "Why We Cover What Politicians Wear" using the same exhausted tone you'd use to explain TikTok to your grandpa.

On the bright side, the idea of a female politician is becoming more normal and is well on its way to being unremarkable. When women are no longer the exception in these roles, it will hopefully open us up to take a clear-eyed look at their views. The "blue wave" of Democratic victories in 2018 introduced more female congresswomen, like AOC and Ilhan Omar, who have made casual dress more acceptable. When Cori Bush was elected to Congress in 2020, she shared her plans to thrift-shop for work attire with her Twitter followers, writing: "The reality of being a regular person going to Congress is that it's really expensive to get the business clothes I need for the Hill." As these new entrants into government have helped demystify the political process for their constituents, they have helped make Beltway style more egalitarian and at least seemed to remove the artifice from it.

Political fashion has also become more practical: As AOC's worn-out shoes prove, the job requires a lot of time on your feet. Comfort has become more of a priority. It's why Kamala Harris might as well have a Converse contract at this point. Some of this shattering of political dress codes is thanks to Wendy Davis, who conducted a thirteen-hour filibuster on the floor of the Texas State Senate while wearing a pair of bright-pink sneakers in 2013. While high heels were the norm, Davis's sneakers were far more appropriate for this political marathon, a quest to block a bill that imposed stringent abortion restrictions in the state. Naturally, they were celebrated in the press to the point of possibly overshadowing the substance of the debate.

The problem is less, at this point, that fashion is obscuring substance and more that it's intentionally edging it out. At a time when politics has all the subtlety of professional wrestling, complete with dramatic tearing up of papers and other moments that seem made for reaction GIFs, over-the-top fashion statements are becoming par for the course. And style takes on a particularly outsized significance when it is the only way to communicate. At the last few State of the Union addresses, clothes became a kind of silent rebuttal. In 2018, a group of Democratic congresswomen wore all black to show solidarity with the Time's Up movement. In 2019, they wore white in tribute to the suffragettes' signature color and as a symbolic move meant to show resistance to Trump's agenda. The choice presented the women in the group cannily, as a mass bloc whose similarities supposedly outweighed their differences. It also called back to legions of female politicians who'd chosen the color for important moments, including Shirley Chisholm, the first Black woman in Congress, on her first day of work and the day she announced her presidential run; Geraldine Ferraro, when she accepted the first-ever vice presidential nomination to go to a woman; and Clinton at many times during her career, including Trump's inauguration.

When *The Guardian* examined which topics garnered the most blocked comments, fashion was at the top of the list, ranking above even the category of "world news." And this is coming from a left-leaning paper. Controversial fashion statements by female politicians certainly aren't limited to our shores. While there have been some who tried to wholly reject it, like Israeli prime minister Golda Meir, who called fashion "an imposition, a rein on freedom," the majority used it to their advantage. Margaret Thatcher, the UK's first female prime minister, softened her conservative suits with pussybow blouses, handbags, and pearls that belied her austerity-obsessed "Iron Lady" reputation. Indian prime minister Indira Gandhi chose to wear khadi, an Indian-made fabric that had been promoted by Mahatma Gandhi as a way for Indians to gain economic independence from Great Britain. More recently, some figures on the world stage have realized that what they wear can help boost their country's GDP—a prime example being New Zealand PM Jacinda Ardern, who often wears local designers to promote the country's fashion industry.

International leaders also haven't been immune to critique. When Theresa May took on the office of prime minister of the UK, she was derided as frivolous for wearing leopard-print kitten heels and £1,000 leather pants. (But if she'd opted for, say, Labour leader Jeremy Corbyn's casual-bordering-on-schlubby tracksuits, she would have never heard the end of it.) When May and the first minister of Scotland, Nicola Sturgeon, met to discuss Brexit, both wearing skirt suits and heels, the *Daily Mail* ran the headline: "Never mind Brexit, who won Legs-It!"

Still, the particularly anti-elitist nature of America means that every elected official is supposed to be a man or woman of the people, despite the reality that these Beltway figures mostly don't come from the working classes. Leaders are supposed to dress like their constituents . . . except not really. Blend that with Washington, DC's conservative style tendencies, and you have a tough tightrope to walk. Politicians may be at pains to distance themselves from the elitism of the fashion industry—but neither party's anti-elitism seems to extend to, say, swearing off hosting events with wealthy donors and kowtowing to powerful corporate interests.

The savviest players of this game know that what they wear *will* be dissected and decoded no matter what. So they are harnessing that power instead of shying away from it. If their style choices are going to be talked about, they may as well make them count. Nowhere was this clearer than at the 2018 swearing-in of the new congresspeople, where carefully thought-out style statements celebrating personal identity triumphed. Representative Rashida Tlaib was sworn in wearing a thobe, a traditional Palestinian garment. Representative Deb Haaland, who is Native American, wore a tribal dress and moccasins. Omar successfully challenged the ban on headwear that had existed in Congress for 181 years, becoming the first woman to wear a hijab on the House floor. "No one puts a scarf on my head but me," she tweeted. "It's my choice—one protected by the First Amendment. And this is not the last ban I'm going to work to lift." At that swearing-in ceremony, Ocasio-Cortez wore a white pantsuit, again nodding to suffragists. Her hair and makeup paid tribute to her Latinx heritage and her Bronx upbringing. She tweeted, "Lip+hoops were inspired by Sonia Sotomayor, who was advised to wear neutral-colored nail polish to her confirmation hearings to avoid scrutiny. She kept her red. Next time someone tells Bronx girls to take off their hoops, they can just say they're dressing like a Congresswoman."

Sure, a political consultant might have told AOC to tone it down. But by that point, she had already won.

PART IV

Moon Boots and Jumpsuits

The Future of Fashion

CHAPTER THIRTEEN

Dress for the Job You Want

The Tyranny of the Uniform

Enclothed cognition" is the fashion equivalent of the timeless art of "acting as if." And science has affirmed that it is actually a real phenomenon. Psychologists at Northwestern University asked students to put on white coats that they were told belonged to doctors, and their performance on a task that required sustained attention improved. But the researchers didn't see the same effects when those coats were identified as painters' jackets. That suggests that it's not garments themselves that hold power and authority, but the identities and associations we project onto them. When the students simply *looked* at the supposed doctors' coats, they didn't have the same reaction; the effect only held true when they put them on. It's not quite as simple as "don a uniform and you *become* a doctor, or a soldier, or an inmate," but the uniform is part of the role, and assuming one for, say, your work or school day involves taking on the identity you project during the week.

While a wide swath of professions, from surgeon to crossing guard, require uniforms, they are coded in our society to mean very different things. They signify not just your position and status but your fealty to an employer or an institution of some kind. From jobs to schools to teams to religions, uniforms are used to reinforce loyalty and keep our individuality in check. And while there seems to be an artificial leveling of the playing field of late—influenced by startup culture, where both the CEO and the lowliest programmer might wear the same nondescript hoodie—the distinctions still exist, they've just gotten more subtle.

Institutions reinforce their values through fashion. Controlling what you wear is a proxy for controlling what you do, how you subsume yourself to the organization. The indoctrination begins early, with school uniforms. Politicians have advocated for them as a disciplinary tool in schools, and not just conservatives. In his 1996 State of the Union address, Bill Clinton said mandatory uniforms were worth adopting in public schools "if it means that teenagers will stop killing each other over designer jackets." In another speech later that year, he called them "one step that may help break the cycle of violence, truancy, and disorder by helping young students understand what really counts is what kind of people they are." This anti-fashion sentiment discounts style as a tool for self-expression and suggests that uniforms may help keep students from being "distracted" by the vagaries of fashion. Their more important, though less readily acknowledged, purpose is to keep students where administrators want them—members of a featureless, undifferentiated mass.

In America, we associate uniforms with private and parochial schools, though they are also worn in some public schools. But for many countries, including Japan and Australia, uniforms are mandatory throughout the school system. A school uniform often attempts to mimic adult professional dress (think dress shirts, khakis, jackets, and ties) as a way to indoctrinate students into the garb of the working world. Students often try to put their own spin on school uniforms—rolling up skirts or adding accessories that broadcast their individual tastes—but the uniform still takes away most opportunities for self-expression at a time when kids are craving it most. When you put on a uniform, your loyalty to the school is expressed over and above any outside loyalties. You can get in trouble for uniform "violations," even if they're simply expressions of your life outside of school or your personal beliefs. In the midst of the Vietnam War, students at an Iowa high school were planning to wear black armbands to class to protest the US involvement in the conflict. Before they could even do so, the school administration found out about it and instituted an anti-armband policy. When five of the students were suspended for wearing their armbands to school anyway, in defiance of the hastily instated rule, the state's branch of the ACLU approached their families about suing. Their case, *Tinker v. Des Moines Independent Community School District*, went all the way to the Supreme Court, where the court ruled that the students' First Amendment right to symbolic speech (in the form of the armbands) superseded the school's rules about dress.

The uniform's hold on us can be seen by the fact that past secondary education, uniforms are rarely required in schools, except at some military and religious colleges. For those who attend it, college marks the time when you're told you can begin to "be yourself." That freedom extends to fashion, even if it means wearing pajama pants to all your lectures. A college campus is probably the last stage of life where you can get away with that, though. When you move into the working world, uniforms of one kind or another tend to pop up. There are uniforms that are functional, like mechanics' overalls, and ones that are more about constricting your identity in the workplace, making sure who you are as a person is subsumed to who you are as an employee. I have held low-level service jobs where I wore a name tag affixed to my polo shirt, which means anyone can informally address you. In a uniform, you are both anonymous and easy to spot, the company logo sitting near your heart, denoting you as corporate property. You become a stand-in for whatever organization you represent, and a target for whatever "I was told by AppleCare" lunatic who walks in to project that rage at the larger company's failings onto you. The sword of Damocles dangling over your head at all times is that if these people know your name, they can report you to the manager. In the uniform, we are allowed to be brusquer and function as extensions of our company, but we are also the target of brusqueness and able to be dehumanized by others. In *The Language of Clothes*, Alison Lurie writes that a uniform "acts as a sign that we should not or need not treat someone as a human being, and that they need not and should not treat us as one. It is no accident that people in uniform, rather than speaking to us honestly and straightforwardly, often repeat mechanical lies. 'It was a pleasure having you on board,' they say; 'I cannot give you that information'; or 'The doctor will see you shortly.' "

Work uniforms, just like school uniforms, are about compliance. They are meant to snuff out any semblance of autonomy. A common piece of career advice is to "leave yourself at the door" when you enter the workplace—cover your tattoos, don't talk about religion and politics, keep mum about your personal life. In alienating jobs like these, it's only when you take off your uniform at the end of the day that you feel free to return to your "real" self.

In the corporate world, the default uniform is still, largely, the suit, and its denizens are sometimes colloquially known as "suits."

In *The Man in the Gray Flannel Suit*, later made into a movie starring Gregory Peck, the narrator looks at the men who streamed into the business world after World War II and says, "All I could see was a lot of bright young men in gray flannel suits rushing around New York in a frantic parade to nowhere. They seemed to me to be pursuing neither ideals nor happiness—they were pursuing a routine." The suit became a symbol of postwar conformity. Corporate America is no longer synonymous with a man in gray flannel; it's now home to women and non-suits, but the suit still predominates as the default C-suite mode of dress. Formal business wear has been shown to increase our capacity for abstract thinking. And it's still linked to hypermasculinity: One experiment that asked participants to engage in a mock negotiation found that casually dressed men registered lower testosterone levels during the negotiations than men in suits did. Still, with the casualization of the American workplace and the increased numbers of people working from home, office dress codes have changed somewhat. In *The Atlantic*, Amanda Mull notes that now that millennials have ascended to higher rungs of the workforce, their affinity for casual clothing may be impacting the overall dress codes. Younger people, she observes, have "started to reshape the meaning of 'work clothes' in their image—upending the very idea of a dress code as a single standard to which all should aspire."

In a hierarchical institution like the military, your rank is clear at a glance, denoted by stars, bars, and medals. Distinctions are more subtle in casual work environments. But just as open-plan offices and CEOs who sit at modest desks unprotected by glass walls and gatekeeping secretaries have not necessarily made offices more equal, lower-key fashion doesn't necessarily erase all the subtle differences between employees. The workplace doesn't magically become an even playing field just because everyone is wearing hoodies. As I've mentioned, Mark Zuckerberg may favor T-shirts, but they're expensive Italian ones his rank-and-file employees likely couldn't afford. The outdoorsy-looking power vests favored by Jeff Bezos and Uber CEO Dara Khosrowshahi are, similarly, more luxe than they might initially appear. Mastering the stealth luxury of the Silicon Valley casual look is not as easy as it may seem; if you're trying too obviously to look good, then you can be shamed. Mull cites a Silicon Valley message board where "a man in his late 30s recalled being humiliated by the CEO at his new job for daring to wear a button-down shirt among his cargo-shorts-clad co-workers." The rules about what's "acceptable" to wear to work have not actually become more flexible, it's just that their specifics have changed.

And the startup dress code only goes so far. When the four titans of Big Tech—Zuckerberg, Bezos, Apple's Tim Cook, and Alphabet's Sundar Pichai—testified in front of Congress in 2020 as their industry faced its "Big Tobacco" moment, they didn't opt for Palo Alto casualwear. When it counted, they were in gray and navy suits, indistinguishable from more traditional CEOs and even earlier business titans. "The reference was, if anything, the men in the gray flannel suits of yore," wrote Vanessa Friedman in the *New York Times*. "That they wore such suits at all was a nod to the mores of Washington, because in their natural environment, denizens of the digital world often see the garments as sartorial shackles that reflect old ways of thinking. But these witnesses' outfits, in their straightforward styling, both separated the chief executives from their traditional camouflage, thus making them seem less subversively Other, and conveyed respect for the office before which the men were appearing."

Early in the coronavirus pandemic, the same week that many white-collar offices began transitioning to remote work, *Washington Post* senior critic-at-large Robin Givhan wrote an essay titled,

"Our clothes tell our story. What happens when the narrative is just pajamas and sweats?" As offices and other public spheres—museums, amusement parks, theaters—shut down, Givhan mused about how these shifts might affect not just fashion, but our sense of self. "An essential part of our identity is rooted in how we relate to the people around us, how we situate ourselves within the social hierarchy," she wrote. "We are defined, in part, by our tribe. We dress to tell a story about ourselves and if there is no one there to hear our narrative, we've been put on mute—turned into mere ectoplasm in pajamas." While some might be celebrating the casting off of binding office clothes and uniforms, others were mourning the loss of who they were in that attire. Givhan has a more positive take on uniforms than what I've advanced here, one that is more community-based. A work costume "identifies one's place in the social order," she writes, "announcing you are participating in the ebb and flow of a community. Most work clothes do not underscore individuality. To the contrary, [they] remind us we are part of something. That uniform, that badge dangling from a lanyard, that congressional pin: They are all reminders of connectivity."

Still, the power of enclothed cognition applies even to the laxest environments. Even freelancers who can work in leggings and pajamas often endorse putting on "real clothes" for the workday as a way to vault themselves into work mode. Another frequent piece of advice is to "dress for success" or "dress for the job you want." By emulating your boss or betters, the idea is that you'll become them through a form of fashion osmosis. But in fact, some of the most successful people in a lot of workplaces tend to be either slobs or people who refuse to abide by whatever vague dress code the office has as a sign of counterintuitive power. (In my experience, they're mostly, though not all, men.) Again, there is research to back up this anecdotal finding. A Harvard Business School study in the *Journal of Consumer Research* found that the "red sneakers effect"—

named for the fact that one of its authors wore a pair of red Converse to teach a class at Harvard Business School—is indeed very real. In certain cases, fashion nonconformity can work in one's favor, giving an impression of prestige. For example, their research found, walking into a luxury store wearing gym clothes can, surprisingly, make you seem more powerful because you presumably don't care about impressing anyone there. "While unintentional violations of normative codes and etiquette can indeed result in negative inferences and attributions," the study's authors found, "when the deviant behavior appears to be deliberate, it can lead to higher rather than lower status and competence inferences." By showing that you're not ignorant of the rules, you just don't care about following them, you counterintuitively command respect. That's the move Zuckerberg pulled when he showed up to meet with venture capitalists in pajamas or to his company's IPO kickoff in a hoodie—a gesture that says, "I don't even care about this meeting." That might have shocked traditional Wall Streeters, but in Silicon Valley, it made him a hotter commodity, emphasizing his relative youth and the college-dorm founding mythos of Facebook. (For Zuckerberg, the red sneakers are Adidas shower slides, the ultimate dorm-core look.) Of course, while the study didn't control for factors like race and gender, my own experience and that of friends in this field suggests that it probably helps to be white, male, and/or wealthy if you want to attempt this feat. In order to selectively reject some signs of status, you need to have stores of it in other ways.

As I've touched on previously, the standards for women's work attire are invariably more stringent than they are for men. For female-dominated industries, in particular, this can be challenging—just look at the imbroglio around various airlines' uniforms, which were making their workforce, including the majority-female flight attendants, ill to the point that some had to carry EpiPens. More than five thousand American Airlines employees complained that their allegedly "toxic" uniforms were causing them to suffer from severe headaches, rashes, and breathing problems, but the uniforms were only recalled after two employees filed a federal lawsuit against the manufacturer. Delta and Alaska Airlines have faced similar situations with their uniforms. The idea of loyalty, as expressed in the uniform, trumped even the employees' health and safety in this case. And one wonders if, had this happened to a largely male group like pilots, the companies would have taken their complaints more seriously. As Heather Poole, one of the flight attendant plaintiffs in the American Airlines case, put it, "We're still a majority of females in this job. And so it's basically shut up or quit. When you have a pretty job, that's the kind of attitude. You don't have a right to complain. You should smile and be thankful."

All too often, women, especially in these "pretty" jobs, have to put up with more revealing or uncomfortable clothing as a condition of their employment, whether they are flight attendants or cocktail waitresses. Female flight attendants have often been required to wear high heels and makeup, and in the old days some airlines fired them once they reached the venerable age of thirty-two. Some were forbidden from getting married or pregnant, because it clashed with the fun-loving "cocktail hostess in the sky" image. Like airborne *Playboy* bunnies, they sometimes had to wear miniskirts or hot pants; in the '60s, Braniff Airways famously collaborated with Emilio Pucci on uniforms that were designed to be removed in a mid-flight "air strip," revealing a more skin-baring look. Attendants were inspected to make sure they'd shaved their legs and were subjected to weigh-ins and girdle checks. They could be fired for exceeding the airline's weight limit by even a few pounds. And even for those who don't wear uniforms to work, there are still restrictions around dressing and appearing workplace-appropriate that are often harsher for women and require them to spend more money (on makeup, hair products, and a regularly up-dated wardrobe that reflects the latest trends while hewing to the ever-shifting bounds of "good taste").

Certain specialized professions still have their own, highly regulated, visual hierarchy. In the military, uniforms carefully delineate one's rank and indoctrinate soldiers into groupthink—it's not a far leap from shining your shoes because an officer orders you to and going along with combat orders you don't agree with. Some religious leaders, like rabbis in Reform and Conservative Judaism or Protestant ministers, are able to wear street clothes most of the time, reflecting the fact that their roles are more in and of the world, while other adherents don religious clothing all the time. Another highly hierarchical profession is medicine, where the highest-ranking members wear white coats whose re-semblance to lab coats suggests both an alliance with science and a reassuring purity. Nurses are usually attired more casually, in scrubs, sometimes with cute designs that make their wearers far less intimidating and thus more approachable than clipboard-wielding doctors. Doctors' white coats suggest a kind of separa-tion from the actual nitty-gritty of medicine—they are not meant to get bodily fluids on them, unlike surgeons' and nurses' scrubs. They're instead about inducing trust and conferring legitimacy. If someone came up to you in a doctor's office wearing street clothes, brandishing a needle, you'd be scared: The uniform lets you know that this person is implicitly to be trusted.

As for patients, they are squarely at the bottom of the power structure. A standard doctor's visit or operation requires a drafty paper gown that depersonalizes the wearer and renders him or her childlike and helpless. For longer-term patients, a hospital gown exacerbates powerlessness when illness is already destabilizing and disempowering enough. Transitioning out of the "patient" uniform can speed the healing process, in some cases. In a sociological study of nurses in a hospital's rehabilitation unit, Michael G. Pratt and Anat Rafaeli found that the clothes the patients wore marked an important transition for them. "We believe that patients who wear pajamas will think of themselves as 'sick,' " they wrote, "and by wearing street clothes, patients think of themselves as moving out of the 'sick' role and into rehabilitation."

Another bastion of indoctrination through fashion is law enforcement, whose uniform has been quantitatively seen to coerce people. In a 1974 study, an experimenter commanded people on the street to do various tasks, such as picking something up from the ground. Unsurprisingly, that person was much more successful when dressed as a cop than as a milkman, or when wearing street clothes. (Impersonating a police officer is considered a federal crime—the powers that be deem disrupting these visual categories literally dangerous to society.) But police uniforms don't just change our perception of law enforcement: They change the way actual cops' brains work, at least according to a 2017 study at McMaster University. Using a similar method as the Northwestern lab coat study, the researchers found that students who simply put on police uniforms altered their thinking and were more suspicious of people wearing, say, hoodies. They concluded that "not only is police culture symbolized in the uniforms worn by officers, the uniform, by virtue of its (paramilitary) style, also influences police culture."

That effect has likely intensified: American police uniforms have become more paramilitary as the police have become more militarized, complete with equipment like body armor, SWAT gear, and tanks. This process began in the '90s as a way to unload unused military equipment and was expanded after 9/11. The transformation of the police into an unofficial wing of the military is a sign of how police forces have become less of a guarantee of public safety (if they ever were that) and more of an oppositional force acting on society. The myth of the "friendly" neighborhood officer has been subsumed in the idea of the military superman. Depending on your view of the police, that might make you feel safer or less safe. A decade after the original enclothed cognition experiment where the subjects wore white coats, one of those researchers, Columbia professor Adam Galinsky, published a story in *Fast Company* examining what he called "enclothed blue aggression." Current-day police now looked "more suited to take on a hostile nation's insurgents than protestors on US soil," he wrote. Writing in *The New Yorker*, Maria Konnikova found that more than 80 percent of this riot gear was not used in response to anything but was merely "proactive." In 2015, in the wake of the Ferguson protests against police violence, President Obama enacted stricter rules about police departments' use of military gear, hoping to decrease tensions between police and the communities they serve. President Trump revived the program in 2017, though lawmakers have tried to push back on it since then, particularly after the murder of George Floyd inflamed nationwide protests and resulted in countless instances of police attacking protesters. The use of these items "may harm relations between police forces and citizens not only because they signal violence but because they may, in some sense, cause more violence," Konnikova writes. "The same cues that signal 'army' and 'conflict' to civilians may affect police officers themselves . . . when donning SWAT gear to respond to a riot, they no longer feel like local law enforcement anymore but like part of a broader military machine." Wearing a face covering may further embolden officers to engage in warlike maneuvers like tear-gassing protesters or firing rubber bullets at them.

In court, another precinct of extreme order, as I examined in chapter 9, the way a plaintiff or defendant dresses can shape our view of their reliability. It's the reason defense attorneys often push for their clients to be allowed to wear street clothes—juries often assume someone in a prison uniform is automatically guilty. But the rest of the courtroom, too, is intensely structured via fashion. Lawyers wear sharp suits, court officers don uniforms that resemble police attire, and judges cover themselves in identical black robes. "I am fond of the symbolism of this tradition," Justice Sandra Day O'Connor once wrote of judges' robes, because "it shows that all of us judges are engaged in upholding the Constitution and the rule of law. We have a common responsibility."

Of course, there is a final group in this law-and-order category that is relegated to uniforms, but in this case, it happens without their consent. When incarcerated people are processed through the system, they are assigned a number and a uniform and separated from their possessions and street clothes. They are now completely subjugated to the institution. Part of their punishment is being denied the comforts of normal life—thus the hard beds and no-frills cells. The standard-issue uniforms are similarly meant to be punitive, but they also stamp out individuality, reducing convicts to one indistinguishable mass. Uniforms are just one of many ways the state acts on the bodies of incarcerated people, and they are in evidence whenever a government has imprisoned people. For example, drone footage has shown Uighur Muslim prisoners in China wearing identical blue uniforms and shaved heads.

And just like lab coats or police uniforms, prison uniforms are subject to enclothed cognition. They, too, can markedly change the way we behave. The Stanford prison experiment, conducted in 1971 by Stanford professor Philip Zimbardo, randomly classed students as jailers or imprisoned people based on the flip of a coin.

The latter were "arrested" at their homes, strip-searched and de-loused, and given numbered uniforms (they were actually dresses, chosen as a way to emasculate the all-male group, Zimbardo later told *The New Yorker*'s Konnikova). The guards were given khaki uniforms. Immediately, both factions began playing their roles to the hilt, with the guards abusing the imprisoned people, who wholly submitted to the treatment. The experiment got so out of control that while it was supposed to run for two weeks, it had to be shut down within six days. While the study has since been re-examined and found to be flawed, it does seem to establish that uniforms play a strong role in shaping our behavior.

Prison uniforms were brought into general use in the late 1700s, just as prison surveillance was becoming more sophisti-cated. In an article for the fashion journal *Vestoj*, Anja Aronowsky Cronberg notes that they were introduced around the same time that the philosopher and social reformer Jeremy Bentham cre-ated his Panopticon, which allowed prisoners to be watched con-tinuously from all angles. While inmates once wore striped suits whose pattern mimicked the iron bars of a cell, the style has been largely discontinued. Loose jumpsuits, sometimes in a bright shade of orange that makes the prisoners stand out in the "straight world" and would make escaping incognito a challenge, are now more common.

The clothes worn by the imprisoned are not a far cry from the attire required by communes and utopian communities, which of-ten exert some kind of fashion domination over their members, too. In the mid-eighteenth-century Oneida Community, which emphasized "free love" in the interest of breeding a supposed supe-rior race, women wore simple bloomer-like costumes and bobbed their hair. The Shakers, an offshoot of the Quakers founded in the eighteenth century, wore subdued, practical clothes, reserving ri-otous patterns for the insides of their garments. Like the furniture they became known for making, it was free of embellishment. For the group, this lack of ornamentation was meant to quash internal conflict. An 1866 Ministry circular decreed that "uniformity in style, or pattern in dress, between members, contributes to peace and union in spirit, in as much as the ends of justice are answered, and righteousness and justice are necessary companions." Given that celibacy was one of the Shakers' tenets, they also wore clothing that deemphasized their bodies. For women, that meant square bodices that hid the natural waist, neckerchiefs or capelets (called "berthas") that obscured the wearers' breasts, and caps and bonnets to cover up their hair. Members of the Transcendentalist commune Fruitlands, cofounded by Louisa May Alcott's father Bronson, wore uniforms of linen and simple canvas shoes; they were banned from wearing cotton because it was produced by slave labor, and from wearing wool or any other animal products, as all the residents were vegan. These groups often followed "mortification mechanisms" like mutual criticism and expelling deviants, and uniform clothing helped establish this in-group versus out-group dynamic. The sociologist Rosabeth Moss Kanter's research found that in the nineteenth century, 89 percent of successful communities of this nature required a uniform, while only 30 percent of unsuccessful ones did, suggesting that homogeneous clothing helped cement their values.

With the upheaval of the '60s came a revival of these types of communities, many of which came with their own accompanying fashion doctrines. At Twin Oaks in Virginia, members jointly owned a wardrobe that was known as "community clothes." Converts to the Source Family, a mystical group founded in the '60s by an eccentric health-restaurant owner who called himself Father Yod, were given new first names and all took on the surname Aquarian. They, too, wore communal clothing.

The emphasis on sameness only intensifies when it comes to

cults. Followers of Synanon, the Santa Monica drug rehabilitation program that became a utopian community in the '60s before devolving into a violent cult, shaved their heads and adopted a coed uniform of denim overalls, meant, according to Kanter, "to express their common interest in work." As documented in *Wild Wild Country*, members of the Rajneeshpuram wore monochrome outfits to display their loyalty to their leader, Bhagwan Shree Rajneesh. Many of the members were yuppies who had renounced a beige, consumerist existence; when they arrived at the commune, they left not just their names but their street clothes behind and began dressing in shades of red, orange, and purple, the colors of sunrise, "which was supposed to reflect a new start, a new day," filmmaker Maclain Way told the *Wall Street Journal*. The warm tones certainly made them stand out in their home of rural Oregon, full of farmers in denim overalls. The group even had an in-house store where new acolytes could buy clothing in the correct hues, including orange jeans that were the result of an exclusive deal with Levi's. The members of the Heaven's Gate cult all ate the same food, sported shaved heads, and wore unisex uniforms of black and gray. They also famously wore box-fresh Nike sneakers and identical outfits for their mass suicide, which they believed was a passage into another world.

In some cases, cults have gone to extreme lengths to show fealty to their leaders. Female members of the NXIVM cult were branded with cult leader Keith Raniere's initials, denoting them as his property. And the Japanese doomsday cult Aum Shinrikyo (Supreme Truth), which carried out the 1995 sarin-gas attack on the Tokyo subways, wears white robes and has marched with masks of their leader Shoko Asahara's face over their own faces, signifying total submission to his views.

But despite the emphasis on sameness, there is always a

pecking order, even among supposedly egalitarian groups. In the NXIVM cult, for example, members wore scarf-like sashes whose colors corresponded to their status in the group and followed what was called "the stripe path" to collect stripes on their sashes and graduate to a new level. Members of Scientology's elite Sea Org wear naval-style uniforms whose decorations correspond to their status.

Oddly, the fashions of groups like Rajneeshpuram and the Fundamentalist Latter-Day Saints, who wore retrograde costumes of high-necked dresses and French braids, came to exert an influence over their polar opposite: coastal-elite hipsters. Monochrome outfits in warm tones could be seen on the runway after *Wild Wild Country* aired on Netflix, while FLDS's influence was evident in the ruffled, high-necked Urban Prairie Girl style (as coined by Chloe Malle in the *New York Times*) that emerged among brands like Batsheva and Dôen. Perhaps, in pampered lives where there were no new frontiers left to chart, the staunch fashions of the pioneers looked fresh again. Or maybe the idea of belonging, even to something suffocating, felt enticing—why else do people stand in blockbusting lines at Supreme?

There has been a recent trend, especially when it comes to personal essays about style, of restricting oneself to a personal "uniform" or "capsule wardrobe" as a way to exert order amid a lack of structure. Almost inevitably, the experiment is found to be freeing. While artists and other office-independent types have long had their own working uniforms—Picasso's striped shirts or Sontag's dark turtlenecks—the renewed emphasis on uniform dressing in an era when you can mostly wear anything may be a response to the chaos and entropy of the modern gig economy, a yearning for enforced simplicity. Even when at leisure, we slip into designated uniforms. Whether it's a sports team, a sorority, or a boutique fitness class, it has become trendy to signal your involvement in a group even when you're not actively participating in it. It's why sports fans show up to the stadium (and often elsewhere) in their jerseys and caps, emulating their favorite players. Or why proponents of Greek life cling to their fraternity and sorority gear long after graduation. Music merch, which has become more explicitly fashion-oriented in recent years, is worn to advertise your taste and membership in a fan group. Myriad boutique gyms and exercise classes now offer merch, too, so you can proclaim your loyalty to Barry's Bootcamp or SoulCycle at the grocery store.

As uniforms have come to swallow up our off time, our work clothes have gotten less regimented. But that doesn't mean that work is more relaxed—if anything, it's the opposite. The difference between a job and a cult might seem to be an extreme one, but careers now demand so much more of our loyalty—working late hours, responding to emails 24–7, eating all our meals at the job (as in startup culture). Work was once something that you left at work. Don Draper's real-life counterparts had to wear suits, but they could take a three-martini lunch and leave at 5:00 p.m. to catch the train home to the suburbs. Most "cool" jobs no longer require you to wear a tie, but they exert a choke hold just the same. Now, that division of one's life into "me time" and "the job" is something apps like Slack have made impossible. For all the recent emphasis on work-life balance, this is mostly beyond an individual's control, whether they're a minimum-wage worker who is at the mercy of shift-scheduling software or a white-collar type who's expected to respond to every "urgent" message no matter when it clatters into their inbox. And the overarching philosophy, especially when it comes to the latter, is perhaps more damaging: It comes all while insisting on our common values and the pernicious idea that "we're all a family." You're expected to have a single-minded devotion to your profession, a "passion" for what you do, and to be in agreement with your company mantras. Corporations' external control over their employees' fashion may be a thing of the past, but that has been replaced by control over every other aspect of one's working life. Once, you could shrug off your suit or uniform at the end of the day. Now, there's no such thing as clocking out.

CHAPTER FOURTEEN

Basic Instinct

Why We're All Starting to Dress the Same

I SAT DOWN TO watch *Blade Runner* for the first time in November 2019. The movie was one of those perennial fashion reference points that I had, embarrassingly, never actually gotten around to watching. The synchronicity of the title card stating the month and year I was currently living through felt surreal. The movie had correctly predicted a few things: a climate change–choked planet lashed with Biblical rain; reliance on voice recognition technology; street food as haute cuisine. But that was mostly it. To watch any futuristic narrative in the time it was originally set in is to marvel at the ways the seams between the imagined present and the real one show.

Some of the same ambivalent pleasures can be found in examining what we used to think the future of fashion would look like. People have always dreamed about futuristic designs; an 1893 article called *The Future Dictates of Fashion* predicted the styles of the upcoming century, imagining voluminous breeches and donut-shaped hats becoming all the rage in 1965. But the idea reached its optimistic peak in the actual 1960s, specifically in France, where three designers—André Courrèges, Pierre Cardin, and Paco Rabanne—became known for a Space Age aesthetic that would end up being highly influential. Their bold geometric shapes and high-tech materials shook up a moribund fashion landscape. In 1965, Courrèges showcased his latest designs in a gallery, with the models standing in for works of art, surrounded by whirling mobiles and kinetic sculptures. His compatriots Cardin and Rabanne were the Buzz Aldrin and Michael Collins to his Neil Armstrong, planting their flag into the outer-space unknown and presenting their gleaming vision of the future. In some cases, it literally gleamed: They favored futuristic materials like vinyl, lenticular plastic, and Lurex. Cardin even created his own fabric, Cardine. Synthetics are now looked down upon for being far from eco-friendly, but at the time they represented the cutting edge.

The '60s imagination of the future turned out to be as illusory as any other futuristic aesthetic, and if anything, the modernist design of that time has become a hallmark of the Establishment. Movie stars snap up Case Study houses in Los Angeles; midcentury modern furniture is priced like rubies; and the fashions of the era are now collectors' items living out their days in climate-controlled storage units. Think of the modernist houses in *Parasite* or *Ex Machina*, whose polished veneers presage doom.

As for the era's predictions about the future of fashion, the reality of what most of us wear is a lot more prosaic and casual—Uniqlo instead of unitards. The Tomorrowland fantasy of the Space Age designers and their descendants is fun to look at but ultimately just that—a fantasy. If Courrèges and his cohort could teleport from the '60s and see what we wear today, they'd probably be sorely disappointed. Today, fashion is, largely, moving toward sameness and away from singularity. The predictions about intergalactic It girls in go-go boots have not come to pass. The ones about people wearing identical jumpsuits turned out to be more on the nose. You can go to any major city and will see regional differences in style—New Yorkers wear more black, Los Angeles is casual, Paris traditional— but increasingly, thanks to globalization and the internet, a uniform has sprung up. The future, as it turns out, is not plastics. It's athleisure, simple separates in neutral colors, all-occasion sneakers. We may not be *Blade Runner*–style cyborgs, but our clothes have taken on clone-like qualities, merging into one mass.

Nowhere was the geographic convergence of style into a single, indistinguishable horde more evident than with the advent of normcore. In a 2014 *New York* magazine story titled "Normcore: Fashion for Those Who Realize They're One in 7 Billion," Fiona Duncan identified a growing trend: Her cool, individualistic young New York peers were dressing like dads, or tourists, or dads who were also tourists. "Clad in stonewash jeans, fleece, and comfortable sneakers, both types looked like they might've just stepped off an R train after shopping in Times Square," she wrote. "When I texted my friend Brad (an artist whose summer uniform consisted of Adidas barefoot trainers, mesh shorts and plain cotton tees) for his take on the latest urban camouflage, I got an immediate reply: 'lol normcore.' " The unfamiliar term came from the trend-forecasting group K-Hole, though its contemporary use is a bit controversial. As K-Hole later clarified, the "normcore" identified in the article aligned more with another K-Hole-coined term, "acting basic." "Normcore" was more of a behavioral trend, while "acting basic" was more of a fashion trend. However, since "normcore" came to stand in for the latter, I'm using that word here in the sense in which it's come to be colloquially used.

In her story, Duncan defined the term as "embracing sameness deliberately as a new way of being cool, rather than striving for 'difference' or 'authenticity.' " It found its source material in what she called "ardently ordinary clothes. Mall clothes. Blank clothes. The kind of dad-brand non-style you might have once associated with Jerry Seinfeld, but transposed on a Cooper Union student with William Gibson glasses." Normcore enthusiasts favored the kind of anonymous garments you might find in packs of three at Kmart: stonewashed denim, dad caps, unbranded sneakers, fanny packs, and windbreakers. Defiantly uncool, the movement drew from style icons like '90s-era Seinfeld and Steve Jobs or present-day Larry David.

It's no accident that normcore flowered as street style, personal style blogs, and Instagram were becoming less about individual self-expression and more about creating opportunities for corporate sponsorship. Every major magazine and website featured street style, and the medium quickly minted its own celebrities. Style bloggers were getting clothing deals; Instagrammers were getting #sponsored. The imperative to carve out your own totally individualistic personal style suddenly felt like a psyop on the part of Big Fashion. The only possible reaction was to dress as generically as possible. Normcore annihilated the idea of personal style and its emphasis on individuality. A kind of radical purism affected this worldview: These generic garments are the only ones untouched by the hands of capital-F fashion, and thus okay to wear. Duncan quoted Jeremy Lewis, the founder/editor of the influential zine *Garmento*, who called normcore "one facet of a growing anti-fashion sentiment." He was given to wearing khakis, fleece, and New Balances. Once, this might have felt like a way of blending in, but "Lewis says his 'look of nothing' is about absolving oneself from fashion, 'lest it mark you as a mindless sheep.' " K-Hole's Emily Segal clarified that the trend wasn't "about being simple or forfeiting individuality to become a bland, uniform mass," but rather "welcoming the possibility of being recognizable, of looking like other people . . . seeing that as an opportunity for connection, instead of as evidence that your identity has dissolved."

Duncan notes that the look had some references to the '90s, when many of its practitioners were growing up. "The aesthetic return to styles they would've worn as kids reads like a reset button—going back to a time before adolescence, before we learned to differentiate identity through dress," she writes. "The Internet and globalization have challenged the myth of individuality (we are all one in 7 billion), while making connecting with others easier than ever. Normcore is a blank slate and open mind—it's a look designed to play well with others." She cites the photographer Corinne Day's images of Kate Moss wearing Birkenstocks in 1990 and the art collective Art Club 2000's early-'90s series of photos titled *Commingle*, depicting its members posing in Gap clothing. In one, shot in arguably the world's most normcore place, Times Square, they wear identical shredded denim ensembles, bandannas, and sunglasses; in another, they lounge in a furniture store in matching madras shirts and khakis. Art Club 2000 member Patterson Beckwith told the Smithsonian's *Threaded* blog that the series was a comment on the increasingly corporate landscape of cities, which had gone from Jane Jacobs–approved clusters of independent businesses to an uninterrupted chain of, well, chains. "The early '90s were a time in New York City when we were first starting to see Starbucks on every corner," he explained. "The Gap had recently opened on the corner of Haight and Ashbury in San Francisco and on St. Marks Place and Second Avenue near Cooper Union. They'd just opened twenty locations in Manhattan and there were loads of ads in bus shelters—it was kind of in your face and we were responding to that." The group members later told *Artforum*, "There's a big difference between 1993 and now. New York, certainly downtown, has been swabbed in vanilla. And khaki. And it sucks."

Despite the fact that it sold proto-normcore, basic clothing,

Gap's ad campaigns emphasized individuality. Once a counter-cultural San Francisco shop, founded in 1969, its name came from the generation gap between hippies and their staid elders. Soon, it evolved into a purveyor of simple, conservative clothing whose selling point was the people who wore it. In the '80s, at the height of yuppiedom, Gap introduced its Individuals of Style campaign, which included Joan Didion, Spike Lee, and the gallerist Leo Castelli as models. In the early '90s, its Who Wore Khakis campaign used archival photos of iconic people, including countercultural figures like Miles Davis and Jack Kerouac, wearing the bland style. (Gap attempted to reclaim this turf with a "dress normal" campaign in 2014, after the initial normcore story was published in *New York* magazine.) When I look at the Art Club 2000 photos, the uniformity of the group's fashion makes me focus on the differences between its members. Similarly, the highly stylized, somewhere-north-of-middlebrow Gap ad portraits shot in black-and-white by big-name photographers force us to fixate on the individual characteristics of the person pictured. The clothing is an afterthought, a blank slate that sets off a personality.

From beatnik offshoots to the Pepsi Generation to millennial-focused startups, so much of advertising has consisted of generational identification and, sometimes, pitting one generation against another. Art Club 2000 positioned itself as anti-categorizable. Normcore, when it came along, was less stridently against commerce. It was more about surrendering to the corporate, Gap-on-every-corner reality and letting yourself fall, heedlessly, into the Gap. The revelation that you're one in 7 billion can induce, depending on the context, alienation or pleasure. As Duncan writes, "Normcore isn't about rebelling against or giving into the status quo; it's about letting go of the need to look distinctive, to make time for something new." One person photographed for the story's accompanying portfolio said, "Everyone's so unique that it's not unique anymore.

Especially in New York." Looking boring was now the only way to stand out, so it became celebrated. A tweet from K-Hole proclaimed, "#Normcore finds liberation in being nothing special, and realizes that adaptability leads to belonging." The agency expanded on this further in its report *Youth Mode: A Report on Freedom*: "It used to be possible to be special—to sustain unique differences through time, relative to a certain sense of audience. As long as you were different from the people around you, you were safe. But the Internet and globalization fucked this up for everyone." Generations were now generalized, and "belonging to your generation becomes an inescapable truth—you're a Scorpio whether you believe in astrology or not. At the same time, responsibility for generational behavior is partial at the max. ('It's not you, it's your whole generation.')" There is pleasure in dissolving yourself into a crowd, in outsourcing your personality to astrology (OMG I'm such a Virgo!) or an age group (Only '90s kids will get this!). At the risk of disappointing the snobs, nothing is niche anymore: Now, chances are, someone is listening to the same obscure song on Apple Music as you, and they may well be in Berlin or Mumbai. Normcore rejects the marketing philosophy of "you are what you consume," opting out of the prevailing idea that what you wear or buy necessarily says anything about you.

If Think Different was once the slogan for one of the largest corporations in the world, how can difference really be subversive? According to K-Hole, striving for difference was now our default mode of being, and had become something to rebel against. Instead of smoking under the bleachers at the pep rally, decrying its cheesiness, the Normcore-ites are in the stands cheering along with the crowd. "Once upon a time, people were born into communities and had to find their individuality. Today people are born individuals and have to find their communities," K-Hole's report continues. "In Normcore, one does not pretend to be above the indignity of belonging." The way the internet has splintered our worldview makes people long to be in the middle of a mass event. You can feel that kind of glee as people live-tweet the Oscars or the Super Bowl halftime show, some of the few remnants of monoculture still available to us. Middlebrow culture was once something to escape from—a few network channels, movies, and magazines dominating the landscape—and now it's an escape *from* the world of ten thousand channels (or, increasingly, streaming services) and nothing to watch. Nicheness and specialization have become a tyranny of their own, and wanting to stand out feels like a boring default option. Sometimes it's just easier to turn on the TV and zone out.

Of course, nothing gold (or greige, in this case) can stay. Like any other trend that reaches its saturation point, normcore eventually became ubiquitous. You couldn't walk through Bushwick or Echo Park without hitting a dad cap or a socks-and-sandals combo, to the point where a browser extension promised to remove all mentions of "normcore" from your feed. Still, normcore persists, just as a feature rather than a bug in the fashion landscape. The normcore influence can be seen today among a slew of labels, notably post-Soviet designers like Demna Gvasalia and Gosha Rubchinskiy. Though he has rejected the normcore label in interviews, Gvasalia has become known for using real people on runways and for reinterpreting normcore brands like Hanes and Champion. He has attributed his aesthetic to the "delayed cultural formation" of his upbringing—fashion and capitalism were unknowns to him until the Soviet Union collapsed in 1991. For Rubchinskiy, globalization also played a part. Discussing a uniform-inspired collection, he told NowFashion, "Kids [today] can see what's going on around the world through the Internet, through Instagram, through all this new technology, and that's why it's easier to stay in the same mood all around the world, in this kind of uniform."

In 2017, Gvasalia held a show for his label Vetements that was organized around archetypes. Models were dressed as, say, a bouncer in a slick leather jacket, a chic Parisian woman in tweeds and pearls, or a dowdy office worker. Rather than present some underground vision meant to overthrow the norm, Gvasalia did something that felt more subversive—he dug into the idea of what "normal" really means. The designer told *Vestoj*:

> A lot of people, or rather a lot of fashion people I talked to afterwards, thought it was too simple. Not *fashion* enough. And that's even though the collection included forty-five different design concepts, like a wedding dress as a jogging suit. In most collections you have one concept—like, this season the concept is "Greece" and the whole collection is about Grecian goddesses. I had forty-five, and still fashionistas found it simple. They found it simple because my trench coats were beige, or because a model in jeans and a shirt reminded them of a neighbour. To me, that was the whole purpose of the show.

Eckhaus Latta designers Mike Eckhaus and Zoe Latta also play with the aesthetic of normalcy, elevating "ordinary" clothes like turtlenecks and acid-wash jeans on their runway. Even Kanye West's Yeezy line presents its own future-minimalist vision of normalcy: clothing the world in matching, neutral-colored, vaguely dystopian uniforms. And Gen Z–beloved resale apps like Depop allow teens and twentysomethings to trade normcore-gone-cool looks among one another, recontextualizing items that might have once read as lame or out of date. These pieces, dredged up from the detritus of long-past trends, also seem like a response to an epoch of climate catastrophe and social apocalypse, when no new things are created and we're left clinging to the vaguely nostalgic flotsam and jetsam of prior eras like a life raft.

Normalcy, once a grim fate to be avoided at all costs, has become an unexpected luxury. Zoomers have flocked to shows like *The Office* and *Friends* because the small foothold they promise—a steady office job, even if it's at a foundering paper company; a circle of friends that has infinite time to linger over coffee-shop couch hangs—genuinely feels like a luxury good in a world where that's slipping away. The '90s dominates so much of normcore fashion not just because it was a pre-internet time, but because it marked the last era when the structure of American society still felt sturdier than a three-legged coffee table, and being, or remaining, middle-class seemed like an achievable aspiration.

Normcore was positioned as both anti-fashion and anti-cool. Still, the style required you to be in on the joke. The movement was supposedly inclusive, but a suburban dad couldn't have dressed normcore and been celebrated. (Or at least, celebrated unironically.) Truly normie style found its apotheosis in the "basic bitch." In the same year that Duncan published her normcore story in *New York*, Noreen Malone delineated the difference between hipster normcore and lame basicness in the same publication. "We have arrived at an odd cultural and lexicographical moment," she wrote. "To dress 'normal' is the height of chic, yet to call someone 'basic' is the chicest put-down, one that shows no signs of disappearing." The term originated in the hip-hop world, aimed at women who lacked authenticity and defined themselves by their proximity to luxury brands. (Specifically women. Men can be bros or himbos, but they're rarely described as basic.) The Game's song "Basic Bitch" gives a working definition: "She gotta fake Louie, fake Loubies, fake booty, so she a Basic Bitch." Kreayshawn, whose hit "Gucci Gucci" took aim at label-loving basic bitches, told *The Fader*,

"She likes those normal brands and wears them all the time because that's some basic shit." The YouTuber Lohanthony, who made a viral video decrying basic bitches, defined the term in *Paper* as "someone who does what everyone else is doing and isn't their own person at all." In The Cut, Maggie Lange flagged a key basic bitch attribute: openly enjoying feminized, mass-pop products, like *Sex and the City*, Taylor Swift, pumpkin spice lattes, and prepackaged Skinnygirl margaritas. Liking the mass-market items you're *supposed* to like was uncool for women, even though liking a laundry list of their male equivalents (off the top of my head: *Entourage*, Drake, whatever caffeinated nightmare Ben Affleck is ordering at Dunkin' Donuts, and Coors Light) would not be tarred with the "basic" brush.

Accusations of basicness always highlight the anxiety of the person calling out the basic bitch, whose insecurities take shape in these attacks, while the basic bitch herself remains serene. So why was being normcore cool and lauded by the same quarters that scorned the basic bitch? In a word: class. Malone notes that while the term "pretends to criticize . . . unoriginality of thought and action, most of what *basic* actually seeks to dismiss is consumption patterns—what you watch, what you drink, what you wear, and what you buy—without dismissing consumption itself. The basic girl's sin isn't liking to shop, it's cluelessly lusting after the wrong brands, the ones that announce themselves loudly and have shareholders they need to satisfy. (The right brands are much more expensive and subtle and, usually, privately owned.)"

Inevitably, even basic bitch culture went from terminally uncool to cheekily ironic, with Eckhaus Latta and Telfar collaborating with Ugg and Vetements collaborating with Juicy Couture. There are no unmediated items of clothing anymore. Even mass culture is eventual fodder for high-end or indie brands to turn into something niche. Increasingly, we actually *want* to blend into a herd, to sink into the pleasure of sameness. Amid millennial burnout and the collapse of hustle culture, fashion-as-lifehack has emerged as a salve for our collective overwhelm. As the fashion historian Anne Hollander points out, adult clothes are beginning to look more and more like playclothes, which, she writes in *Sex and Suits: The Evolution of Modern Dress*, express the fantasy of "no responsibilities outside the self . . . freedom from the burdens of adult sexuality." As we slide into our Uniqlo Garanimals, we may be trying to compensate for our lack of access to other "burdens" of adult life—like pensions, 401(k)s, home ownership, and even the haziest promise of continued employment.

In recent years, "viral" fashion items have popped up, turning everyone into clones of each other: There was a nondescript "Amazon coat" that, according to The Strategist, had "taken over" the Upper East Side, a leopard-print skirt that quickly wallpapered the streets of SoHo, and a TikTok-famous strawberry-printed dress that, too, found many imitators. There seems to be a two-pronged formula behind creating these moments. First, the trend must originate in some teasingly obscure way—a coat that people just happened to find on Amazon, giving it a sense of discovery, as opposed to something that was pushed on us via the runway or ads. And second, it must be instantly legible, via a color, pattern, or shape that renders it immediately recognizable in the urban landscape. Like the songs and shows we stream, fashion is now undergirded by algorithms, molded by the machine learning of our tastes, and tailor-made for prime digestibility on the platform that hosts it (i.e., clothes that show up "well" on Instagram). Like Muzak, it's calculated to hit all of our pleasure centers without overriding our existing preferences. Men's fashion wasn't immune—the blue-checked J.Crew button-down, redolent of so many finance bros, became a meme of its own.

Instagram encourages slight but superficial differentiation.

The Instagram account @Insta_Repeat collates near-identical shots of outdoorsy tropes from different users, whether it's feet stretched out in front of a campfire or a hand holding a bird against a background of landscape. The account's bio reads "Déjà Vu Vibes 🌲 Wander. Roam. Replicate," suggesting that as we go on these John Muir–like outdoor quests for the self, we're not actually embarking on the individualistic project we think we are.

Somehow, many of us still want to get in on those fads despite knowing they mark us as fashion lemmings. They may be appealing because, in a world of broken connections, they offer a tenuous link to other people, a way to participate in something, like the Oscars or a World Cup match or a pep rally, that feels bigger than ourselves despite its inherent lameness. Fashion represents one of the few remaining ways for us to feel like we are a part of something—it's a kind of third place, as the sociologist Ray Oldenburg called locales that are neither home nor work, a kind of agora in which people can mingle regardless of affiliation (like cafés, malls, churches, or bingo nights). As those avenues disappear, we turn to digital connections, but also to the visceral links to others that fashion offers. It's why you caved and bought a "nap dress" despite seeing them replicate infinitely in your timeline, like Tribbles.

CHAPTER FIFTEEN

The Couture Body

A FEW YEARS AGO, I noticed a trend as I surveyed the photos from the latest Met Gala red carpet. Beyoncé, Jennifer Lopez, and Kim Kardashian were all wearing looks that eventually earned the designation "naked dresses"—beyond being skintight, they were selectively see-through and skin-exposing. More strikingly, all three posed completely identically on the red carpet—an angled side view that emphasized tiny waists and ski-jump curves. Not long before, Rihanna had worn a completely see-through gown to accept the Fashion Icon award at the CFDA Fashion Awards. "We've officially entered a realm that you might call post-fashion," I wrote in *New York* magazine at the time. "The body is the new outfit. The gym is the new atelier. Curves and indentations that were once sculpted by corsetry, boning, panniers, strategic padding, or even, more recently, Spanx are now squarely in evidence. Where celebrities once relied on the darting hands of *petites mains* fitting them, designers' clever tricks of tailoring, or stylists' concerted applications of double-stick tape, they now turn to personal trainers (and maybe, in some cases, plastic surgeons) to design their bodies. And they're, in some sense, wearing their bodies just as much as they are wearing fashion."

Fashion, of course, cannot be extricated from the bodies that wear it. As long as there has been clothing, it has reshaped and re-imagined our silhouettes in sync with the prevailing standards of the times. In fact, fashion has often specialized in the containment and control of unruly bodies. Once, clothing did the work of arti-ficially shaping female figures, creating wasp waists and shelflike busts where none existed. Designers saw it as their job to disguise "flaws" and mold women into the beauty ideal of the time. Now, as we've thrown off restrictive corsets and girdles, we've shifted those rules onto the human body itself, with the craze for a slim yet curvaceous figure only achievable through diet, exercise, and often plastic surgery—to the point where "Who are you wearing?" might be a less pertinent question than "Who's your trainer/nu-tritionist/surgeon?" It's a state of affairs that traditional designers have struggled to adapt to.

Right alongside these unattainable body standards has come the advent of athleisure. It's now acceptable in many situations to dress in skintight, studiedly casual workout-wear-as-daywear. At the highest end, these clothes can cost as much as a special-occasion dress. The athleisure revolution, such as it is—with its cellophane-like cling, its strategic showcasing of windows of flesh—has permeated even the design of eveningwear, as seen in the Met Gala looks I mentioned. It is a style that bespeaks cer-tain class and status signifiers, like having enough free time to focus on your exercise regimen. It's also the result of more direct access to the body via social media: people's nearly nude photos, Facetuned bodies in bathing suit photos, and so forth. "The ideal body type right now is a particularly tricky feat of engineering—simultaneously curvy and toned, voluptuous and meager—the Protestant work ethic writ onto flesh," I wrote at the time. "Effortless is no longer the goal—now, a body has to look like the product of *work*. When a celebrity leaves the house, she is always, in tabloid parlance, flaunting her post-baby body, showing off her hard-won abs, or declaring her previously absent corporeal form to be 'back.' (Where was it hiding?) Where we once piled ourselves with gems, we now tote equally fetishized green juice."

The way we dress and present our bodies has always existed at the intersection of technology and politics. New innovations in fabrics and designs, and later in plastic surgery and retouching, have shaped the way we literally shape ourselves. So have changing ideas about women's empowerment and sexuality. Even in medieval times, which you might associate with grimness and sackcloth, people were using fashion to show off their bodies. Women used lacing to turn oversized gowns into showcases for curves. In the fourteenth century, a garment called the cotehardie, which was worn over a chemise but exposed the sides of the wearer's torso, became trendy. The sideless surcoat, a variation on the cotehardie, was considered so scandalous that the Church denounced it as "Hell's Windows."

By the time the modern corset emerged in the sixteenth century, clothes had become both armature and armor, full-on scaffolding meant to shape the perfect body. A 1777 epigram quoted in Karen Bowman's book *Corsets and Codpieces* reflected the myriad beauty modifications of the Georgian era, including the use of cork to pad the derrière. "False rumps—false teeth—false hair—false faces—Alas! Poor man how hard thy case is; Instead of 'woman, heav'nly woman's charms, To clasp cork—gum—wool—varnish—in thy arms.'" Those jibes don't sound all that different from modern-day complaints about fake body parts and makeup. Women are chastised when they go off adventuring into the uncanny valley, often by men who supposedly prefer the "natural look." A 1776 article quoted in Bowman's book asked if a man could sue his wife for, essentially, false advertising if she wore these counterfeit body parts. The anxiety around the deception of these "tricks" suggests a deep-rooted misogyny; the idea that women are cheating their way to beauty instead of naturally possessing it. Worse, this way of thinking mocked women for simply following the fashions that were enforced by others in order to be seen as socially acceptable.

Just as dangerous wellness fads are cloaked in the trappings of health today, corsets were once thought of as healthy, because women were considered to be too weak to hold themselves up properly. But as various forms of "rational dress" became more common, couturiers, too, began to diverge from the corseted silhouette. In 1905, the French designer Jeanne Paquin introduced clothing that didn't require a corset. Her looks featured Empire waists (so named because they referred to the Napoleonic era) as opposed to the typical wasp waist. Madeleine Vionnet was inspired by the Grecian costumes of dancer Isadora Duncan. She preferred clinging, bias-cut styles, for a figure-skimming, second-skin effect. "I have never been able to tolerate corsets myself. Why should I have inflicted them on other women?" she supposedly said. But best remembered and most craterlike in his impact is Paul Poiret, the designer, canny self-promoter, and contemporary of Paquin. He had come to disdain corseted styles, saying that they made women look like they were "divided in two and . . . dragging an anchor." Still, his silhouettes didn't promise complete liberation, either— along with looser chests and waists, he showed hobble skirts, which restricted the wearer's ability to walk. "I freed the bust but I shackled the legs," he later admitted. Coco Chanel took comfort a step further and made loose knits and baggy trousers trendy. The former had mainly been used for underwear; the latter was, until that point, reserved for men. Poiret was not a fan; he supposedly called her disciples "undernourished telegraph boys dressed in black jersey" and called her aesthetic "*misère de luxe*" (luxury misery).

Alongside this more freeing clothing came increased restrictiveness around the body. As the fashion historian Valerie Steele writes in *The Corset: A Cultural History*, the body ideal morphed "from an opulent Venus to a slender, athletic Diana." Around the time of the flappers, many of the prior restrictions in fashion were displaced onto anatomy, becoming less about clothing and more about body type. Steele has argued that as we tossed off the corset, we came to internalize it. Though fashion modifications still existed—to achieve the hipless, breastless flapper silhouette, curvier women wore girdles or even bound their chests to fit in. The novelist Alison Lurie found that women even strove to emulate these body trends in photographs. "Late Victorian nudes protruded their behinds like bustles," she wrote in her landmark study, *The Language of Clothes*. "Twenties nudes adopted a debutante slouch and nudes of the Forties tucked in their tummies and hips and stuck out their chests to produce the flat-bottomed, melon-breasted figure then considered the most desirable." Fashion historian James Laver's theory of "shifting erogenous zones" posits that designers emphasize certain parts of the body until they cease to become exciting, at which point they move on. As we run out of flesh to expose, designers have become more creative—while once a glimpse of ankle was considered provocative, underdog body parts like the early-aughts' lower midriff or the slice of torso revealed by cutouts in the late aughts had their moments in the runways' sun.

After World War II, fashion reverted to the past, or at least to a version of it. In his autobiography, the designer Christian Dior wrote of postwar France, "We were still living in the aftermath of a terrible war. Traces of it were all around me—damaged buildings, devastated countrysides, rationing, the black market, and less serious but of more immediate interest to me, hideous fashions. Hats were far too large, skirts far too short, jackets far too long, shoes far too heavy." A style subculture called Zazou had cropped up. Its emphasis on individuality was a riposte to the fascist occupiers. Zazou hallmarks included short skirts, high platforms, heavy makeup, and dyed hair. Dior called it "half-existentialist, half-zombie," noting that it "originated in a desire to taunt the forces of occupation, and in the austerity of Vichy. For lack of other materials, feathers and veils, promoted to the dignity of flags, floated through Paris like revolutionary banners. But this style was already on the way out."

On the way in was Dior's own creation, which would be dubbed the New Look. The name supposedly came from fashion editor Carmel Snow, who said, "It's quite a revolution, dear Christian! Your dresses have such a new look!" The show where Dior debuted the New Look was so crowded that people were spilling out of his salon and onto the steps. "All around us, life was beginning anew; it was time for a new trend in fashion," the designer wrote. And that's what he gave the assembled hordes. With their strong shoulders, wasp waists, padded hips, and long, full skirts, Dior's women resembled trumpet flowers. The Bar jacket became iconic and is still riffed on by the house today.

Was it reactionary or revolutionary? The answer to both questions is yes. During the war, little fabric was available because of rationing, thus the rage for short skirts. Functional accessories—like snoods that kept your hair out of factory machinery—predominated. The wartime rubber shortage diverted the material from being used for girdles and corsets (that is, until a letter-writing campaign from women complaining they needed them for health reasons forced the U.S. War Production Board to remove the rubber ban).

This freer mode of dressing hung on in the immediate postwar years. In 1946, Dior writes, "women still looked and dressed like Amazons. But I designed clothes for flower-like women, clothes with rounded shoulders, full feminine busts, and willowy waists above enormous spreading skirts. . . . We were just emerging from a poverty-stricken, parsimonious era, obsessed with ration books and clothes coupons; it was only natural that my creations should take the form of a reaction against this dearth of imagination." It was why his clothes used so much fabric. (The Chérie dress, Dior writes, incorporated eighty yards of pleated white faille.)

How new *was* the New Look? The silhouette called back to another time, though imprecisely. The "fragile air" that the designer was going for, he wrote, "can be achieved only by solid construction. . . . I wanted my dresses to be constructed like buildings, molded to the curves of the female form, stylizing its shape." The padding evoked pre-war fecundity and abundance—so many women had starved during the war that curves were almost a status symbol. The look wasn't just a change in fashion; it also made the "old" Venusian body type desirable again.

Like a transitional object a child uses to move from one stage of life to another, the New Look was a passage into a new era. It evoked the values that people had been craving during the instability of the war: traditionalism, femininity, safety, and national pride. Following a craze for Eastern styles, wrote Dior, "people were delighted to be faced with fashions which were European rather than exotic, clothes which were well made, and styles which for the first time in years were 'becoming' and 'pretty.' . . . Girls could safely feel that they had all the trappings of a fairy tale princess. A golden age seemed to have come again. The war was over and no one could foresee what was to follow. What did the weight of my sumptuous materials, my heavy velvets and brocades, matter? When hearts were light, mere fabrics could not weigh the body down." As the feminist theorist Ilya Parkins writes in the *Athenaeum Review*, "Though Dior has been called—and intermittently presented himself as—a 'revolutionary,' which implies a will to the new, his designs derived their revolutionary force from their reclaiming of the past. This was work that turned away from the present." In fact, the style has intimations of eighteenth- and nineteenth-century French fashion, including the reign of Napoleon III and the Belle Époque.

Dior wrote that, despite their historical associations, his creations were embraced by many young people, including the cabaret singer Juliette Gréco, who normally favored existentialist all-black ensembles. The New Look and its representation of an exciting French future were understandably appealing to those who wanted to put the privations of the war behind them. But not everyone wanted to do that. For women who had entered the workforce for the first time and had been temporarily allowed more freedoms (including fashion freedoms), the New Look felt like a return to pre-war constriction. And so some people revolted, violently, against this supposed revolution. A photo by Walter Carone shows older women tearing a younger woman's New Look finest off her in the street. In the UK, the Board of Trade banned British *Vogue* from mentioning Dior by name, out of concern that demand for fabric would go up. Protests sprang up: Women in California gathered in bathing suits, with signs that read "Do We Need Padding?" A group in Dallas calling themselves the Little Below the Knee Club stopped traffic dressed in their grandmothers' clothes. They were accompanied by a band playing old-time music, to reinforce the idea of the clothes as belonging to a bygone era.

When he made the passage to America, the designer recalled in his autobiography, he was greeted as a celebrity. The first person he encountered was an immigration officer who interrogated him about his skirts' length. Shortly after making it through customs, he was hustled into a press conference: "I faced the grave charge of wishing to conceal the sacrosanct legs of the American female, and I had to defend myself on the spot." When he arrived in Chicago, his show "was literally patrolled by embattled housewives brandishing placards bearing the words: 'Down with the New Look,' 'Burn Monsieur Dior,' 'Christian Dior, Go home.' " The language of war used here ("defend," "patrolled," "embattled") doesn't feel accidental—the designer felt that he was defending a front, even a way of life.

The New Look required additional undergarments, like a waist-cinching garment often called a waspie, requiring new levels of body modification. And despite the initial resistance, the shape prevailed. You can draw a straight line from the New Look to the predominant '50s silhouettes of fembot bullet bras, skirt-inflating petticoats, and slimming girdles. That look was a form of social control through silhouette. It combined containment of the female body with a simultaneous fetishization of it. The fads for "sweater girls" and "wiggle dresses" were ways of clothing the body for propriety's sake, while still making its curves hyper-visible. Bras were padded to conceal the nipple, the biological function of the breast. And lurking beneath all this was the shadow of the Cold War–era combat machine; bullet bras and girdles were as sturdily constructed as tanks.

Central to this conceit was the bra, which had been around in some form since antiquity—it appeared in ancient Greece as a fabric band enclosing the chest—but acquired new significance in the absence of the corset. The bra benefited from a new emphasis on (and optimism about) technology, with stretch fabrics that became popular in the '50s. The decade also brought us the "training bra," which became a ritual inculcating girls who didn't yet "need" one into the bra lifestyle. The weird term "training" suggested preparation for a grueling, underwire-filled adulthood. Bras, which had been seen as functional garments, now began to be marketed as sexy in ads—a tool of seduction rather than engineering. Their marketing also started to use the language of empowerment. From 1949 to 1969, Maidenform ran a series of ads that showed women doing traditionally male jobs like bullfighting, firefighting, and house painting. Perhaps the most poignant was an "I Dreamed I Won the Election in My Maidenform Bra" ad from 1952. The ad campaign began post–World War II, as women left the workforce and returned home, making these positions truly feel like dreams as opposed to realities.

Silhouettes loosened in the '60s and '70s, with bralessness becoming trendier. In a callback to the flapper era, rail-thin Twiggy was the high-fashion body ideal. The ideal shape was one of arrested adolescence, with the emphasis off breasts and hips and onto thin limbs. (FORGET OXFAM FEED TWIGGY read a popular bumper sticker of the time.) In the '70s, the wrap dress, as popularized by Diane von Furstenberg, became a uniform for the sexual revolution, fitting for the many fluid roles women were now supposed to play.

Second-wave feminists were frequently described as "bra burners," a coinage that still unfortunately comes up when talking about feminism today. That is a reference to the 1968 protests of the Miss America pageant by a group called New York Radical Women, led by the feminist Carol Hanisch, who coined the phrase "The personal is political." In a manifesto, the group called out the objectification and racism of the pageant. The demonstrators, prominent feminists Flo Kennedy and Robin Morgan among them, threw items they saw as symbolic of feminine oppression—including bras, girdles, eyelash curlers, and women's magazines—into a "Freedom Trash Can." They also tossed in items associated with housework (like mops) or low-paying pink-collar jobs (stenography pads). Before the protest took place, the *New York Post* incorrectly said that the participants would be burning their bras, à la Vietnam War protesters who were, at the same time, burning their draft cards. The organizers have maintained that no bras were actually harmed in the making of this event. Still, the idea was quickly picked up by other media outlets and became a handy way of dismissing the nascent women's movement as shallow provocateurs.

With the feminist movement targeting bras as a symbol of oppression and many women abandoning them, the garment was threatened. Research done by Wonderbra determined that women didn't, in fact, want to eschew bras completely. They simply wanted "less bra." This new concept marketed the garment as freer and more natural. For example, the 1974 ad for the Dici by Wonderbra line has the tagline, "Let it be Dici. Dici or nothing." The commercial shows an unadorned white bra flying out of the box on a beach and transforming into a seagull as a woman sings softly about feeling the wind on her body and feeling free. The trick of this style was taking something unnatural and manmade and positioning it as being as much a part of nature as a bird. Another strategy was to associate bras with high fashion, as in a Richard Avedon–directed 1979 Wonderbra commercial that shows bra-clad models getting ready for a fashion show.

Despite flagging public interest, designers still wanted the bra to be relevant. A capitalist conundrum reared its head. If women prefer no bra, what do you sell them? What about . . . selling them "no bra"? In 1967, Rudi Gernreich came out with the "no bra," which was, in fact, a standard bra, but a sheer, wireless style that looked like something you might pick up from a trendy direct-to-consumer lingerie brand today. It was made to make the wearer look like they were not wearing a bra, which is . . . not something you really need a bra for? The whole thing was redolent of the way supposedly oppressive garments are cast off, then resold to us in a new form. Corsets would be reborn as waist trainers; girdles were reincarnated as Spanx.

By the '70s, the draconian dictates of fashion fully displaced themselves onto the body via a robust diet culture and an increased emphasis on fitness. In her 1972 essay "Fitness," Kennedy Fraser wrote, "In order to be fashionable—a state only tenuously connected with propriety or comfort, and one avowedly at odds with contentment—most women out of their teens need to diet and take exercise. . . . And it is clear that supple clothes that offer no camouflage to middle-aged bulges are in style once and for all." The growing openness about sex and nudity had led the fashionable to wonder "whether it isn't more important to create a good impression in the skin than in clothes."

By the '80s, aerobic exercise had become a religion and muscles were the "It" accessories of the moment. In *American Psycho*, the narrator extols women he calls "hardbodies"; Jane Fonda in her workout videos embodied the hard-bodied ideal. The constricting styles of the time, like "King of Cling" Azzedine Alaïa's skintight designs and Hervé Leger's bandage dresses, rewarded, maybe even required, serious gym time.

As the next decade rolled around, the gym rat was replaced by the waif, the epitome of heroin chic in her tiny slip dress. Robin Givhan called the aesthetic "a nihilistic vision of beauty that mirrors the wasted silhouettes and pinched faces of drug addicts." While it's true that it was influenced by the drug culture of the time, there was something else that conferred status on the extreme-waif look. It was much harder for most women to emulate than the hardbody: It couldn't be achieved through the labor of workouts, or even through standard dieting.

A fusion of ultra-thinness and curves marked the mid-'90s. Even the ur-waif Kate Moss was touting the push-up Wonderbra by 1994, saying it was the only one that gave her cleavage. In 1999, *Vogue* heralded the "return of the sexy model" in a story about Gisele Bündchen, who, while still very thin, had a curvier frame than Moss and her fellow waifs. *Sex and the City* popularized a waxed, gym-toned, perpetually sex-ready body that was a triangulation of grooming, dieting, and exercise. By the aughts, even the girdle had somehow managed to become "empowering." While working as a fax machine saleswoman, of all things, Sara Blakely hit on an innovation that would turn out to be a lot more popular than what she was selling. By cutting a pair of control-top pantyhose into a makeshift girdle, Blakely came up with the product that would make her a billionaire: Spanx. (She told *The New Yorker* she wanted a name with "virgin-whore tension.") Supposedly, her invention liberated women from the body vigilance necessary to reach an increasingly rigid ideal. The names of products like Power Panties and lines like On Top and In Control underscored the empowerment message. The boxes bore messages like "Don't take yourself or the 'rules' too seriously," and "Re-shape the way you get dressed, so you can shape the world!" Blakely was hailed as a feminist hero in some quarters, named to the Time 100 list, and graced the cover of *Forbes*. The press around her often mentioned her natural trimness in a way that implied a plus-size woman would not have met with the same universal approbation. As Katie Couric put it in her Time 100 writeup, "The comic irony of Spanx is that the woman who became a billionaire after inventing them doesn't even need them."

Lingerie, too, had been tagged with the "empowerment" label. Victoria's Secret, with its super-sexy, unattainable image, had long been the standard. But the rising body positivity movement was reflected in newer, millennial-targeted lines like Rihanna's label Savage x Fenty, launched in 2018, which catered to a wide swath of bodies and used a diverse group of models, and Aerie, which had been around since the mid-aughts but in 2014 began releasing unretouched ads showing celebrities in a range of body types wearing comfortable-looking bralettes. According to the *New York Times*, "letting the breasts be gives the bralette those social media bona fides: body positivity, inclusivity, authenticity. (One more reason Victoria's Secret and its va va voom push-up bras are on the wane.)" In 2016, Victoria's Secret capitulated to the craze and started pushing its bralette offerings. Signs in its store windows read NO PADDING IS SEXY NOW! A commercial, reminiscent of the '70s Dici push, touted the look as "Being free." (At least this one didn't star an animated seagull.) But bralettes are tricky. They don't offer much support, which means they work better on small-breasted people, who tend to, broadly speaking, be thinner. Kendall Jenner wears bralettes as daywear and is lauded as a trendsetter, but were a larger-framed or larger-breasted woman to do that, it would be seen as trashy. They were hardly the universally liberating underpinning they claimed to be.

Meanwhile, as the bralette soared, the corset was also undergoing a revival. Less than a century after the corset was retired from most women's lingerie drawers, it reemerged, though in a disguised format: the waist trainer. These were advertised as a way to achieve the hourglass figure that was, once again, prized. As with corsets, they were progressively tightened in order to slim the waist. And like corsets, they could cause organ damage and other health issues. Still, they were everywhere, especially since Kim Kardashian and Kylie Jenner advertised them on Instagram. A picture of Jenner, Kourtney Kardashian, and Khloé Kardashian all wearing waist trainers over cute, trendy workout clothes epitomized the shift in our thinking. We're more transparent about the work we are doing on our bodies, coyly letting everyone backstage and behind the scenes of our "transformation." That might initially seem like a refreshing instance of radical candor, but it doesn't give us permission to break the draconian body rules. Jenner positioned waist trainers as a way to "snap back," or return to an acceptable degree of slimness, after pregnancy. Kim Kardashian, who previously endorsed waist trainers on Instagram, pivoted to selling them as part of her Skims line of shapewear, or, as she calls it, "solutionwear," a neologism that frames the female body as a solvable problem.

It might seem like now we're freer, but we've just offloaded the responsibility for living up to a beauty standard from fashion to various realms outside it. Worse, as the philosopher Heather Widdows outlines in her book *Perfect Me*, "the beauty ideal is transforming into an ethical ideal" and pursuing it has become "a moral duty." She gives as examples the way people frame themselves as "good" for refusing desserts or exercising, and the way " 'letting yourself go' is morally bad, shameful and disgusting. Shame is doing the same work in accounts of beauty failure as in traditional accounts of moral failure," even though "letting yourself go" really just means letting nature take its course.

The minister and writer David Zahl coined the term "seculosity" to describe the way we have displaced our religious fervor onto other segments of life, from food to parenting. The language of virtue and vice has accrued to weight and exercise: "good" and "bad" foods, being "bad" by skipping the gym, even extreme fasting that evokes the behavior of religious adherents. There is some kinship between today's gym rats and the "Muscular Christianity" movement of the Victorian era, in which self-improvement through physical exertion was twinned with faith—and associated with moral correctness. And being fit and eating healthy are now pillars of status that have supplanted more traditional class markers. Look at the sweatshirt that reads KALE in the Yale font—it was once a sign of social standing to wear an Ivy League sweatshirt; now the ultimate prestige is advertising that you're a fan of leafy greens.

In an episode of *The Marvelous Mrs. Maisel*, set in the late '50s, the characters struggle through an arduous calisthenics class. Watching, I found something delightfully retro about their open distaste for exercising. Now, you must claim you're doing it for yourself—as part of self-care, self-empowerment, or a "wellness journey." The standards have not actually become more flexible, it's just that their underpinnings have become more insidious. Now we have to pretend that working out, and every other part of the bodily bildungsroman we call our "journey," is something we're doing for our own betterment and pleasure. Club music blasts in boutique workout studios; as spiritual-erotic group activities go, planking alongside strangers has largely replaced sweatily dancing along-side them.

In *The Care of the Self*, Michel Foucault writes, "The final goal of all the practises of self still belongs to an ethics of control." The energy that might have once been spent on clothing our bodies is now focused on training them, breaking them like recalcitrant horses. And athleisure, according to Jia Tolentino in *Trick Mirror*, is the ultimate uniform of optimization, a form of "late-capitalist fetishwear . . . tailor-made for a time when work is rebranded as pleasure so that we will accept more of it—a time when, for women, improving your looks is a job that you're supposed to believe is fun." In this mode of thinking, diets, exercise, Botox, fillers, and plastic surgery are all methods of weatherproofing the body against the coming winter of age—arresting its youth and firmness in amber. When we live in such a visual culture, it makes a kind of business sense to attend to your body in this way, not just for ac-tresses, models, and influencers but for ordinary people, too. We are all tilling our own fields, hoping for a harvest. When we do this work—and it is work—we are engaging in what the sociologist Eliz-abeth Wissinger calls "glamour labor," defined as doing "both the body work to manage appearance in person and the online image work to create and maintain one's 'cool' quotient."

Glamour labor extends to exercise, which we're now encour-aged to professionalize and approach like athletes. We do the body work (running the half-marathon, hitting the gym, taking the hike) and supplement it with the online work (the selfie at the fin-ish line, the contours of your run posted to Instagram stories via a training app, the couples lifting shot hashtagged #Swolemates, the fist-pumping photo at the summit). The online work is sup-posed to show that you don't take things too seriously, that you're "fun"—maybe you're chugging a beer at the finish line, or making a dumb face as you run that last lap. Perhaps you shoot an "Instagram versus reality" diptych to show you don't take your image that seriously. There is room for looseness and irony in the online self-presentation, but not in the physical work.

The inherent contradiction of athleisure is that it feels comfortable and constricting at the same time. It's a serious uniform for self-optimization, a kind of business suit you wear to the gym, but it's also casualwear. Like wearing no-makeup makeup, it still involves effort—not to mention the additional effort required to make it all seem perfectly effortless.

While technology has replaced so many human-performed tasks when it comes to, say, housework—eliminating the drudgery of sweeping the floor or washing the dishes or doing laundry by hand—beauty work has been the opposite. The functions once performed by corsets and girdles are now offloaded onto *us*, and the hurdles are raised ever more slowly. Even celebrities, with trainers, nutritionists, and infinite resources at their disposal, struggle to adapt to increasingly specific and ever-shifting body ideals. One way to hurdle them is through plastic surgery. Few celebrities will admit to their procedures, but they're now out there for the world to see. Popular Instagram accounts like @Celebface chronicle the plastic surgery transformations of the famous (or the simply Insta-famous). They can be read as an exposé or as a manual, to take to your plastic surgeon as casually as you show a celebrity photo to your hairstylist. We used to reserve our most dressed-up, made-up selves for special occasions; now we have to, like celebrities, be camera-ready at all times. And since we all exist on the same platform as celebrities and models, we're now on the same playing field as them, forced to keep up not just with the Joneses but with the professionally beautiful. There is more transparency about what we're doing: like celebrities, regular people show off our diets ("what I eat in a day" videos are popular on TikTok) and our exercise regimens. But there is less transparency about *why* we're expending so much energy on this, and whether or not it's actually worth it.

Trends in bodies, at this point, nearly outpace trends in clothes. They are as impossible to keep up with, and even more costly. This is why the thin, gym-toned body has become such a class signifier—it alerts everyone to both the money and time you have to spend on your looks. Between microtrends in bodies like the thigh gap, or the YouTube workout videos devoted to eliminating arcane corporeal flaws like "hip dips," there's always something new to fixate on. In this way, we're always aiming for an ideal that shape-shifts before we can actually arrive at it. The cultural theorist Meredith Jones has written about the concept of "makeover culture," which "dictates that bodies, selves and environments must be in constant states of renovation, restoration, maintenance and improvement," almost like a home we're perpetually trying to overhaul before putting it on the market.

Which brings us to the question: What does this mean for fashion? If fashion has become, increasingly, about physiques and not clothes, will designers someday be superfluous? Will the plastic surgeons who redesign our bodies replace them entirely? What does the arc of fashion history bend toward? It may be that we've taken steps both forward and back. With the advent of body positivity and an increased push for diversity, the beauty ideal has both contracted and widened. Beauty is at once more diverse and harder to live up to. As America becomes less and less white and our culture becomes more globalized, we have moved closer to a multicultural beauty ideal that is both welcome and overdue. At its best, it redefines what beauty is and includes more people in the "beautiful" category. But it also puts more pressure on people to be all things. Writing about beauty standards in *Bossypants* (and admittedly leaning quite heavily on stereotypes), Tina Fey observed, "Now every girl is expected to have Caucasian blue eyes, full Spanish lips, a classic button nose, hairless Asian skin with a California tan, a Jamaican dance hall ass, long Swedish legs, small Japanese feet, the abs of a lesbian gym owner, the hips of a nine-year-old boy, the arms of Michelle Obama, and doll tits. The person closest to actually achieving this look is Kim Kardashian, who, as we know, was made by Russian scientists to sabotage our athletes." Fey wrote this in 2011, in Instagram's infancy; the challenges have only increased since then. For every "brave" selfie showing stretch marks or cellulite, there is a person Facetuned to look like a Bratz doll. For everyone pushing back against the unrealistic pressures on new moms' bodies, there is a Kylie Jenner selfie promoting a "snap back package."

We can theoretically see more kinds of bodies through the window of social media, but the ideal has narrowed at the same time. Even as we expand our definition of what the perfect body looks like, old-fashioned restrictions still remain. For example, the writer and fashion blogger Nicolette Mason has written that despite the growth of size inclusion on the runway and in ads, "Almost every time we see a woman above a size fourteen in magazines, in advertisements, or on the runway, she's a perfect hourglass shape." Ashley Graham, the most successful plus-size model currently working, and regrettably often the only one represented in a given show, has this body type, which has surely contributed to her mainstream success. Advice like wearing "flattering" clothes or wearing a waist-cinching look is still given to plus-size women. Mason concludes that "the fashion world celebrates only perfect proportions—and thus implies that even though it may finally be OK to be above a size fourteen, your body still needs to have curves in all the right places." "Perfect" and "right" are used aptly here—we still assign moral value to shapes and sizes, and differentiate between "good" bodies and misbehaving ones.

If the body has become our ultimate currency, can we ever

really divest from it? What began as the body positivity movement has shifted to the quest for body neutrality—to be able to regard our physical forms as just another neutral element in space. But as long as bodies take up so much of our mental real estate, and as long as we live in a culture where the mandate for constant self-improvement lives rent-free in our heads, we may never truly be able to do that.

If, to extend Zahl's idea of seculosity, self-care has replaced religion, it might be said that the obsessive brand of self-care we now practice is the opiate of the masses that Karl Marx decried. It involves the same cyclically performed rituals, the same rigid value system, and the same unquestioning allegiance. As distinct from Audre Lorde's conception of the term—which sought to strengthen the community by encouraging individual members to care for themselves—it's become a distraction from our communities and a retreat from the wider world. The commercial conception of self-care feels like a canny rebranding of good old-fashioned glamour labor. The algorithm rewards diligence and repetition. It encourages us to disappear down a vortex of the endlessly echoed self, but it's done less in service of the self and more in compliance with what the world around us wants to see. The purpose of discipline, wrote Foucault, was "making the body both docile and useful. The human body becomes a machine, the functioning of which can be optimised, calculated and improved through the internalization of specific patterns of behaviour." In our attempt to become shiny, perfectly functioning cogs in this confusing Rube Goldberg machine, we abandon our place in society and become independent contractors of the self.

That's why the fixation on self-care versus community care has recently loomed large. Few systemic problems can actually be fixed by self-care. As community organizer and researcher Nakita Valerio put it, "Shouting 'self-care' at people who actually need 'community care' is how we fail people." Organizers are stepping in where governments and churches have failed; for example, creating community fridges for the food insecure or shelters for unhoused people in their neighborhoods. Neoliberalism wants us to endlessly confront the self. Community care asks us to look outside it. And stepping outside of ourselves en masse is, very possibly, how we free ourselves from the narcissistic trap that self-care has become.

The more challenging part may be reprogramming the constant ticker tape of physical self-improvement narratives that streams through our psyches. Something I've struggled with, particularly as someone with an unruly, perpetually untrendy body in an industry that fetishizes appearance, is how much of what I'm doing is for my own enjoyment and how much is to fit in and keep up. Once, that "keeping up" might have been confined to the hermetic world of other fashion editors, with writing and editing still being the primary duties of the job. Now that our images and bodies are front and center in public life, it's common for editors to be offered, for example, free personal training services or fitness classes, with the knowledge that people are grooming themselves for Instagram. This isn't merely a vanity-driven enterprise: There are tangible job rewards to be gained by being the kind of person who can fit into sample-size clothes, post themselves wearing said clothes on Instagram, gain followers by doing so, and render themselves more employable in the process. This all admittedly falls under the category of "first world problems," but as more arenas become celebrity-adjacent, there is intensified pressure not just to keep up with beauty standards at an A-lister's pace, but to shape the narrative arc of one's life on social media in the way a celebrity does, using relationships, weddings, babies, and other life events to keep your "public" interested—all while appearing effortless and transparent. Now that everything is a visual medium,

I would imagine more professions are becoming like this, or soon will. To declare, "I will completely step off the treadmill of self-advertisement and self-disclosure" is to make, say, promoting a book or working at a publication more challenging in a way it wouldn't have been in 1995. (In fact, anyone who promoted themselves IRL in 1995 the way the average person does today on social media would have come across as tiresomely deranged.)

This never-abating firehose of pressure is why a less challenging, sanded-down, aesthetically consummated, and, yes, smaller version of myself is always hovering just ahead of me, taunting me to keep up. (And at the same time, why I fantasize about just being a brain in a jar that occasionally goes for a bracing walk in the woods.) Even as I'm professionally situated to understand just how hard it is for models and celebrities to maintain their "perfect" bodies, divesting from the self-actualizing mindset proves virtually impossible. Intuitive eating and exercising is a worthy goal, but how do you approach it when your intuition has been shattered by a lifetime of conditioning in the opposite direction? When I swim or hike, I keep thinking, in the horrible voice of an aughts fitness magazine, "If I do twenty laps of this stroke, it'll melt away my back fat" (good) or "Scaling these hills is going to bulk up my calves" (bad). The jailer has invaded my own brain. While I like being outside and enjoy the mental health payoff that exercise brings, I can't seem to completely divest from the idea of fanatical self-improvement and go back to my preteen self who simply loved to move and be in nature without a care. Then I enter a vortex of feeling bad *about* feeling bad about my body, because body positivity! I suspect I'm not alone in the quandary. The denial that we're all on a collision course with decay and atrophy is powerful. And to completely separate oneself from this mode of thinking might be as impossible as separating oneself from a society where these are our concerns. I imagine it's worse for a younger generation, who didn't even experience an analog period of time where they were more concerned with pursuing their own passing interests than building themselves into a human brand. We are now expected to be corporations of our own; we're now the CEO, creative director, social media manager, and janitor of our own bodies, simultaneously.

This fanatical emphasis on our corporeal selves as distinct from the things we own has not been liberating. That's why the relatively recent fixation on perfecting the body, as distinct from the clothes that shape and ornament it, doesn't sit well with me. It might initially feel like progress: Contrary to what the fashion industry has told us for centuries, we don't need expensive, regularly updated wardrobes to be on-trend! Clothing alone is no longer the status symbol it was. But one status symbol has merely been exchanged for another; the "ideal" appearance is just as much of a luxury good as the ideal wardrobe, maybe more so. After all, which is more unattainable, a red-carpet dress or the body that wears it?

All the People Who Tell the Truth Are in the Last Rows

Bill Cunningham's Anti-Fashion Style

B ILL CUNNINGHAM, THE longtime *New York Times* fashion photographer, ushered in the modern-day concept of "street style." He saw fashion even in non-fashion spaces—in the '60s, he left an Oscar de la Renta runway show to take pictures of what people were wearing at a Vietnam War protest outside. Now, of course, street style has become a marketing tool like any other, but for Cunningham it was an anthropological project by a fashion outsider. As I wrote in his *New York* magazine obituary in 2016, "That kind of self-separation is rarer and rarer in fashion, where the chroniclers now want to be part of the story. Cunningham's detachment from the elites helped him connect to the part of fashion where the real energy was contained: young people, eccentric outliers, and the denizens of the street."

Now that follower counts have outpaced genuine personal style and self-expression, blogs and social media have become as advertising-driven as traditional media, and even authenticity and flaws feel like marketing gimmicks, it can be hard to get excited about fashion's future. Even the much-vaunted "democratization of style" that occurred around the turn of this century ultimately just meant that we all have access to the same low-priced basic items. In an essay for *n+1*, "The Accidental Bricoleurs," Rob Horning makes an important connection between two technologies that have promised democracy through capitalism: social media and fast fashion. Both give us endless modular options that supposedly allow us to "express ourselves." Instead, they end up making us look and seem more and more the same.

Fashion can feel like an oppressive set of standards to measure up to. In this technology-tethered era, we're constantly performing our visual identities to fit in and look like everyone else. Even our bodies and homes have become subject to the kind of trend roundelay we've previously seen in fashion, constantly requiring us to project ourselves as being effortlessly cool and to reinvent ourselves regularly. The data on what we're wearing, watching, consuming, and buying is then fed to advertisers who will offer us more of the same, creating an endless feedback loop. It's not exactly a recipe for creativity or transgression.

Yet true style comes from the kinds of factors that can't be quantified. As I mentioned earlier in these pages, some of our most beloved style icons evolved their distinctive looks as a response to the conformity around them. In a world of bland sameness, our eyes will be drawn to the artfully disheveled, the challenging, the real. And, most importantly, to the new.

It's probably ludicrous to apply the term "democracy" to any consumerist pursuit. But there's still something egalitarian about the way the fashion industry, at its top tier still admittedly a hermetic elite, thrives on the contributions of outsiders and even weirdos: the punks, goths, and theater kids at the proverbial edge of the cafeteria. The next wave of style will not come from an algorithm. It will come from the kinds of transgressors Cunningham loved and appreciated, who explode the concept of what "looking good" means and challenge our traditional ideas of gender and self-presentation.

That new wave is already breaking over us, stirring up fashion's norms and changing the way we think about beauty, our bodies, and what it means to look "aspirational." Though we certainly have a long way to go, racial, size, and gender representation in traditional fashion media has broadened even in the past couple of years, and I'm hopeful that will only improve in the future. We're also entering an era that I think will resemble the '90s in its rejection of our current moment's anodyne slickness and conformity. Identical Instagram-ad sneakers and athleisure and the equally bland facades of influencers will start to seem passé, and resistance, rebellion, and self-expression will rush in to fill the void. Rather than trying to "hack" the daily grind of getting dressed, maybe there's a shred of hope that we'll start engaging with fashion again.

In this book, I wanted to focus on the way fashion intersects with our everyday lives. Waiting in the wings of that discussion are the many problems of the fashion industry, from the deleterious environmental impact of producing clothes to the fast-fashion castoffs choking landfills to the reliance on underpaid labor. I'm as troubled by fashion's sins as anyone else, but I've always found it challenging to talk about capital-F fashion as a monolith. The word can refer to everything from a couture atelier to a fast-fashion giant, or a young designer in Lagos, Sydney, or Seoul determined to create a new world in their image. It's the last group that I want to concentrate on.

So much of luxury has been built on the idea of "heritage," the concept of elite lineage being acquired through consumption rather than genealogy. Buy this expensive item, the rationale seems to be, and you'll be included in this exclusive group. Young designers of late have, happily, given the lie to that practice. Design collectives like Vaquera and Hood by Air have eliminated the "auteur" concept and included people from all different walks of life in their happening-like shows. The Brooklyn designer Telfar Clemens, whose approachably priced "It" bag became known as the Bushwick Birkin, pushed back against the exclusivity and wait-list-driven nature of the luxury industry. And designers of all kinds continue to push the bounds of gender expression, self-presentation, and inclusivity.

It's become a cliché to say that fashion is moribund and broken, that nothing will nudge us out of our monotone sweatpants. But if fashion history has taught us anything, it's that this is a realm that thrives on new ideas. As Cunningham knew, change never originates from the Establishment. It will come from the kids, from the show crashers. It will come from the people in the last row.

Acknowledgments

I AM SO GRATEFUL to Monika Verma for seeing the statue inside the unwieldy chunk of marble I slapped onto her desk, and for patiently counseling me through the full roundelay of first-time author crises. Huge thanks also to Dominic Yarabe, Rebecca Rodd, and the peerless team at Levine Greenberg Rostan.

Once I met Mary Gaule, everything fell into place. She immediately got what I was trying to say and it was such a relief to find a kindred spirit who understands that, no, fashion is *not* a niche interest! I treasure her and everyone at HarperCollins who took on this project with such enthusiasm and good humor: Lisa Erickson, Amy Baker, Heather Drucker, and Viviana Moreno. Thank you to Joanne O'Neill for the stunning cover.

Everyone at *ELLE*, especially our fearless leader Nina Garcia, has been so supportive about the book, and has helped make me a better writer, editor, and colleague.

Credit is due to the talented editors who helped me develop some of the ideas in this book when they were mere articles, including Molly Fischer (who helped me birth both the term "millennial pink" and the essay that introduced it) and Isabel Wilkinson (for the essay on the couture body). Big thank-yous are owed to Ann Friedman and Rachel Antonoff for sharing your insights, to Mary Mann for nimble fact-checking, and to Meredith Jenks for my deceptively attractive author photo.

Thank you to my friends, especially the long-suffering individuals who follow: Adrienne Gaffney, Alix Sternberg, Caitlin Collins Haynie, Chris O'Donnell, Colin Shepherd, Diane Vadnal, Elana Fishman, Elana Rakoff, Erin Lisowski, Jennifer Chun, Julie Vadnal, Kathleen Hou, Laura Hallett, Maryam Maleki, Nojan Aminosharei, Phil Fry, Piper Gray, Rachel Krupitsky, Rahsaan Kerns, Richard Lonsdorf, Yailett Fernandez, and, of course, the entire revue crew. Thanks for making New York feel like a small town and the world at large feel like a friendlier place. Special plaudits go to Kathleen, Alix, and Adrienne for reading assorted rough drafts.

To Diana Goldstein, for reading to me way back when.

And finally, to my parents, whose enduring love and support thankfully outweigh any lingering puzzlement that this is what I've chosen to do with my life.

Further Reading

Roland Barthes, *The Fashion System*, 1967

Simone de Beauvoir, "Brigitte Bardot and the Lolita Syndrome," *Esquire*, 1959

Edward Bernays, *Propaganda*, 1928

Anja Aronowsky Cronberg, "Docile Bodies," *Vestoj*, 2013

Elizabeth Currid-Halkett, *The Sum of Small Things*, 2017

Aria Dean, "Closing the Loop," *The New Inquiry*, 2016

Christian Dior, *Dior by Dior*, 1957

Fiona Duncan, "Normcore: Fashion for Those Who Realize They're One in 7 Billion," *New York*, 2014

Michel Foucault, *Discipline and Punish*, 1977

Kennedy Fraser, *The Fashionable Mind*, 1981

William Gass, *On Being Blue*, 1975

Tavi Gevinson, "What Instagram Did to Me," *New York*, 2019

Dick Hebdige, *Subculture: The Meaning of Style*, 1979

Amanda Hess, "Celebrity Culture Is Burning," *New York Times*, 2020

Anne Hollander, *Sex and Suits: The Evolution of Modern Dress*, 1994

bell hooks, *Black Looks: Race and Representation*, 1992

Rob Horning, "The Accidental Bricoleurs," *n+1*, 2011

K-Hole, *Youth Mode: A Report on Freedom*, 2013

Audre Lorde, *A Burst of Light: and Other Essays*, 1988

Alison Lurie, *The Language of Clothes*, 1981

Amanda Mull, "It's All So . . . Premiocre," *The Atlantic*, 2020

Laura Mulvey, *Visual and Other Pleasures*, 1989

Jenny Odell, *How to Do Nothing*, 2019

Venkatesh Rao, "The Premium Mediocre Life of Maya Millennial," *Ribbonfarm*, 2017

Georg Simmel, "Fashion," 1904

Kassia St. Clair, *The Secret Lives of Color*, 2016

Jean Stein, *Edie*, 1982

Judith Thurman, "The Misfit," *The New Yorker*, 2005

Jia Tolentino, *Trick Mirror*, 2019

Heather Widdows, *Perfect Me: Beauty as an Ethical Ideal*, 2018

About the Author

VÉRONIQUE HYLAND IS the fashion features director of *ELLE* magazine. Her work has previously appeared in the *New York Times*, *The New Yorker*, *New York* magazine, and even in a few publications without "New York" in their title. She lives in Manhattan with an orchid that will probably be dead by the time you read this.